S.F.

IN
TELEKI'S
FOOTSTEPS

IN
TELEKI'S
FOOTSTEPS

An East African Journey

TOM HEATON

MACMILLAN
LONDON

First published 1989 by
MACMILLAN LONDON LIMITED
4 Little Essex Street London WC2R 3LF
and Basingstoke

Associated companies in Auckland, Delhi, Dublin, Gaborone,
Hamburg, Harare, Hong Kong, Johannesburg, Kuala Lumpur,
Lagos, Manzini, Melbourne, Mexico City, Nairobi, New York,
Singapore and Tokyo

A CIP catalogue record for this book is available from the
British Library.

ISBN 0-333-51777-6

Typeset by Rowland Phototypesetting Limited
Bury St Edmunds, Suffolk

Printed and bound in Great Britain by
Richard Clay Ltd, Bungay, Suffolk

To Jackie for believing it was a good idea

Contents

List of Maps

Prologue

Count Samuel Teleki von Szek returned to Vienna in the spring of 1889 after spending two years exploring East Africa. Throughout that period he kept a diary, which is extant but remains unpublished. In it he describes East Africa as he saw it then: a land full of violence and strife. He also describes it as teeming with wild animals and how he killed many of them. Motivated by a mixture of an unfulfilled hankering for adventure, a nagging curiosity and sheer recklessness, I retraced Teleki's route by bicycle and on foot between 17 February 1982 and 4 December 1983. The pages which follow describe my experiences.

Publication was delayed because, at the outset, I failed to present these experiences coherently. My first attempt to put them together was rejected by ten publishers. By mid-1987 it looked to me that what I had written was likely to share the fate of Teleki's diary. As a last resort, and on the spur of the moment, I sent the manuscript to an old friend, Andrew Blake of Marondera, Zimbabwe, asking him to comment on it. He did, and ended up helping me transform it into its present shape. For this I owe him an immense debt of gratitude.

I also thank Mike Duffield of Raleigh for lending me a bicycle (which to this day sits on my veranda awaiting his summons); Professor Godfrey Muriuki and Tony Avirgan for helping me obtain official clearance to carry out my journey respectively in Kenya and Tanzania; Dr Richard Leakey for giving me permission to travel through the Sibilot and Lake Bogoria game parks; Batuk and Clare Jethwa for helping me before and during my journey; and Priscillah Wanjugu for typing the manuscript.

Lastly, and most importantly, I must pay tribute to my companions, Lobun and Sayya, without whose assistance and loyalty I would never have made it through north-western Kenya.

Ngong, 16 December 1988

Introduction

'This is not the way I used to travel in the old days when I was District Commissioner Stephens's orderly,' said Orogai. 'Mr Stephens used to ride a horse. Him and me and fifteen soldiers, all on horses. And six camels to carry our gear. Everywhere we stopped, Mr Stephens had his tent, table and chair, and his special canvas washstand. His cook would make food for all of us – and not just a few miserable bits and pieces like we've just had. You should have seen us! We were smart and got respect wherever we went. None of this scurrying unarmed through the bush, driving three wretched donkeys loaded with a few bits of old rubbish.' He rammed the blunt end of his spear into the sand.

Orogai was almost totally bald, but at sixty his body was still as slim and straight as a young man's. During that day's march he had also proved his stamina. So hard had he forced the pace that I had found myself begging him to halt. Only for those brief moments had he allowed the poor donkeys respite from his ever whirling stick. Under such a relentless assault, it was a miracle that their strength had not given out. Now, looking down at me with his old bird's eyes, hooked nose wrinkled in contempt, he shook his head in deprecation. 'Tom, why did you insist on camping in this forest when there's a perfectly good village over there? All we've got here is insects and snakes and a good chance of a load of thugs coming in during the night and polishing us off. Ah well, it's your own funeral.' With that, my guide Orogai wrapped his black cloak around him, stepped out of the firelight and vanished.

After a while I gave up searching the shadows for thugs and snakes and instead began asking myself what I was doing in such a dismal place massaging a pair of wrecked feet. How does a supposedly sane man of middle age, used to hot baths and soft armchairs, find himself sitting on a torn tarpaulin in a deserted no man's land between two mutually hostile tribes in the west of Kenya?

For a while I raged at myself, but then, as I lay back to watch the constellations, which seemed only an arm's length away in the velvet night sky, my mind drifted back to a morning in Nairobi early in 1979.

1

Before me on the table lay cassettes of a speech which Sudan's President, Numayri, had broadcast in his characteristically turgid Arabic the previous night. Translating excerpts from it with the help of earphones, transcriber and the notes I had taken was going to be a piece of routine drudgery of the sort I had performed hundreds of times by then. Perhaps the coming days would become more interesting, as Kampala radio had announced the invasion of Uganda by the Tanzanian army. It would be exciting to capture the news of Amin's fall when it came, as it inevitably would.

But, for some reason, on that day, I could not concentrate. Instead of getting down to the convolutions of Numayri, I found myself looking around at the men working with me. I saw my fellow editors and monitors fading grey with boredom and pictured myself with them, scribbling the years away, scribbling and shrinking. There just had to be something else. But I was fifty, and if there was to be such a something it would have to be soon.

By midday I was in a spiral of black despair and had been through a severe inquisition. Most of the questions I had asked myself had been about Kenya, which had been my home for the best part of a decade, yet so much remained a mystery. Living in a cocoon of luxury, I had learned next to nothing of the harsh realities outside that cushioned niche of mine behind the shield of the BBC. It was then that the idea of a journey came to me – a slow journey with time to stop and stare for as long as my resources of time and money would permit.

Experience had already shown me that the motorist misses too much by flying past things at high speed; and when, in a country like Kenya, he stops, he is often regarded as an intruder from outer space or as a man with many possessions all more interesting than himself. If he wants to stay at a small countryside lodging or settle down under a tree, he becomes suspect. What does he want here when he can easily drive to the next town and find himself a hotel commensurate with his status? My journey would be by bicycle and on foot. That way I would be more likely to arouse sympathy than envy, less likely to meet with suspicion than with curiosity.

The search for a suitable route took longer than the journey itself. It became a kind of Holy Grail. The ideal route existed, but where? I spent evenings, beer-quenched and pensive over maps, index finger jabbing as I retraced in my mind the great trade routes of East Africa. I hungrily devoured every book I could lay my hands on.

One day deliverance came in the form of two obscure nineteenth-century ghosts, one Hungarian and the other Austrian. I found myself reading *The Discovery by Count Teleki of Lakes Rudolf and Stefanie,* written by the explorer's travelling companion and amanuensis, Ludwig von Hoehnel, and published in 1894. Not only had Teleki, the Hungarian, and von Hoehnel, the Austrian, cut across Kenya from end to end, but they had been the first Europeans to pass through Kikuyuland and penetrate the area north of Lake Baringo.

What particularly attracted my attention was that their journey had been made just one hundred years before I could expect to do it myself. In that century the peoples first encountered by them went through every trauma known to history – slavery, colonisation, myriad forms of economic exploitation and finally wars of liberation and the pangs of political independence. In the space of little more than a biblical life span, the illiterate spearmen of Teleki's day, who had never seen a wheel, had become today's computer programmers, teleprinter operators, pilots, mechanics, architects and doctors, as well as bank robbers, fraudsters and drug addicts. In less than a century they had learned to accept what had taken the West nearly twenty centuries to develop.

Nairobi, an uninhabited swamp at the turn of the century, is now a sizeable industrial city by African standards, but within twenty miles of it many Masai still live much as they did before it came into existence. Yet one of these same Masai will stow his spear, shield and blanket in a corner of his cow-dung hut and don a suit and cowboy hat for a trip to town.

It was clear to me that on the surface the people had taken up their modern role with much success, but how well had they adjusted psychologically? Were they still in a state of shock? To what extent had the mechanised era made itself felt in the countryside, the remoter parts?

As an idea the journey was very attractive, but how to find the time and money for it? I had no savings to speak of and only a month's leave in hand. No one in his right mind would sponsor a greenhorn traveller like me. The only way was to take early retirement. The lump sum that went with it would hopefully suffice both to support my wife, Jackie, during my absence and to meet my own expenses. That was what I decided to do. It was now or never. I put in my notice.

My friends said I was crazy. You will never get through, they said. You are deluded by the male menopause, said one. The thugs of Kikuyuland will pounce and strip you naked, another predicted. You will be eaten by lions in Masailand or die of thirst in the Loriyu Hills. You will be speared by the Hamar Kuke from Ethiopia and your testicles turned into necklace beads. I argued that I might be just as easily beaten to death by skinheads or run over by a bus in Oxford

Street. But what I did not confess to anyone at the time was my most real fear – that of losing my nerve at some stage and finding myself running home with my tail between my legs.

I retired from the BBC at the end of October 1981. No one but Jackie approved.

My Travelling Companion

Teleki and von Hoehnel started their journey by taking a dhow from Zanzibar to Pangani on the mainland of what is now northern Tanzania. A few days later, on 28 January 1887, armed to the teeth and accompanied by hundreds of locally recruited men, they were off along the old slave and ivory route into the interior.

Their journey could be broken into five distinct sections. The first was the march from Pangani to Mount Kilimanjaro and Meru. Next was the push from Taveta through Masailand to Ngong, a few miles west of the future site of Nairobi. They then fought their way through the land of the much-feared Wakikuyu, attempted Mount Kenya and reached Baringo.

Then came the most daunting part of all, the long and very arduous walk to the northern extremity of Lake Turkana and the southern shores of Lake Chew Bahir. An outbreak of smallpox pursued them back to the southern end of Turkana, from where they headed north-west to the Lodwar area before returning to Baringo. The final section was the return to Ngong and from there to Mombasa, which they reached on 24 October 1888 after covering in all between 3,500 and 4,000 miles.

To follow this route was not going to be easy. Cycling through Tanzania and Masailand would probably present few difficulties other than those germane to a hard slog. The trail through Kikuyuland led north-east across more than seventy streams and rivers, all flowing south-east. Food and water would be no problem, but that section would have to be walked. And security – or rather the lack of it – was something to be reckoned with. Ever since first arriving in Kenya I had been repeatedly warned about rampant crime in the area; the prospect of crossing it was tinged with real trepidation. As for the rough country north of Lake Baringo, I had been warned that it was likely to be even wilder than in Teleki's day, because instead of bows and arrows the local warriors now had automatic rifles. It was also very sparsely populated, and the availability of food was unpredictable. Again it would have to be walked, but hopefully I would be able to buy donkeys at Baringo to carry my supplies.

On the last lap to Mombasa I would be able to revert to the bicycle.

After spending a month in London to put my affairs in order, I returned to Nairobi on 16 December 1981. I brought what I thought would be essential: a copy of von Hoehnel's book, an American army water bottle, a Swiss penknife, maps, a compass, a sleeping bag, a pocket radio and a bicycle generously supplied by Raleigh, who also gave me a letter certifying they had lent it to me. Why I had felt it necessary to import a bicycle from England now escapes me, but on the plane I had rehearsed every possible question-and-answer sequence that Kenya's customs men might ask. However, I was unprepared for the opening line: 'Why does an old man need a bicycle?'

This was indeed a good question and one that I was to ask myself several times before I actually got on the saddle. Now I could only mutter, 'Special tour,' in reply.

The customs man scanned my document with one distracted eye. The other eye scanned the customs hall for more succulent prey. 'You will have to see our old man,' he said as his eyes fixed upon a heavy-paunched Asian businessman.

His 'old man' was grey haired and looked kindly. Cursorily he scanned the letter and waved me through. But what followed was like Kafka's *Castle* – over three months of cutting through the bureaucratic bush in pursuit of papers authorising me to cross the border with a vehicle; permits from the Tanzanian and Kenyan police; customs declarations; valuation certificates; insurance policies; export licences – the list is too long to be worth recording.

In Teleki's day paperwork was minimal. All that was needed was plenty of money and a well-stocked armoury. It was a state of affairs that suited Count Samuel Teleki von Szek very well. Born in Saromberke in southern Transylvania (now part of Romania) in 1845 into a famous family of Hungarian aristocrats, and as heir to extensive estates, he was a man of ample means. What motivated such a man to mount an expedition so fraught with hardship and peril? Von Hoehnel's explanation is that Teleki was 'imbued with a passion for research' and dominated by 'the fascination exercised by the unknown'. Perhaps he was, but there was also another reason, which von Hoehnel out of loyalty to his friend does not mention.

Teleki happened to be an intimate friend of the Austrian Crown Prince, Rudolf. He also shared Rudolf's political views, which at the time were regarded as dangerously liberal. Rudolf's conservative court disapproved of these ideas and suspected Teleki – a bachelor reputed to be a libertine as well as a liberal – of exerting an undesirable influence over his royal friend. In 1885 it came to light that Teleki had committed what has been described as 'a minor social indiscretion' with Rudolf's wife, the Princess Stefanie. Whatever the nature of this 'indiscretion' might have been, Rudolf – whose romantic inclinations were attracted by women other than Stefanie – condoned it. The court, however, did not, and banished Teleki from Austria until such time as the matter could be suitably forgotten.

Teleki, a passionate devotee of blood sports, decided to go to Africa on a hunting trip. Rudolf persuaded him to make it in the continent's last remaining unmapped tract and to add to the thrills of the chase the tasks of scientific exploration. But Rudolf knew his friend well enough to realise that if the scientific aspect of the expedition was to succeed, Teleki – whose eye was more familiar wih the rifle barrel than with the sextant – needed a suitably qualified travelling companion. The candidate Rudolf had in mind for the role was Ludwig von Hoehnel, a young lieutenant in the Austrian navy and a graduate of the Fiume naval academy. Rudolf and Stefanie knew him well and liked him very much.

Von Hoehnel records that early in 1886 he 'happened to be off the island of Lacroma on His Majesty's yacht "Greif", which had been placed at the disposal of Prince Rudolf'. Rudolf seized the opportunity to invite Teleki aboard and then persuaded him to accept von Hoehnel as travelling companion. Von Hoehnel's scientific and cartographical skills subsequently served to lend Teleki's expedition a significance it would otherwise have lacked.

I did not think I would need a travelling companion until I encountered a logistical problem which could only be solved by finding one. It was that to start I would first have to go to Tanzania, which I had never visited. Very little information on conditions there was available in Nairobi, because the border with Kenya had been closed for the past four years. The amount of time I would be able to spend in Tanzania was limited by a punitive exchange rate. Bicycle was therefore the obvious means of transport. But although I had kept fit by jogging two miles a day for ten years, I had no idea how I would stand up to long hauls of cycling. I knew no one in Tanzania I could turn to if I was hurt in an accident or fell sick. For these reasons I decided to take my Land-Rover as back-up. I would load it with essentials and send it ahead; if I failed to catch up with it at set points, it would turn back to look for me. For this, however, I needed a driver.

I met Desmond, as I shall call him, at a Nairobi dinner party. He was tall and dignified with silvery hair and humorous bright blue eyes. In conversation he revealed an impressive breadth of reading and experience. Here is a real old Africa hand, I thought. That same evening I confided in him about my proposed journey. He smiled when I said I intended calling it 'The Teleki Project'. Perhaps he found it a little pompous, but he listened carefully and, unlike so many others I had talked to, appeared genuinely interested.

I already knew that Desmond was, among other things, an author who had written much about East Africa. He told me about the financial problems he constantly faced and how in order to keep going he always needed to teach – even at the age of seventy. At the time he was working for a crammer. He said he was about to make a brief visit to England, after which he would return to teach again, hoping at the same time to gather material for yet another book.

In a moment of sympathy and daring, I said, 'I have an idea, Desmond. Have a rest from teaching. Why don't you be my back-up man in Tanzania? I could keep you going. You could just poodle through my route ahead of me.' To my surprise he was eager. I was delighted.

When Desmond returned from England, Jackie and I went to see him at Sam's Inn, a sleazy downtown hotel in the garden of which he was living in his uninsured, South African-registered camper. It was just getting dark. Sam's regulars were sitting round a table heavy with bottles. Their latest girlfriends lounged on the arms of chairs and ate fried eggs using greasy fingers. But Desmond was not with them.

We found him at a separate table a little back in semi-darkness. In front of him was a tray of tea. He was sipping gingerly from his cup and, when we greeted him, stared up with unexpected coldness. I was put out, but we pulled up chairs and asked about his trip. 'Tiring,' he said. 'Cities exhaust me.'

He seemed only then to realise who we were. He talked about interviews he had given, going to see his family, how London seemed so grey and the people dowdy. I offered him a beer, but he looked sad and shook his head. Then he told us that he had had a heart attack in London. He had been rushed to Middlesex Hospital and kept there a week. He said his memory was damaged and that he kept forgetting where he put things.

We realised then how ill he looked; fear had battered his confidence. We spent the rest of the evening desperately struggling to restore the morale of an ageing adventurer. I wanted to dispel any fear he may have had that I would no longer want him. By the time we had walked him back to his camper he was even making a few jokes against himself. On the way home I tried to lay aside the nagging image of turning up at some agreed place to find the Land-Rover with Desmond dead inside it.

Soon after that I invited him to dinner. He could spend the night in his camper near the house to save himself driving back in the dark. On the appointed day he rang me. 'Would you mind if I brought a person?' he mumbled down the phone.

The 'person' was Flora Muzito, a wide-eyed Muganda. She was aptly named; *muzito* in Swahili means 'heavy one', and it took two of us to ease her out of the camper. Desmond then told us, by way of introduction, that she had been his mistress for twenty years.

Flora had a nature that some might describe as bonny, and she liked her beer. We spent a pleasant evening discussing arrangements for the journey. Later Desmond dominated the conversation with travel stories which went back half a century – of Turkish valour, what Poland was like before the Second World War, climbing the Ruwenzori Mountains in Uganda and hunting with pygmies in the Bundibugyo Forest on the border with Zaire. Truly, I thought, I have found the right man. At ten he said he would leave us and go to bed. Flora made no move to go with him.

All through his monologue she had sat as still as an artist's model, moving only to lift her glass to her lips, saying nothing. But moments after his departure she burst out laughing. 'You going to Tanzania with Desmond? With Desmond!' She choked, and Jackie had to pat her back.

'Of course,' I said, suddenly rather nervous.

She leaned down to take another swig. 'You don't know Desmond,' she stated with authority. Then, easing herself into a more comfortable position, she began telling us about her life with him in Kampala.

Idi Amin's licensed thugs found him writing a book in which he had said things Amin objected to. He was arrested and locked up and came close to being executed. She, too, had then been arrested and beaten by the police, who had broken nearly every bone in her body. She was a spy, they said, who had supplied Desmond with information. Her house was looted by soldiers. In the end she had been rescued by her children and taken to Nairobi, where she had spent six months in hospital.

That had been eight years before. She had not seen Desmond again until they had met, quite by chance, a few days earlier. She drained the remains of her bottle and rubbed her shoulder. I noticed a bluish mark and that beneath the layers of flesh her body seemed somehow twisted. Offered another beer, she nodded and started laughing again.

The door flew open with a loud crash. A puce-faced Desmond,

9

wild-haired, his creased pyjama jacket open to the waist, lurched most alarmingly into the room. 'What the hell is this?' he shouted. 'Don't you people ever go to bed? What kind of a house is this? Don't you realise that I need my sleep?'

My God, I thought, he's like a Victorian grandfather. Flora had gone silent, but there was no surprise on her face. 'But, Desmond,' I said, 'we're only sitting talking. How can you expect us to tell Flora to leave?' He hardly listened. The outburst was subsiding. Grumbling, he marched out. Flora, helped by Jackie, regained her feet and waddled after him. For a moment they hovered by their little shell, both of them large and sick and growing old, having loved and damaged each other, possibly beyond repair.

It was as if a shadow had been laid across my path.

The shadow lengthened during the long sweaty drive south to Pangani a few months later. When we stopped for food at a wayside restaurant, Desmond refused to eat and muttered, 'Typhoid', in my ear.

Late that afternoon, by the Mandera bridge over the Wami River, I turned into what seemed an ideal camping site in the shade of well-spaced trees. Some European overlanders were already there, spreading out their things. 'I will not camp near those people,' a voice stated coldly. I halted the vehicle, turning in my seat in disbelief. Desmond was glaring with eyes like torches at the little group. 'They have dirty bottoms,' he said knowledgeably, 'and their women are always showing their knickers.'

'Don't look at them, then,' I replied, but he was adamant.

'If we are going to camp,' he declared, 'we shall do so in the bush, in the clean grass, not near the middens these people leave.'

I lit a cigarette and swallowed smoke instead of blowing my top.

Two miles on, Desmond directed me to turn into the bush and halt in a patch of knee-high grass and thorny acacia. He was suddenly happy. He climbed out and unfolded his threadbare camping chair. 'This is the place,' he said with euphoric finality. 'Marvellous. Just listen to those birds! Now smell the air.'

I could hear cattle lowing, and the grass stank of their urine.

Two Masai dressed in clean, ironed cloaks called *shukas* told us we were camping in their meadow, where we were most welcome to be, but would we sell them the bicycle? They were perfectly serious and, as members of one of the richest groups in Tanzania, certainly in a position to pay.

Desmond stood up and thrust out his jaw at them. 'What do you want here? Go away,' he told them in settler-Swahili.

Stony stares replaced their smiles as they turned on their heels.

At that instant my image of Desmond as an old Africa hand vanished, and a deep apprehension took its place. I should have taken him straight to Dar es Salaam airport and sent him back to Nairobi and would have done so but for the bond that had been forged that evening, months earlier, at Sam's Inn.

Teleki had come to Tanzania with von Hoehnel as expedition organiser, amanuensis and scientist. I had Desmond – a potential cardiac case and someone who would have to be repeatedly outwitted if I was to accomplish my main objective of meeting the African people along the route.

Pangani

Pangani was where the journey began. Not just for me, of course, but also for Teleki and von Hoehnel, and nothing epitomised the passing of a century more than our divergent attitudes to the place.

Von Hoehnel contemptuously dismissed it as 'a number of dark loam coloured huts among which are a few conspicuous looking stone houses'. This was a rather brusque dismissal considering that he was to see no town worthy of the name for the next two years. But compared with the magnificence of the Vienna of his day, Pangani must have seemed an unworthy gateway to the mysteries that lay ahead.

For me, at that moment of arrival a century later, Pangani was so perfect a blend of history and unspoiled charm that it turned all the attractions of cities suddenly sour. I thought of Nairobi where I had lived so long and happily and saw it for what I had always known it to be, but never admitted – a stop beside the railway line, an African Slough with palm trees. And I saw London as I had always thought of it – a city smothered by its own vastness, dirty and polluted. Small really is beautiful, I told myself and conveniently forgot that I lived within reach of a city for the same reasons that most of the world's population did. Instead I indulged in a dream of Arcadia – the colours were so bright, the sea not blue but turquoise, the sand as white as icing sugar, the tropical vegetation every shade and half-shade of green on a bewildering canvas of shapes and textures.

Feverishly I unpacked the bicycle and sped off like an undergraduate on his first ride to the university, von Hoehnel's book balanced on the handlebars to guide me to the places that greeted Teleki in Victoria's jubilee year of 1887. Round and round I went, taking in the smells as well as the sights. One corner of the town obviously contained a copra mill, for the air lay sweet and heavy with the familiar smell of the oil. In a dark alley, somewhere in one of the shuttered houses, someone was making halva with ghee and cardamom. That was a smell as old as Ibn Batuta, the fourteenth-century Arab traveller and writer. But every now and again Africa reasserted itself – as with the acrid smell of sweat as I passed a porter struggling under his load; and once I was stopped in my tracks when a sudden gust of wind enveloped me in a cloud of dust redolent of desiccated cow dung, a smell so evocative of Africa that it can halt you in an English country lane and drag the sun out of the clouds.

No part of Pangani lay more than five hundred yards from the waterfront, a line of stone houses still exactly as depicted in von Hoehnel's photograph. The largest with its twelve windows overlooking the estuary had been the customs house. Painted green now, it had become the local party headquarters. Next to it squatted the prison, where some porters who had deserted the explorers had been tied naked to a post and flogged by the Sultan's soldiers. The prison now served as the post office. Beyond it straggled the row of square Arab-style houses inhabited once by Pangani's slave-merchant bourgeoisie and now by their bureaucrat successors. The main street was lined on both sides by low rectangular houses, shops and bars, all time-worn and tawdry with decay. At the very end a tiny mud-and-wattle hut advertised itself as the 'Lala Salama Hotel' – the Sleep-Easy – but it was only a teahouse, and any sleeping there would have to be done by day.

Opposite gaped an abandoned ruin. The word 'UHURU' painted in large letters across its frontage had been rent asunder by a yawning crack. *Uhuru* is a Swahili word derived from the Arabic noun *hurr* – a free-born person. Frederick Johnson's 1939 *Standard Swahili–English Dictionary* defines *uhuru* as 'freedom from slavery'. After the Second World War the word evolved to embrace also the ideal of emancipation from foreign domination. *Uhuru* was born as a reality twenty years before I stood there in the dust that the British had shaken off their heels, but by now its message seemed more in keeping with the broken wall it was written on and the less than glorious history of the town than with the splendid ideal world of Nyerere's dreams.

In the torpor of a tropical afternoon, Pangani slumbered, heedless of time. There was no traffic. The inhabitants sleep-walked through the narrow streets just as they had done each day for a century either side of Teleki, cocooned by Islam in a rhythm of life as steady and predictable as the tides.

For almost a thousand years Omani Arabs had maintained toeholds such as Pangani on the fringe of Africa and sent out caravans groping like tentacles into the far interior, each one a work of adventure and exploration in its own right. I reflected that when Teleki arrived he had stepped into a midden of blood and greed into which the slavers and ivory traders had transformed the interior. Their practice was to arm the rulers and encourage them to capture those ruled by others, thus turning the whole of what is now mainland Tanzania into a battlefield.

Once this sombre recollection had crossed my mind, it became inevitable that the bicycle would roll me out of my Arcadian dream to show me another, sadder aspect of Pangani.

As I rode, I greeted people. Quite often I passed them a second time and greeted them again. Some of them probably thought I was mad, but others might have recognised the euphoria and manic energy of a traveller about to set out on a long journey; in this at least the townsmen had pedigree.

Suddenly the bicycle took me into a vast garden of feathery casuarina and flamboyant trees heavy with scarlet flowers. Beneath the canopy of branches lay a curiously unfinished-looking building, single storeyed at one end and double at the other, the two parts linked by a covered veranda. A sign over the entrance read 'Mawenzi Bar and Hotel'.

A light-skinned young woman dressed in slacks introduced herself as Halimah, the landlady. Her leopard walk and confident eye disclosed that she was boss, organiser and maker of rules. Yes, we could camp in the garden, and all facilities were at our disposal. Yes, she could have supper prepared for us provided we paid in advance for the ingredients. Desmond asked about security. Halimah looked surprised. It was not a problem, she said, but we could hire her watchman, Abdullah, a dour thin-lipped Makonde, for 30 shillings a night – the price of a bottle of beer.

Desmond was delighted, but would not seek out the bar with me. The camp could not be left with only the watchman in charge.

The little ground-floor bar was deserted but for Halimah and two men, who abruptly stopped talking as soon as they noticed my white man's face. One looked at his watch and hurriedly left. Halimah emerged from behind the counter and sat down beside me. 'This is Ali Ahmad,' she said.

'That's right, and the fellow who just left is the district commissioner's clerk. Seeing you made him fear I might ask him the sort of questions he wouldn't care to answer in front of you.'

'People in Kenya advised me to watch my tongue in Tanzania because of police informers,' I said, immediately wishing I hadn't; for all I knew, this Ali Ahmad might be one of them.

'Quite right, but we know who they are and when they turn up we just keep quiet until they go. So, how are things in the colony?' he asked with a wink.

'Colony? What about *uhuru*, what about Kenyatta?'

'What I mean,' Ali said brusquely, 'is that you people are still there. Kenyatta didn't throw you out, so everyone's still making money.

Here? Comrade Julius got rid of the Europeans and told us that showed we were getting real *uhuru*. Then everything fell to bits. The shops emptied, people were pushed around the countryside and forced to live away from home, and beer went up to 20, even 30 bob a bottle. Julius Nyerere kept telling us it was the price we had to pay for real *uhuru*. But truly, we would rather be like you people in Kenya. If you want to buy a shirt, you go to a shop and pay a reasonable price, but here – if you want anything you have to get it through *choromchoro*.'

Choromchoro, Halimah explained patiently, was the Tanzanian version of the *magendo* of Kenya and Uganda: smuggling, black-marketeering and racketeering. It was a term derived from the Swahili word *chora-chora*, which means scribbling or writing illegibly. *Choromchoro* was inevitably something I had to learn about during my very first conversation with a Tanzanian, because it was an aspect which affected them all.

'Before I started with the fish trade,' Ali went on, 'I used to do *choromchoro* full time. I'd go to Mombasa and buy clothes and sell them here at five times what I paid. Then they tightened up the border and I got scared.'

A lanky, bearded Arab came in. Halimah passed him a bottle. They leaned over to each other in a whispered conversation. Ali caught my eye and flared his nostrils. The Arab drained his beer in long gulps, then approached me, hand outstretched. 'I'm Muhammad Ahmad,' he announced, his ingratiating face wearing half a smile, 'head of the regional trading company here. If anyone tells you there are shortages, don't believe him. If you need anything – cigarettes, sugar, whisky – just come to me. Halimah knows where my office is, OK?'

'That's right,' sneered Ali as soon as the man was out of the door. 'He's got everything, just as he says. And probably if you went to him he'd sell you what you wanted. He'd give you a receipt too, showing a third of what you paid him. They all do it. Everyone knows, except of course Nyerere. His auditors just see the copy receipts, the accounts balance up and Julius thinks everybody's getting things at the proper price.

'The proper price is what people are prepared to pay for something they want, not a price fixed by the government,' he declared in a voice hot with capitalist fervour.

'But how do they get away with it?' I asked indignantly.

'It's like this. That Muhammad Ahmad, for example, is a popular man. When a shipload of, say, needles arrives from China, the government fellows sitting down there in Dar divide it up and Muhammad Ahmad gets his allocation. As soon as the goods arrive, he tells his friends. They go to his office very early in the morning and buy the lot at five times the fixed price. Then the people who have made orders are told that the company has already sold out to people who made orders before them. All they can do then is go to Muhammad's friends and pay ten times the proper price. That's the way it works.'

A couple of evenings later the Mawenzi was milling with visiting officials from Tanga, large bespectacled men with important-looking beards. The watchman, Abdullah, sidled up and whispered in my ear, 'Bwana, I've taken some beer to your camp. You can't drink it here, because those bigwigs have been told it's rationed and we don't want them to get angry.'

I went out and sat on a log behind the Land-Rover, out of sight. The light was slowly fading into photographic shades. Now, at the end of a blistering day, the air had become delightfully cool. A frail breeze had stolen up from the beach, trailing a balm of jasmine as it came. Then a lithe form pressed itself beside me and breathed upon my ear a warmer and more potent perfume. Soft, coffee-coloured fingers closed over mine like a benign trap.

A long silence held us motionless, hearing no sound other than the distant boom of the surf from a shot-silk sea. A full moon, rising as abruptly as the darkness had fallen, lit up our faces like a white parachute flare. In that witching garden it seemed as if the night was stealthily putting out tendrils, weaving around us a phosphorescent web of dream-like lassitude. For a while we sat quietly.

The first to break the silence was Halimah, but when she spoke she was no longer Halimah the manageress. Her voice came husky, toneless, so different from that other confident voice I had heard so often during the past few days. 'Here we can do nothing,' she wept. 'It is hopeless because no one is allowed to make an honest penny. I used to have a life once, a future too, but it ended three years ago. Now all there is left for me is this broken-down old place where we can't even make someone a meal unless he pays in advance.'

A hint of self-pity clinging to her words fell on my ear like a caution. Had she decided that I was potentially something more than a passing stranger? Was she casting me in the role of some sort of entrepreneur, a person more affluent than appearances suggested? Had there not been talk that same afternoon during a conversation with Ali Ahmad of what would be needed to make the Mawenzi attractive to tourists? Perhaps she saw in me a potential source of capital.

A patch of cloud reached out and switched off the moon, leaving us shrouded in darkness. She pressed my hand hard. Interpreting this as a command to ask about the way of life she had lost, I complied. What I

17

heard was in its way so typical that its veracity could hardly be doubted.

'It all began in 1975,' she said. 'That was when I was married to a Ugandan Anglican clergyman called Crispin. We went to Masaka, up there in south-western Uganda. It was the Amin time, but things were quiet and we lived reasonably well. I had two children, a boy and a girl. Then, in February of 1979, the Tanzanian army came. It was at night. The noise from their guns was very loud and the electricity had gone off. We were all sitting close together in the front room. I wanted to run away, but Crispin said it was no use, we were in the hands of God. Amin's soldiers were still moving around outside. Those were the ones we feared.

'From down the street we could hear glass breaking and wood being smashed. Suddenly there was a kick at the door. Crispin told me to take the children into the kitchen. Almost at once, then, I heard the door break and shooting from a machine-gun. I didn't wait. I rushed the children out of the back door and we hid in the reeds at the bottom of the garden.

'In the morning I found Crispin's body on the floor, naked. He had been shot many times. The house was empty except for a few broken things. By that time the Tanzanians were in the town and they helped me to get to Mazinde, where my mother lives. There was no work there, so I left the children with her and came here to help my sister, who is the real manageress.'

Halimah's arm crept possessively around my waist, anchoring me to herself. She knew I planned to leave next day and that once I had gone it was unlikely that we would ever meet again. 'Stay a little longer,' she whispered in a voice full of appeal now. 'Why are you in such a hurry?'

Anyone who has lived in Africa comes to realise sooner or later that sex is looked upon as little more than a handshake. The cart of a meeting of bodies is almost invariably put before the horse of a meeting of minds. I knew that, but caution was already groping in the crepuscular mist of beer where temptation hid alertly poised to strike. A tiny demon danced up like a firefly. 'Why not agree,' he seemed to whisper, 'why not just stay and while away a few more days on this delightful shore?'

Then, as I gazed out over the dark swell of the sea, a flicker of breeze caressed my face like a gentle reminder, and with it came, all but lost in the drifting perfumes of Pangani's flowers, a whiff of ether. Suddenly I could see myself standing at the beginning of the road ahead, but between me and it a shape reared up and raised a hand in an unmistakable gesture of dismissal. That spectre of failure had often

18

haunted me, but this time it galvanised my mind and restored its focus. The firefly demon flitted back into the shadows.

There could be no postponement, no delay, I told Halimah. But by way of a parting handshake, we spent the night in her room. The first thing I noticed there was a 90 kilo sack propped up in a corner. 'What's in that?' I asked her.

'Sugar,' she replied. 'I sell it *choromchoro*.'

Off and Away

The day of departure began with a brief pilgrimage to the shore of the great bay where the explorers had made their first landing. The beach lay deserted and serene under the rustling coconut palms.

Slowly in my mind I coaxed the scene into life. Boats laden to the gunwales began grinding their prows into the sand, and from them sprang a multitude of men. They splashed ashore in an uproar of shouting. Surging backwards and forwards then, they piled up the baggage brought by their masters – two and a half tons of camping gear and instruments, one and a half tons of ammunition, one and a half tons of preserves, soap, tobacco, sugar, tea and coffee, a quarter of a ton of alcoholic drinks, no less than ten tons of cloth, glass beads, iron wire, cowries and other trade goods, plus over three hundred rifles and hand guns. These were Teleki's supplies.

My impedimenta were less complex. My bicycle was ready. The saddle bag contained a water bottle, toolkit and puncture-repair outfit, map, compass, penknife and an orange.

Teleki followed the old slave route between the Ruvu River and the Usambara Mountains. He passed through the gap between the South and North Pare Mountains and, after walking the length of Lake Jipe, reached Taveta, the rear base for his attempts on Mount Meru and Mount Kilimanjaro. All that took him six months. To climb the mountains before the rains started and my money ran out I had six weeks.

Teleki's main problem was administering his rabble of over three hundred guides, guards, donkey drivers and porters. Disorderly conduct by the porters was understandably frequent, since each was expected to carry a 77 lb load on his head. In addition to several incidents of this kind, Teleki constantly had to be on his guard against pilfering by unfriendly or hungry tribesmen.

My main worry was Desmond. He had already left to stop somewhere on the way to Lewa. He would certainly drive well and protect our possessions to the point of fanaticism, but his uncompromising attitude and tendency to be gratuitously impolite made him a potential trouble-maker. Because he had been robbed over and over again in the past, he had come to regard every black face with grave suspicion.

Driving alone through Tanzania must have seemed to him like running a gauntlet of hands reaching for his pockets.

But now it was time to go, for 'mighty is ever the fascination exercised by the unknown', as von Hoehnel stoutly declares. My immediate destination was Mauia on the left bank of the Ruvu, where he and Teleki had made their first camp. I glided down a sandy track through groves of palm and pawpaw glistening green in the morning light. Carmine bee eaters swooped and gyrated like flying jewels through the dappled shade. 'Onward to Mauia,' I sang, pedalling gently; 'you cannot fail.'

Buoyancy came to an abrupt end when the track turned into a derelict road made of lumps of coral. It was hemmed in and made gloomy by a jungle of kapok trees. For several miles I had to walk. Then the road inexplicably dissolved into a dilemma of four paths all pointing in different directions. Forgetting to consult my compass, I chose one at random. A few minutes later I glimpsed the river through the trees, and it was on my right. I was on the way back to the starting point.

Leaving Pangani was proving harder than I had imagined. Was some devil or witch luring me into returning? In a moment of confusion I laid the bicycle down in the grass and took refuge under a mango tree. It was something Desmond had told me never to do. All mango trees, he maintained, are infested by a fly which cunningly drops its eggs on men. The larva burrows under the skin, forming an ulcerous cyst. Out of this it eventually pops in an explosion of pus. But the days of paying heed to Desmond's advice were already over.

A duiker darted off at my approach, but a covey of guinea fowl ignored my presence as they bustled towards the water, crowing stridently. They could not have been very thirsty, for all the way down they zigzagged or ran around in circles. Intermittently a couple would break off for a quick fight, or one would mount another for an instant of fulfilment. Guinea fowl are formidable. I have seen a covey easily outstrip a runner of Olympic standard pursuing them with a twelve-bore. When, as a last resort, they take to the air, they shoot up like tufted cannon balls in a low trajectory.

As I peeled my orange, the surrounding bushes were mysteriously and surreptitiously invaded by golden-breasted starlings. Soundlessly those lurking, shy birds of paradise flitted from branch to branch, burnished nuggets draped in mantles of royal blue, ever on the move. Their passing was a moment of pure ecstasy. Never before had I succeeded in getting close enough to see the whites of their eyes — literally, for their eyes are as white as diamonds.

It felt good to be so far away from the incessant jarring noises of the man-made world. This was a place to spend a month in, I thought, wishing I did not have to go on. The unique privilege of that brief sojourn became truly clear to me only when I counted up the hours I had spent commuting in the London underground, my feet in the fag-ends.

Then ecstasy was put to flight by consternation. I could not find the bicycle. It was like forgetting the name of the street after parking the car, with no police to help you look for it. The great journey, hardly even begun, was turning into a shambles. In a rage bordering on hysteria, I thrashed through the elephant grass for half an hour. By the end of it I could not even recall which of the many mango trees it was that I had rested under. Where was the blasted machine? Had it been charmed away by evil spirits? *This is the sort of thing that happens to inexperienced fools blundering thoughtlessly into the bush.* I could visualise Desmond saying the words. That was something I could not face. But what to do?

'First, pull yourself together,' I said out loud. *Face away from the river and walk in a straight line until you find the path. Mark the spot and walk a hundred paces in each direction.* I did not find the bicycle. A trick of light did it for me by providing a quick flash of handlebar. But for that it might still be lying there.

The second track led into a wide plain of black volcanic soil covered with yellowish grass. Here the morass of last year's rains had cracked into a vast network of fissures. The ride was a veritable buttock-basher, but at last I reached the edge of the Ruvu valley again, and it was on my left.

Tyres crunching the sand, continually braking, I came to a baobab. Old, bloated and lonely, it sat on a mound, its stubby branches festooned with sticky-petalled flowers. The explorers had camped at Mauia under just such a tree and on such a mound, but was this really Mauia? A young man appeared from nowhere and confirmed that it was. Asked if he had heard about some Europeans who had camped here long before, he looked at me in pity. 'I don't know anything about them,' he said, indulgently adding, 'but would you like to meet some Arabs?'

At the gate of a compound of solidly built houses stood four men and a youth, all wearing white skullcaps and patterned sarongs – the standard dress of South Arabia, where I had lived for more than ten years. A tide of *déjà vu* engulfed me. I felt suddenly as lost in time as I was in place.

Their leader, tall and black-bearded, whose steady grey eyes and long nose brought Egypt's long-gone Nasser to mind, was Shaykh Ahmad bin Haydar. He took my hand, showed me into an open-sided shelter overlooking the river and invited me to rest on a circular reed mat. A kettle of cold water came.

After five glassfuls, I made to go. Shaykh Ahmad's hand pressed my shoulder. 'You came as a stranger,' he stated gravely, 'but now you are an honoured guest, whom we cannot release until all his needs are satisfied.'

How odd, I thought, that after bumping for hours through the bush, expecting at best a drink of river water, I had chanced upon this island of hospitality. Etiquette required me to go through the motions of refusing the invitation. In observance of the same rules, he insisted on acceptance. 'We cherish your presence in our house,' he declared. 'What is the matter with you? Haste belongs only to the devil. Will you not spare the time to talk with us? By God you shall not leave until we have eaten.'

Shaykh Ahmad said he considered himself a Tanzanian, although his ancestors were from Rustaq in Oman. For him Oman was a foreign land, which he had never seen and had no plans to visit. His Arabic was fluent and correct, but his companions knew only a few words and spoke in Swahili.

He owned a coconut estate, which had mercifully escaped the interest of the government. 'Instead they throttle me slowly,' he complained. 'Lack of spares prevents me from shipping my copra to Pangani. Having to use a lorry now, I lose money.'

The youth laid before us two large trays of goat curry and rice, saucers of chopped onions steeped in lemon juice and baskets full of bananas and pawpaw. They soon noticed I was out of practice eating with my hand and gave me a teaspoon. The meal was the best I ever ate in Tanzania.

At the end of it I apologised for being 'a heavy guest'. Literally this term indicates irksomeness. I explained that under present circumstances it means that having arrived hungry and empty handed I was now leaving with a full stomach. Shaykh Ahmad translated the pun, and I sped off, pursued by laughter.

Released from the Arab embrace and having reached the lip of the valley, I found myself pedalling straight into the maw of an African fire. Hiding under a bank of thick smoke, it was eating its way over the tree-dotted plain ahead, diagonally towards the path. Blackened shreds of leaves and bark began hitting my face. The wind that carried them was hotter than the sun on my back. Hardly twenty yards away now, tongues of flame snaked up the silver trunk of a towering kapok and detonated its canopy. Branches snapped like gunshots and crashed into the grass. The edge of the path was alight, and I had to pedal frantically. Seconds later the fire swallowed everything behind me.

Late in the afternoon, after a hard ride over miles of ridges and gulleys, I found Desmond under a wide-branched tamarind in full orange blossom. 'Hello,' he said, smiling. 'So it's worked. You've found me and see what a splendid campsite we've got. Have a cup of tea; I've just made some.'

It seemed too good to be true.

But first a bath. This was done standing naked on a car mat pouring water over the body from the small bowl which also served as cup and component of the puncture outfit. No sooner was I poised to start than several score of bees descended from the tree. These were the bees of Africa, the most dreaded of all the beasts of the bush. As I knew only too well, if panicked into making a suicidal mass attack, African bees will try to sting their victim to death. He has no defence unless he can submerge himself in water, of which there was none but the pathetic bowlful in my hand. There was no escape, and I was terrified.

They were buzzing round my ears, burrowing into my hair, dancing on my eyebrows, scrabbling around my nostrils, even digging into my armpits and the fold between my buttocks. Had they decided to swarm on me? Then more would arrive and carpet me from head to foot. I stood absolutely still, praying for steadfastness while every nerve shrieked for relief from the titillations of tiny clutching feet.

Steeling myself against the sudden blazing pain of the first barbed hypodermic, I recalled that it was in this vicinity that Teleki's men were routed by bees. 'Bearers and loads lay about the ground in hopeless confusion,' writes von Hoehnel, 'the men quite motionless, with faces buried in the grass, while here and there a donkey, trembling convulsively in every limb and panting for breath, stamped about, every now and again kicking out wildly.' The heads and faces of the men 'were so fearfully swollen that their eyes could scarcely be seen at all'.

But ten long minutes later I was still unscathed. Gradually I realised that it was not only feet that I could feel, but tongues. The bees were lapping me like a host of minuscule puppies. They were drinking my sweat. At exactly five p.m., as if in response to a signal, they all flew away.

Exultation replaced fear. I had lost my bicycle and my way, but found them again. I had won the race with the bush fire. The descendants of Teleki's bees had not stung, but quenched their thirst. Unlike Teleki, I had travelled light, but had come to the end of the day safely. I had defeated the witch, and now only sleep remained. That night a hyena whooped faintly in the distance and lulled me into oblivion on a patch of soft sand.

The Church Teleki Missed

Desmond's voice ordering visitors out of camp heralded the morning. Intervention was pointless. The main thing was to get away before our would-be guests returned with reinforcements, demanding to know why we were trespassing. I quickly struck camp. Desmond drove off eagerly to Muheza. His 1968 *Official Touring Guide to East Africa* promised 'à la carte meals' at a hotel called Chez Zoe. As soon as his dust trail had settled, I discovered I had forgotten to fill the water bottle. What if I had a puncture? Use dust, I supposed, or walk.

At Lewa, on 6 February 1887, Teleki's porters celebrated their escape from the bees with an orgy of drunkenness and desertion, forcing von Hoehnel back to Pangani to recruit replacements. I celebrated mine with a drink of water at its only shop, one of a handful of poor huts sprinkled on an ocean of blue-green sisal, which engulfed every horizon.

Lewa means 'to get drunk'. Why such a curious name? 'I have no idea,' said the shopkeeper. 'Perhaps the first man ever to settle here was a drunkard.' She had never heard of Teleki, and I found no one else who had until I got to Marangu on the slopes of Kilimanjaro.

Beyond the sad monotony of the sisal estate, I rode into mixed bush dominated by white-trunked borassus palms up to eighty feet tall. There was no sound other than the scraping clash of their fronds in the wind and the high-pitched hiss of the cicadas. The track remained empty of people and the sun relentless until the bush gave way to a closely cultivated area, where breadfruit, domestic kapok, citrus and pawpaw trees grew in profusion among the coconut palms. Dwellings appeared on both sides of the road and beyond, mostly mud huts neatly thatched with coconut frond. In well-swept yards, women and girls sang softly as they rhythmically pounded grain in stone mortars or sat quietly braiding one another's hair. Legions of chickens flurried away, the cocks a beautiful shiny black or, like bantams, rust red, dark green and brilliant orange. Here, as in Pangani, time seemed to have stood still since Teleki marched through.

This was the Bondei village of Mkuzi, past which I had driven on my way down to Pangani. What had intrigued me then had been tins nailed to palms about six feet off the ground. They were for tapping palm toddy, Desmond had pronounced. But what were they really for? A group of schoolboys did not know, but from behind them emerged a middle-aged man, who said, 'They are part of a West German aid organisation's experimental campaign against an insect pest. The tins are filled with various substances to determine which will attract the greatest number of pests. But most people don't understand what they're for and even take them down and use them as urinals.'

It was the first time in Tanzania that I had been addressed in faultless English. Luke Bukhayti's name suggested he was a Christian with a Muslim father. Wasn't this very unusual? 'Not at all,' he said. 'There are many people with names like mine. You see, in the old days there was a lot of prejudice against Muslims and the only way a young man could hope for a good education and a job was to turn Christian. That was what my father advised me to do. By the way, did you see our church when you rode in? It was built by Anglican missionaries in 1884.'

If that was so, von Hoehnel must have walked right past it, yet he makes no mention of a church. What is certain is that he was more interested in killing wild animals than in talking with missionaries.

People kept greeting Luke with the word *shikamoo*, which was new to me. It was the standard salutation, he explained, a contraction of *shika moyo yangu*, meaning 'Take hold of my heart'. This was an affirmation of vassalage the Sultans of Zanzibar used to expect from their subjects and slaves. The conventional reply was the Arabic *marhaba*, a gracious condescension equating to 'Certainly, if it pleases you'.

'Strange to hear such frankly feudal notions being exchanged by citizens of what professes to be Africa's most democratic state,' I remarked.

'You can change the things of olden times quite easily,' Luke replied. 'You can abolish old laws or replace old buildings with new ones. Getting rid of old words is much more difficult. Nyerere told us we must address each other as *ndugu*, or comrade. How many people have done that to you?'

'No one so far. They've all addressed me as *bwana*, just as they do in Kenya.'

If the notion of *shikamoo* was strange, St Peter's Church was even more so. Immutably compact and built throughout of reddish stone, it might have been lifted bodily out of a nineteenth-century English village and set down here amid the palm trees: Gothic arches supported the roof; bats nested on top of the pillars; plain glass windows. The heavy teak doors were decorated with large Zanzibari-style brass studs. Coloured prints depicting the life of Christ lined the walls of the interior. Duncan Bajzi, the young priest in charge, pulled a white cloth off an altar fashioned of polished wooden panels, each bearing the delicately carved motif of a grapevine entwining a fleur-de-lis.

The bell hung from an iron bar supported by the fork of a tree. About two feet in diameter at its base, the bell was inscribed 'Charterhouse, J. Warner & Sons, London, 1882'.

Duncan proudly showed me registers going back to 1912. In a 'Diary of Church Events', the Reverend Stuart Watts had written on 19 June 1930: 'Today I cancelled the annual dance with the agreement of the headmen and elders due to drunkenness and worse last year.' Another tome turned out to be a record of confessions. Having always believed that a penitent could rely on his sins going no further than the priest, I was surprised to read in black and white that 'John K came to me and admitted sinning with Catherine M for the second time'. Duncan said this record had lapsed after the departure of the last of the English missionaries.

An atmosphere of dusty weariness hung over the church. It was a relic of those men and women who had laboured here to instil a set of values as alien as the church itself. Yet their parishioners had preserved as best they could every material thing left behind. Nothing had been vandalised, nothing taken away. Even the Victorian range lay in its kitchen, no longer in use, because the mission house had become uninhabitable. 'The church is too poor now to maintain it,' Duncan said apologetically.

Luke lived in a house of unfired brick under a sheet-iron roof. The concrete floor of the living room was bare, and the walls were unplastered. Time-yellowed photographs of his life's ceremonial occasions hung in passe-partout frames from nails under a colonial-style topi. 'That,' sighed Luke, 'is the last symbol of those days that are now dead – those other days when I used to walk proudly into my station, wearing a starched uniform with shining brass buttons, polished belt and shoes, and that stupid thing on my head.'

He had spent a lifetime working for the railways, and his last post had been as station-master at Moshi. Now he lived on his pension and three acres of citrus trees.

His son brought in a bulky parcel which smelt strongly of DDT. 'This has a story,' Luke said. 'One night a few weeks ago I heard the chickens squawking as if they were about to have their throats cut. I got a torch and a *panga*. A python had got in through the window of the hutch and was concentrating on swallowing a bird. I burst in and, with a single blow, chopped off the snake's head. I leaped out and slammed the door. A second's silence was followed by one almighty crash. Then crash, crash, crash until I began to fear the whole structure was going to collapse. The monster was catapulting itself to the roof like a hippo-hide whip come to life. It went on lashing the whole night. In the morning we found it lying limp on the floor, but still quivering.'

We undid the parcel and measured the skin. It was fifteen feet long. Luke wanted me to take it with me as a souvenir. I managed to decline it, but was not allowed to leave before I had drunk to the last drop the juice of two coconuts fresh off the tree. Anyone who has not drunk from green coconuts is deprived. It tastes like non-alcoholic gin and is the finest of all thirst-quenchers. The flavour of it stayed in my mouth all the way to Muheza.

Muheza is an ancient place in African terms. In his *Travels and Missionary Labours in East Africa*, the famous German evangelical explorer J. Lewis Krapf described it in 1849 as a village being built on a hill by Kimweri, the king of the Usambara country. Kimweri's reign is regarded by historians as the apogee of Bantu civilisation in Tanganyika, but by the time Teleki arrived unruly descendants had already dismembered the kingdom.

What I rode into was a sprawling slum that looked as if it had not seen a paintbrush since the German railway reached it in 1895. A scattering of brown residential houses with rusty roofs sagged tiredly around a bus terminal, a couple of petrol stations and a colonial-style produce market. A few shops stocked nothing of much use to anyone.

Chez Zoe, now called the Athenaeum, perched on Kimweri's hill. 'A la carte' was a thing of the past, as were the bedrooms, which now served as repositories for piles of broken furniture. Desmond was on the patio under a massive wild fig tree overgrown by cascades of mauve and orange bougainvillaea. He was morose, wishing he was elsewhere. Yet what a pleasant place this must have been in the days of Zoe, when red-necked planters sat around the oval bar, while their wives knitted on the patio, chatting about children, motor cars and servants. Such is the price of democracy.

The only other European there that evening was a large, pink-faced man with long white hair and powerful arms. We speculated on his identity. Desmond was sure he must be a priest or missionary, because his face was expressive of kindness and patience. I judged him by his hands and guessed he was the mechanical superintendent of a sisal estate.

We were both wrong. He was a miner, a Dane named Hansen, who had lived in Tanzania for the past thirteen years. His interest lay not in precious stones and metals, but in minerals easily found and disposed of. He was working on a deposit of silica, loading it into lorries to take to the railway station, thence to be consigned to Dar es Salaam.

'In my opinion this country is ruined,' Hansen said grimly. 'It is riddled with crime and corruption, and the people are resentful of *ujamaa* socialism and hate the government. All the storage facilities the government has built for agricultural produce have been a waste of money. The officials steal whatever is brought there. Now the people have become unwilling to sell their produce to the government, because half the time they don't get paid.'

Desmond told him about my carelessness and how I would drink from streams and rivers. Hansen shook his head disapprovingly. 'That is very bad. There is bilharzia almost everywhere in Tanzania. I never drink any water unless it has been boiled for at least ten minutes.'

I changed the subject and asked him about my proposed route around the North Pare Mountains. Hansen frowned. 'I would not do that if I were you,' he said. 'I have been in that area several times. It is rather uninteresting agricultural land and the security is not of the best. As it is very near Lake Jipe and the Kenyan border, the area is infested with smugglers and criminals. It is much better for you to be sure of keeping out of trouble by just going straight up the main road to Marangu.'

I said my mind was already made up.

'Well, I think you're being very foolish,' Desmond put in tartly. 'It's high time you learned to listen to the advice of experienced Europeans. The day will come when you will remember what I said tonight.'

When confronted by two convinced pessimists attacking in tandem, there is only one course of action for a traveller, and that is to retire from the fray. I went to bed early and writhed the whole night long in the grip of Luke's python and Hansen's gloomy warnings.

The Taste of *Hamna*

East Africa's most common tree is the acacia. It thrives at all altitudes between sea level and about 8,000 feet. Growing in various permutations, its forty-plus species range from small shrubs, climbers and bushes to trees up to 70 feet high. At least ten species are of the 'umbrella' variety, 'apparently placed here by beneficent Nature as a shelter to the traveller from the intense heat and glare of the sun', as von Hoehnel says.

A characteristic shared by all acacia indigenous to East Africa is horridness. Their thorns, spines and prickles can be up to three inches long. These defensive weapons are shaped, according to species, like pikes, rapiers, sabres, daggers or fish hooks, but all are pointed.

Worst of all is the wait-a-bit. A shrub of up to twenty feet in height, it presents a soft, almost velvety appearance, but behind those small, bright green leaves hide countless tiny, razor-sharp barbs. To stray into their clutches inevitably results in torn clothes and deep, very painful scratches.

The second characteristic which this acacia shares with all others is being the cyclist's worst enemy.

The first time I mounted my bicycle in Tanzania I did not even make it to the gate at the end of the driveway. The machine itself was sound and gave little trouble, but the tyres supplied with it were meant only for tarmac. Luckily I was able to buy a pair of Chinese covers, but, as I was to discover, even these were not tough enough for the job.

The road out of Muheza was good, although mostly uphill. Sweat was soon streaming down my legs. All around, under an overcast sky, sisal draped the undulating land. Its dullness was relieved only by the trunks of kapok standing like chalk strokes stippled on an olive screen. Ahead the Usambara range juddered in a blue haze.

Mruwazi was a half-ruined village of rain-scarred huts at the foot of a devastated spur of Mount Tongwe. Refugees from the sun – men and women alike all naked to the waist – lay comatose in every bit of shade. Mruwazi had been Teleki's first stop after Lewa. He went on along what is now the main road to Korogwe, where he was delayed by a fracas caused by 'the carrying off by a Paris belonging to our camp of a black Helen from the village'. A serious gun battle ensued in which Teleki had to intervene 'not without great risk to his own life' and not before nine men had been killed and many more wounded.

Von Hoehnel followed him along the left bank of the Ruvu River until they met up again at Same. I decided to follow Teleki through Korogwe as far as Mombo. Then I would turn west to Mkarama and follow von Hoehnel to Same. Mkarama had been the capital of the Zigua tribe. It was not on the map, but there was a Mkalamo, which I supposed to be an alternative version of the same name.

The road degenerated into a series of raggedly parallel ridges of tarmac dodging around deep gashes and potholes more suited to trench warfare than to traffic. My balancing efforts to ride these ridges were repeatedly frustrated by drivers who, instead of keeping to the left, concentrated exclusively on the least ravaged patches of the road.

An oncoming bus suddenly charged me like a furious rhino. It gave me a split second to fling myself and the bicycle off the road. I snatched a glimpse of the driver. He was grinning like a demented ape, and I felt sure his expression would not have altered if he had squashed me flat. A toothless old bystander tottered over, asking if I needed help. Before I could reply, a car missed us by inches. 'Maniacs!' the old man shouted, shaking his fist. 'We suffer in this sun, but what do they care, those rich people? They just rush past as if we didn't exist. And all they ever give us is their dust.'

Was this, too, part of the necessary price of democracy?

After that I took care to get on the verge every time I saw or even heard a vehicle. Fortunately – for me at least – the traffic was light. The chronic shortage of spares made sure of that.

A passer-by at an unsignposted junction told me Mkalamo was fifty kilometres away. The left-hand fork would soon bring me to the Ruvu. Thirsty, as usual, I turned left.

The track broadened into a red laterite dirt road through ragged savannah cringing under the bitter whip of the dry season's tail end. The sun was burning holes in my head, but I became hypnotised by the straightness of the road and could not stop. The river became more compelling with every stroke of the pedal.

Cattle stopped me dead in my tracks. I lit a cigarette and gave one to the herdsman. He was a Mgogo from Dodoma, far to the west beyond the Masai Steppe. 'I just look after government property,' he told me dourly. 'I have to get up at dawn, graze the cattle all day, take them to the river and then it's back to the ranch. All I get is 480 shillings a month – hardly enough to buy my maize meal. What kind of a life is that with nothing to enjoy?'

How different he was from the Mpare goatherd of a few days before. 'They are all mine,' he had said proudly, thrusting out his stick over the sleek backs of his bell-tinkling herd. His shirt and trousers were without a tear, and he was shod in stout sandals made of motor tyre covers. Slung over his shoulder were a gut-strung bow and a leather quiver full of poisoned arrows for killing buck. 'Here,' he said, seizing a kid. 'Why don't you take it for your supper? I'll let it go cheap.'

That had been a man of property, a man full of incentive. There was in him none of the Mgogo's dejection. He strode off whistling, confident in the possession of an essential adjunct to happiness – freedom to dispose of his property.

I pressed on. The laterite became black cotton soil. A cyclist sweats as much to cover four miles of tarmac as he does to cover two miles of laterite or one mile of black cotton. I reached the river reeling with heat exhaustion. There was no village, nothing, just a signpost at the far end of a wooden bridge pointing to places the map did not show. A cattle track leading upstream ended in an impenetrable wall of wait-a-bit thorn.

The silty-brown river swirled powerfully past banks of reeds bright with fireball lilies. The urgency of thirst made Hansen's gloomy warning redundant. I filled the bottle until it bulged, and drank like a camel in the Empty Quarter after a four-day march. An overwhelming lassitude sent me collapsing into the grass, only to remember Hansen's other warning – that the river was full of crocodiles slavering for sleeping men. I made another bed further inland between the exposed roots of a tree and passed out. An hour later a loud snuffling jolted me awake. Shock jerked up my head and butted my nose into the wet muzzle of a cow.

That put paid to my search for von Hoehnel's route. Thwarted and depressed, I turned back.

Sustenance came in what I can do no better than describe as a tea hovel. Mud walls rain-pitted, its thatch had slipped over the entrance like a hippie girl's fringe. Around a table in the semi-darkness inside, eight bright-eyed boys intently watched a ninth trying to mend a radio. Bicycle pedals made of wooden blocks, grass serving as bicycle tubes, sisal-twine shoelaces, tyre-rubber door hinges, safety-pin buttons: all these I had seen, but a transistor repair kit of twigs, never.

One boy with a topper-like palm-frond hat on his head told me he wanted to go to secondary school, but had failed the entrance examination. The only remedy was a fee-paying mission school. To get the money for this he was growing maize and coconuts. But what was I doing? Nine pairs of eyes focused on mine as I explained I was following the route of the explorer Teleki.

When I put money down for my tea and doughnuts, they sternly ordered me to pick it up. Why? Because I was their guest. 'Go well,' they said, helping me on with my rucksack. 'Go well, go safely with God on your journey.'

They were all in rags, and there was not a pair of shoes between the lot of them. But as much as Tanzania was riddled with shortages, the boys proved to me once again that there was never a shortage of generosity.

As I lifted my leg over the crossbar, a miraculous voice floated out of the hovel. 'Here is the news from Radio Tanzania, Dar es Salaam.'

In Mombo there was a lodging house called Kagera after the invasion by Idi Amin's army of the Kagera River basin at the end of 1978. A mural covering a wall of the lobby recorded the event. It showed the Ugandans, having shot down Tanzanian women and children, being counter-attacked and mown into pools of blood. This event was very well remembered in Tanzania. It led to the Tanzanian invasion of Uganda in 1979 which overthrew Amin. But the invasion was regarded by several people I discussed it with during my journey as having been a catastrophe for both countries. Typical was the view of a soldier on leave who helped me repair a puncture. 'Imagine the dollars the government must have spent sending all those chaps up there, all the food they ate, all the uniforms they wore out, all the petrol and oil the lorries burned up, all the shells and bullets they fired. Where did the money come from? Us, of course, the ordinary people. But did they ask our permission? Did they ask us if the invasion was a sensible thing to do? Of course not. They never ask us about anything, even if it's strictly our business and none of theirs. So we are having to pay for what the government did by doing without so many of the things we need. That's the way things are done here. The big fellows just get together in Dar es Salaam and decide what is to be done. The rest of us just do what we're told. And where did the whole thing get the Ugandans? Nowhere. They got Obote back and everyone knows he's even worse than Amin. They're in a mess, we're in a mess and who's to blame? Well, you know that just as well as I do.'

In the Kagera resthouse, I wheeled the bicycle into a room containing a truckle bed with clean sheets, a chair and a small table. There was a single red bulb to deter mosquitoes. Its light revealed that my only pair of trousers had split at the crotch. The girl at the desk had a needle, but only nine inches of thread.

At a *duka la jumla,* a government wholesaler's I mistook to be a general shop, a woman behind the counter said the word '*hamna*' with heavy emphasis. That meant, 'There isn't any.' As if to ensure that I had understood it, a shirtless man loomed up from behind her, holding a Kalashnikov assault rifle at the port. I fled.

A small shop nearby offered cough medicine, skin tonic, tomato ketchup, rice and toilet paper, of which I bought a roll. 'There is not a single needle or reel of cotton to be had in this town and probably nowhere else in Tanzania either,' I was informed. 'There are no clothes to buy that the poor can afford and, even if there were, there is nothing to mend them with when they wear out.'

Back in Korogwe I had been warned to watch out for *majonzi*, mountebanks who rob people in the streets at night. That evening found me chatting with a half-caste (German father, Tanzanian mother), and I brought up the subject. 'Just look around this bar,' he said. 'They all look like *majonzi*, don't they, every one of them. Torn shirts, no buttons, sleeves through at the elbow, arses sticking out of their trousers, shoes falling to pieces. But this is Tanzania. If you're smart here, you're either a thug or a government official.'

I cobbled up the trousers with the girl's bit of thread and rewarded her with half my cake of toilet soap. She held it to her nose and cradled it in her hands. 'God,' she exclaimed. 'Do you know, I haven't held a thing like this in my hands for over four years!'

That night she washed and ironed all my clothes and refused to accept a tip I offered in the morning.

The day began with a long, steep hill, on which I passed a stream of women, each carrying a pail of water on her head. Every pail was full to the brim, but not once did I see a drop fall. I was astonished: where did they get the strength from, they all looked so small and frail? Had I to carry one of those pails thus, I would – like the majority of my own race – have been stopping every few paces to catch my breath, and most of the water would have been on the road before I reached the top of the hill. The sight of women like these striding out, laughing and calling out to one another as if oblivious of their loads, was one I witnessed in one form or another almost daily throughout my journey, but my admiration for their grace and poise never flagged.

The Usambara range, now gradually sloping away to the north, looked high and cool, its stately gazelle-dun buttresses jutting out as though through rents in a vast curtain of gold, blue, orange and green velvet thrown loosely over its mass. The hazy summits beckoned with the hope that one day I would be able to explore those faraway fastnesses and the deep, rain-soaked valleys tucked between them. As for now, my tyres were drumming the hard black road. No more coconut palms here, but many fig and acacia trees, and brown fields sprouting bushy mango trees looking like giant tea cosies balanced on sticks. More tough uphill gradients past villages of square houses, walls of ochre laterite or brick, and all with sleek grass roofs – Kimunyu, Kwenangu, Msufuni, Goha and Kibaoni – all the villages of Mkumbara district, which von Hoehnel called Kumbaja. Two busty girls sitting on bundles of firewood called out to me in English for a drink of water. 'Sorry,' I called back, 'but I need it for punctures.' I had no idea where next I would be able to fill my bottle.

'OK then, but can you give us some money?'

'And what will you give me?'

Peals of provocative laughter. One of the girls sprinted after me like an athlete, but was soon exhausted. I waved and pedalled on.

After Hedaru, the bush stretched endlessly ahead in dull green undulations. The acacia were stunted, the ground beneath them ripped by erosion. At last I reached a long descent through a devastation of derelict sisal to Same, which lay across the end of the broad valley between Mounts Umari and Kwizu. I could see its administrative headquarters on a low hill to the west of the town with the road passing between them. Desmond met me on the flower-bordered driveway of the Elephant Motel with the incredible news that the bar had cold beer. I had two immediately, and they tasted as delicious as the cold shower felt that followed.

From Same, Teleki and von Hoehnel skirted the western foothills of the South Pare Mountains, then crossed the saddle between them and the North Pares towards Lake Jipe, the shore of which they followed up to Taveta. But because Taveta was now in Kenya, I could follow the explorers only as far as the border, from which I would then have to turn westwards to Kifaru.

At Mgagau, a few miles north of Same, I was to turn right for Butu, the waiters at the motel had told me. As I was asking for directions from a throng of Masai on arrival at the village, a slight, narrow-shouldered man wearing a white skullcap wheeled up a bicycle old enough to have survived both world wars. 'I'm about to leave for Kwakoa,' he said quietly, 'and that's on the way to Butu. You can come with me if you like.'

Side by side we turned into the bush of the broad saddle. What began as a track soon became a sandy footpath overhung with branches so low that time and again we had to get off and push our bicycles. My new companion Msheri's bicycle had been welded at the bottom fork and at the crossbar joint. It had neither mudguards nor brakes; to slow down he had to press the sole of his sandal on the front tyre. A cotter pin was loose and we kept having to bang it back into place with a stone.

'There are still many elephants and rhinos on those slopes over there,' Msheri remarked, pointing in the direction of the South Pares. 'That's where they hide, and at night they go down to the marshes near Lake Jipe. Sometimes they even invade the villages.' There were signs of elephant damage everywhere, but their dried-up dung showed they had not been around for many weeks. Dead trees lay in the red dust; others, still standing, dangled withered arms fractured at the shoulders. The country was stark, ash dry, crackling in the glare.

Ahead a great clump of fig trees, some as high as 150 feet, promised refuge, but the mean brook beneath them proved to be full of tadpoles and slimy with sewage. My rear tyre was flat. I had set off without replacing it with one of the Chinese covers I had managed to buy in Pangani – a piece of laziness I was soon to rue. Msheri helped me mend two acacia thorn punctures, his rapid movements testimony of a lifetime's experience. Then he stripped to wash in the foul water. His body was as lean and angular as a locust's.

The trees disgorged us back into the furnace of the plain, but not for long. A gentle downward slope took us into groves of banana, pawpaw, fig, avocado, mango and wild kapok. We stopped outside a neat hut. A chair was brought for me, then an earthenware jug of cool water. Msheri's tiny fieldmouse mother came to greet me, then his wife with a baby girl, who stopped crying as soon as she was in her father's lap and began scrutinising him with wet-lashed eyes. 'She's been very sick with diarrhoea,' Msheri said, looking down with concern, 'but luckily we have a good missionary clinic here, so she's better now. By the way, if you're not in a hurry, why don't you stay to lunch?'

'I have come back to a water problem,' he said as we ate. 'Our village cistern has been cracked open by thirsty elephants. They are still rampaging in the fields and some of my neighbours have already lost the whole of their harvest. Why those beasts don't just go down to the lake is something I shall never understand.'

From Kwakoa I rode into some of the most beautiful country I have ever seen. The burly shoulder of Kindoroko was upthrust behind me, the barren northern extremity of the South Pares lay to my right and, straight ahead, a strip of tinsel in a cordon of papyrus, Lake Jipe. Beyond it, far away, the Taita Hills bulged out of Kenya's brown Serengeti Plain. The path bisected the plain between the base of Kindoroko and the lake. A dark forest of well-watered trees enfolded me. Many people ambled past. No haste here, none of the scurrying with the drawn face and tight lips of industrialised man. Around Butu lively streams cooled in mountain waterfalls gushed across the path. When I knelt to drink out of the whirling pools, men stopped to talk and offer breadfruit and bananas. I felt confident that when I came to spend the night under one of those great trees, my sleep would be undisturbed.

And so it was, until a spitting shower awoke me before dawn; but the rain was transient and I slept a little longer under the morning star bright in its heaven of Atlantic black. My destination that day was Kifaru, where Desmond was to meet me. The morning was cool. The shower had washed the leaves and I could smell the earth's breath. Msheri had told me it was about thirty kilometres to Kifaru, but he had never done the trip, so it might be half that or double. The state of my tyres worried me, and when I thought of them yesterday's carefree mood suddenly evaporated and Hansen's forebodings took its place.

Beyond Butu the forest ended. There were no more friendly villages. The freshly graded track proved impossible to ride on. Nothing now but typical *nyika* – acacia scrub – and mile after dreary mile of it. By noon the heat was astounding. As I crouched to rest in the diluted shade of a miswaki (toothbrush bush), two boys ran up to stare. Sweat had turned the dust on me to mud, and my face swarmed with flies I could not bother to brush away any more. Transparently taken aback by the sight of such a pitiful creature, they told me Kifaru was only twenty kilometres away. Shorten the traveller's journey if only in his imagination – that is a principle of African etiquette.

I stumbled on along the edge of the road, steering the bicycle along the narrow groove left by the grader between the murram and the verge. A root snatched my ankle and hurled me flat on my back with the bicycle lying on top of me. As I lay there, winded and bruised, a surge of self-pity told me to stay put until help came.

I had not toughened up yet, and defeat plucked at me. I began recalling the abortive ride to Mkalamo, which I had imagined would lead me to a beautiful and peaceful riverside village like Mauia. There would be tea houses serving hot curry and rice on breezy verandas. But all I had found was a signpost indicating nowhere. I had been barred from following the river by the wait-a-bit. Von Hoehnel had faced a similar barrier in the same area. But he had with him a sturdy porter, who 'with the cry "Follow me!" placed himself at the head of the caravan and calmly forced his way through the thorns, which tore his clothes to pieces'. I had not got through because I had lacked the guts to try. The same sense of bitter disappointment swept over me again. Would this be the time when I would run back like a whipped dog?

Questions began to surge through the fog of apathy in my mind.

What are you trying to prove? What are you doing here, dirty, hungry, thirsty, a fool out of place, floundering helpless and alone? My friends of the pin-stripe brigade seemed to be whispering: halfwit, told him so, laughable, pointless exercise, serves him right.

Derision came even from the birds calling over the flat hum of the sun-drowned afternoon. Perched on an umbrella acacia, a hornbill bobbed up and down, its curved beak raised high. 'Weg, weg, weg,' it piped in German, 'weg weg weg, weg weg weg.' A dove struck up an Irish-accented croon: 'Fock orf, fock orf, fock orf!' As it came to the end of its ditty, a chorus of mousebirds shrilled, 'See? See? See?'

I realised then that they were not deriding but advising. Yes, I did see. I had no food and water, and this was not a motorway patrolled by kindly men on motor cycles, but a place where I might rot a week before anyone came.

I staggered to my feet and continued barging down that purgatory of a road. Every means had been used to smash its passage through the bush. Huge aristolochia, those strange oval triffid-like plants von Hoehnel describes, had been torn bodily out of the ground. They lay on their sides like the bloated carcasses of cattle. Every few hundred yards fire had been used to gouge out the scrub, leaving gaping holes full of cinders and charred tree trunks.

Just when the sledgehammer of the sun had so crushed me that I felt almost too weak to drag one foot in front of the other, I reached the end of the grader's havoc. But no sooner was I in the saddle than both tyres went flat. Drunk with exhaustion, I lurched to the side of the road and fell into the dust. Everything was hazy now, as in a dream.

Suddenly I could feel hands touching me. I looked up to find myself surrounded by young men and girls. Well, if these were Hansen's thugs, they could have me. A girl handed me a glass of water. 'I am Mrutu,' said one of the boys. 'You will come to my house.'

Gently he led me to a three-roomed mud-and-thatch hut in a clean, unfenced compound. The bicycle stood against a wooden bed. Beside it, on the bare earth floor, lay my rucksack. The room must have been Mrutu's bridal chamber. The wall bore a mural of flowers painted in whitewash, captioned in Swahili 'No joy can equal the joy of love'.

Like all the Wapare I had seen, Mrutu's mother was diminutive and frail. Somehow girlishly dressed in the conventional bodice and sarong, she weakly took my hand and bade me welcome. Her manner was that of a distant aunt I had not met for years. I was in a home of homes where I had a perfect right to be. 'You'd better have some milk,' she said. 'You look as if you need it.'

It was a bowl of curds, the very thought of which was usually enough to send me retching. At that moment it tasted like honey, and with it energy returned.

Questions from all sides now. How did life in England compare with Tanzania. No shortages? How marvellous! But the cost of English food, housing and transport raised cries of disbelief and wonder. What, 400,000 shillings for an ordinary house! You people in England must all be millionaires living in a sort of paradise. Why, Mrutu's house only cost 10,000 and even if he'd used concrete it wouldn't have been more than double.

I remembered then that Paul Theroux in his book about travelling in England remarked that not once during his journey had anyone invited him to spend the night. He found that very curious. Yet here these poverty-stricken peasants had taken in a stranger as ragged as themselves and treated him like a prodigal son. As I have said before, there is no shortage of generosity in Tanzania.

Supper was a mound of maize porridge and a common bowl of thin stew with one small tilapia fish floating on the surface. Food was a serious business in Tanzania. We ate in silence, using fingers to break off small pieces of the maize and dipping it in the stew. Etiquette dictated that the fish be left for the next person, so we all watched it swim around on its side until, at the end of the meal, it was beached. Mrutu picked it up with thumb and finger and laid it in my hand. 'You are the guest,' he said gravely. 'So eat it.'

Dawn brought murmurings of adults, stirrings and moans of children, creaking doors and clattering pots. Mrutu stood outside, scouring his teeth with a twig. He had already mended my punctures.

After breakfast he saw me to the road.

As soon as his figure had faded out of sight, my front tyre hissed itself flat. I pushed for fifteen scorching miles, but at Kifaru there was no sign of Desmond. I remembered how Flora had laughed so much the night she heard Desmond was to be my travelling companion.

Standing there at the bus stop in my fetid shirt and filthy, sweat-soaked trousers, almost broke and my tyres in shreds, I nearly wept.

Marealle

Desmond's disappearance remained unsolved for several perplexing and problematical days. He had gone to the European-managed Marangu Hotel on the slopes of Kilimanjaro. There I found him, deep in an armchair, in the old-world veranda lounge, admiring a bougain-villaea-bedecked gazebo in a sunken garden. Around him hung photographs of the peaks and their conquerors.

One picture showed a plus-foured European in a broad-brimmed hat standing on the saddle between Kibo and its twin peak, Mawenzi, hand on hip, right foot firmly planted on a boulder. He was surrounded by Africans swaddled in blankets.

Desmond had forgotten our arrangement that he was to have set out to look for me if I failed to arrive in Kifaru as planned. He had spent a day in Kifaru beside the vehicle, birdwatching. Toothache had struck, and he had driven to Moshi in an abortive search for a dentist. That night he sat 'on guard' outside a Moshi hotel. Only mosquitoes and prostitutes had noticed him. 'No sleep and nothing to eat,' he said triumphantly.

'But why didn't you stay at the hotel?' I asked, astounded by his forgetfulness and what seemed to be sheer masochism.

'Can't risk that sort of place. Too many thieves.' His eyes were clear and blue; the great mane of grey hair nodded indulgently.

On the second day his toothache was gone, so he drove back to Kifaru. What he did not know was that one of Tanzania's biggest barracks is near Kifaru. After watching a European peering through binoculars for two days, the soldiers got suspicious and arrested him. He was taken to a police station and questioned for several hours. Not until after our documents had been thoroughly examined was he released. He then booked in at the Marangu Hotel and went to ground.

But there were other mysteries to unravel in Marangu. I hunted down several descendants of the characters von Hoehnel mentions in his book. Of these, the son of Marealle was by far the most interesting. Not only had his father befriended Teleki, but he also became involved with the notorious German adventurer, Carl Peters.

Marealle was one of the most important chiefs of the interior in the late nineteenth century. He was of the Chagga tribe, which inhabits the southern and eastern slopes of Kilimanjaro. Teleki and von Hoehnel visited his 'windowless' house built by stonemasons from the coast.

While making their final preparations to climb Kilimanjaro, the explorers became Marealle's guests. Had he opposed their plans, they would have got no farther; but befriending European travellers was part of his plan to extend his power. The stronger he could make himself, the safer he would feel, for he had many enemies as ambitious as himself. In spite of being motivated by such considerations, however, he seems genuinely to have liked his visitors, whom he helped in every way and on whom he lavished hospitality and gifts.

Marealle was about twenty-five at the time and at a critical stage in his career. In von Hoehnel's words, he was 'a young man of a highly nervous temperament, intelligent looking with very little of the Negro in his mobile features. He wore in the pierced lobe of the right ear a round bit of wood some four inches long and about the thickness of a lead pencil, whilst in the unusually distended lobe of the left was a decorated wooden ring some four inches in diameter. Round his neck he had only a string of blue beads.'

Like all his peers, he was, of course, a pitiless killer and slave trader. But the slaving game was tricky. It depended upon ostentatious displays of strength and desperate alliances with unlikely bedfellows. One slip and the African slaver suddenly became a slave.

At the very time that Marealle was entertaining the explorers, the Germans were busy empire-building. The initiator and prime mover of this process was Carl Peters. Peters hoped to be made governor of Tanganyika, but Bismarck did not like him. As a sop, he was given the post of 'Imperial High Commissioner for Kilimanjaro District'.

Four years after befriending Teleki and von Hoehnel, Marealle befriended Peters – with the same motives – and persuaded him to make Marangu his headquarters. Peters describes his task as 'bringing Kilimanjaro District under the aegis of the Royal Majesty', which entailed the exercise of 'full powers', even 'the power of life and death'. His job was not 'a gentle comedy', he says, but one he would either do or die in the process of doing.

While Marealle intrigued and extended his realms under Peters's protection, Peters had a man and a woman hanged from a tree outside his house. He does not tell us why, but vehemently insists that the two cases were unconnected and that a period of six months intervened between the executions.

He asserts that his passionate devotion to the advancement of German interests in East Africa aroused the hostility of the British, who forged 'a weapon to blow up my position sky-high'. They had accordingly contrived through the British mission in Moshi to have a report sent to Dar es Salaam 'that I had deliberately hanged my servant and a concubine for acts of a sexual nature'.

An official inquiry conducted at Peters's request in 1892 cleared him. But like the case of Brigadier Dyer's role in the famous Jallian-wallah massacre of 1919, the affair refused to die down. In 1893 Peters was recalled to Germany, indicted and sacked from the colonial service. He reacted with loud protestations of innocence. He compared himself with Dreyfus. He had the matter debated in parliament, saying he had been unjustly deprived of his life's vocation to serve German East Africa. He gnawed and worried this bone for the next eleven years, but never managed to crack it.

After the downfall of Peters, Marealle's fortunes waned. By 1904 the Germans began to suspect him of plotting against them. On finding out that his arrest and probable execution were imminent, Marealle fled to Kenya. He later returned, but did not regain his former power. He remained chief of Marangu, however, and became one of the first Wachagga to grow coffee. After his death in 1916, he was succeeded by his sons, first Mlanga and then Petro Itosi Marealle.

Had I had the sense to consult the telephone directory, I would have found Petro's name in it. As it was, all I could think of doing was search for the site of his father's house. In spite of my ineptitude as a detective I found both the house and Petro.

Petro was an upright old man with plenty of black hair – dyed perhaps – a small straight nose and a firm chin. People still greeted him as '*mongi*', although in democratic Tanzania he was no longer chief. He lived in a modern bungalow on a hillock west of the hotel. His tastefully furnished living room was crowded with photographs. One was of his mother, a dignified lady with dark circles under her eyes, wearing a full-length dress. The picture was a blurred sepia print, but even a century had been unable to efface the nobility of her expression or the enigmatic little smile on her lips.

'She was my father's second wife,' Petro explained. 'He had sixty altogether. The senior one was the daughter of Mandara, the chief of Moshi, but she was sterile.'

Asking him about his family history was like priming a pump. His wife, Mama Simba, a heavy beauty much younger than he, brought coffee, after which I just sat back and listened to his measured, correct English.

'First of all I must tell you,' he said, 'that my father's name has been incorrectly rendered. The name given to him at birth was Ndeguruo, but later the Masai, who admired him and whose language he spoke fluently, called him Meliari, which means 'the indefatigable', in recognition of his prowess as a warrior.

'Our clan was originally from Kitui in Kenya's land of the Kamba tribe and settled on a spur of Mawenzi about ten miles north of here. Gradually over the years they moved down the mountain, always marking their southern boundaries with stones. According to legend, the inhabitants were pygmies who fled to the Bundibugyo Forest in Uganda, where they still live. But when we came up against the Wachagga of Moshi and Kilema, we found people we could not dislodge and became as one with them.

'The first of the Lutheran missionaries, who came hard on the heels of Peters, looked upon us as heathen savages. They thought they had brought us God in a basket, refusing to believe that we already knew Him as Ruwa. We told them we also had our heaven called Ahera, where the departed spirits lived. The missionaries said that was hell. So, when they first arrived, people didn't go to the missionaries to be shown God, but for other reasons, such as being oppressed by relatives or chiefs, or wanting work and material things.

'Another thing the missionaries and the other Europeans ignored at first was that we had a sophisticated social system. Not only had we a well-constructed network of irrigation canals but properly constituted rules of landownership, under which everyone knew exactly where his boundaries were.

'The custom the missionaries hated above all we still practise. We periodically exhume the skulls of our former chiefs. Then we sacrifice goats and cattle and pour their blood over the skulls. But because we are Christians now, we can only perform the ceremony in secret.'

Petro explained that what I had thought of as the house that Teleki saw was in fact the third to occupy the site since then, but the original stone boundary still surrounded the compound.

His own *baraza*, or court, where as chief he had acted as judge, sitting on a special stone no one else was allowed to use, was a low building with an open veranda. It was now the local party hall, and a meeting was in progress. 'Even I can no longer go in there without special permission,' Petro remarked wryly as we passed it.

A gnarled mbindyo tree at the edge of a field marked the 'charming camping ground' his father had allotted to Teleki on 13 April 1887. It remained, in von Hoehnel's words, 'a meadow with soft greensward, watered by a little gurgling brook about one foot wide, and surrounded by banana trees'.

Petro had several photographs of his father, one showing him resplendent in the uniform of the Kaiser's cuirassiers with feathered hat and heavy cavalry sabre, sitting next to the German trader, Foerster, and behind them rows of ostrich-plumed warriors holding spears. There was a picture of Chief Mandara of Moshi in bed, wearing a Victorian-style night cap. There was also a dated photograph of Hans Meyer, taken after his successful first ascent of Kibo in 1889. But of Peters there was none.

About his father's relationship with Carl Peters, Petro professed to be totally ignorant. He could not remember his father ever mentioning Peters and possessed not a single document relating to the period. I was absolutely stunned.

Petro had never read any of Peters's writings, yet appeared to be very interested in him. On learning that I knew German, Petro made me promise to search out and send him every mention of Marealle. Was this a genuine request for information or a classic example of African evasiveness? That is a question to which I will never find an answer.

About the executions, Petro said, 'Everyone in Marangu knows what happened. Peters had a mistress. One day he found her in bed with a lover and hanged them both from a tree. I will show you where it was. We cut it down two years ago, because every time we passed it we remembered the cruelty of the Germans and all those people they killed without mercy or justice.'

Peters was not the only German who hanged people from trees. He summed up his own and the general attitude of his compatriots in a monograph entitled *Military Methods and Expedition-Leading in Africa*, published in 1892. In it he defines 'the African' as 'the opponent'. 'He is,' says Peters, 'a born slave who needs his despot as much as an opium smoker needs his pipe. He lacks every form of sophistication. He is hypocritical, given to thieving, false and sly'.

Having presented the German public with such a philosophy, Peters had no choice but to keep any sexual relationship he might have had with an African a closely guarded secret. But was the woman he hanged really his mistress, and what were the circumstances prompting him to take such an extreme step?

On the day I finally left Marangu, I took a photograph of Petro. The picture was not printed until months later. In it he looks down from the steps of his home with a contemplative aloofness in total contrast with the spontaneous effusiveness I remembered of him. Here there was something which must have escaped my notice before – a hawk-like resolve more in keeping with the features of a Prussian warlord than with his gentle and tolerant personality. Where had it come from? It seemed an inexplicable anomaly.

One day I was leafing through Peters's *Wie Deutsch-Ostafrika Entstand*. In it is a pencil sketch of the author. The look on that face sent me reaching for the photograph of Petro. I laid it next to the sketch. My eyes sped back and forth, and unless they deceived me, the identical distant, predatory expression was clearly written on both faces. The similarity in features too was there so clearly that I was driven into a storm of wild speculation. Had I blundered into the confines of a secret, the source of Petro's curiosity about Peters? Was the name Petro more than a coincidence?

Hitler, unsurprisingly, rehabilitated Peters posthumously. Peters's *Collected Works* were republished in three volumes in 1943. They included a sixteen-page chapter of his autobiography originally published in 1918, the year of his death. In it he vigorously defends himself against the accusations levelled at him over the hangings. But in doing so, he fails to specify or even refer to the personalities, places and events essential to the credibility of his contentions. Neither in this chapter nor anywhere else in those three volumes is there a single mention of Marealle or Marangu.

It was not until I read John Iliffe's *A Modern History of Tanganyika* (1979) that I found a clue to throw light on the mystery. Iliffe notes that in November 1891 Marealle 'induced the local German commander to move his headquarters to Marangu. The commander was Peters and the inducements included Marealle's wives.'

I became convinced not only that Peters was the father of Petro but that Petro knew. But it had taken me two years to get a copy of the *Collected Works*, and by that time Petro Itosi Marealle was dead.

The Mountains

Marangu was a very private place, but there was energy here, even bustle. For the first time since arriving in Tanzania, I saw well-dressed people walking as if they knew what they were going to do when they reached their destinations. Their houses were hidden away behind flowering hedges in arcades of ancient trees, groves of coffee and forests of giant plantains. Clear water flowed everywhere between the grassy banks of the famous irrigation channels of the Chagga tribe. Marangu was an oasis of well-being basking at the edge of a wilderness of apathy.

The hotel where Desmond had settled was in a large, well-tended garden full of mango, peach, orange and lemon trees, all bowed down with fruit. Over it towered the two peaks of Kilimanjaro: Kibo a mammoth's grizzled head, Mawenzi the crooked fingers of a wind-battered colossus, everlastingly linked like ill-matched Siamese twins by the great smooth saddle between them. A Chagga legend tells how once they had been on friendly terms, but one day Mawenzi decided to play a prank on Kibo. His fire had gone out, so he went over to Kibo and begged for some embers. Instead of using them, he threw them away and begged for more. Again he threw them away. When he went back for the third time, Kibo picked up his gigantic pestle and beat Mawenzi to a pulp. That, say the Wachagga, is why Mawenzi is so scarred and battered.

The inhabitants of the mountain's slopes are descendants of refugees from various parts of Tanzania and Kenya. They evolved a common language and merged as the Chagga tribe. Kibo, their forefathers' symbol of refuge, became for the Wachagga the giver of abundance and peace. It is the source of the water for their crops and a sanctuary from the hot, malaria-ridden plains below. Charles Dundas (*Kilimanjaro and Its People*, 1924) says, 'Kibo is to the Chagga people the embodiment of all that is beautiful, eternal and strengthening.'

One of the world's fifteen highest peaks, Kibo was first seen by a European in 1848. He was the missionary, Rebmann, to whom it seemed like 'a dazzlingly white cloud'. Europeans who then tried to reach its summit all failed. They included Teleki, who had to turn back at 17,387 feet when his lips started bleeding. In 1889 Dr Hans Meyer became the first to succeed. He scaled the 35 degree Ratzel glacier with twenty strokes of his ice-axe for every step. At that altitude and without climbing irons, it was a fantastic feat of courage and endurance.

Since Teleki had included the mountain on his itinerary, I felt obliged – despite a slothful attitude to mountaineering in general – to get as far as he had and, if I could summon up the energy, to climb to Gillman's Point on the lip of the crater, 700 feet below Kibo's true summit, the 19,340 foot Uhuru Peak. I found a guide, James, and a porter, Moses, and set off. I carried my gear in a shoulder bag with two tins of corned beef and a packet of coffee. Moses's rucksack, fashioned out of a plastic grain sack with strips of tape sewn on it as straps, contained the rest of the food. James was shod in a decent pair of boots, but Moses only had the usual car-tyre sandals. I wore my old elephant-hide boots.

After two hours of forest and a plague of houseflies, we reached the Mandara Hut. This was not one but a number of high-gabled timber buildings grouped around the whitewashed Bismarck Hut, which was built before the First World War. Accommodation was separate for 'tourists' and 'porters'. We had, it appeared, stepped beyond the pale of the classless society into a zone of neo-apartheid.

We passed the huts and pressed on into a forest of moss-bearded trees, which clanked in the wind like skeletons on a gibbet. Then out and up a long shoulder thick with white and yellow flowering *Helichrysum kilimanjari* bushes along a track made ugly by discarded sweet wrappers. We rested in an open expanse of dark green, olive, lemon and silver senecio groundsels, which stood in hooded groups like camouflaged soldiers on battle alert. Looking south-east, I could see the Ruvu River's papyrus fringe and the entire mass of the North Pare Mountains. It was a spot where one could gaze away time and savour the passing of it, but suddenly an icy wind buffeted down from Mawenzi. '*Upepo*,' (wind) the young men said, frowning; it was not a good omen.

Perched on an outcrop at the end of a yawning ravine of sullen grey stone under Mawenzi's spires was the cluster of buildings formerly named after Carl Peters, now known as the Horombo Hut after an early-nineteenth-century Chagga chief. Here too neo-apartheid reigned. The German, American and Japanese inhabitants of this exotic village were all absorbed by machismo and talk of the gravity of the business ahead, the unique feat of climbing Africa's highest mountain. My cheery good afternoons drew only the most cursory of nods. I was allotted a hut to myself, which pleased me, since even I had begun feeling antisocial.

Morning took us through a delightful swathe of pink and white heather to the moon desert of the saddle. Here vegetation dwindled to tufts of grass and clumps of silvery-leafed everlasting flowers, while a hacking wind kept the sky clear and the jeans flapping around my ankles. Ahead, Mawenzi glared balefully at a smiling Kibo.

I felt strong and forged mindlessly ahead until we reached an expanse of fine gravel. The last mile to the Kibo Hut was like squelching through a morass. A solitary black-headed eagle surfed the screaming wind above the iron rocks. Dusk stealthily made off with Kibo's smile, leaving an expression of bleak challenge. I looked up the six-in-one slope, and suddenly my confidence was gone.

In the gloom of the spartan Kibo Hut, whose windows rattled in the wind, I sat on a bunk and panted. A notice describing altitude sickness hung aslant on the wall. The door swung open, letting in a frigid gust and a British couple we had overtaken earlier. They tottered past with painful steps, white faced and worried looking. 'I felt completely smashed when I got here,' I volunteered. They smiled back wanly and wordlessly.

A yellow stretcher leaning up against the wall reminded me of the story Desmond had heard at the hotel. A German diplomat had trained for six months in the Alps before attempting Kibo. He had come down on that stretcher.

James came for me at one o'clock in the morning. Swaddled in every available piece of clothing, I stumbled like a Kamchatka convict out into the frosty moonlight. The climb was not too bad at first. We again overtook the white-faced pair, and a small measure of confidence spurted into my blood. But when the really steep slope began, each lifting of the foot became an enormous effort. A battle of wills broke out between the body and the mind. Each twenty steps was like a 100 yard all-out sprint, leaving me sobbing for breath. Foolishly having forgotten to drink water, I started eating snow. How eagerly I had once looked forward to doing just that, but its effects were those of eating salt.

James plodded ahead, pigeon-footed in his clomping boots. The day before he too had been panting, but now, unencumbered by his load, his movements were effortless. Mawenzi taunted from behind: Worm, you can't even make this easy climb, so you'll never try me!

The ground became soft and infuriatingly restraining. Again and again I fell, panting hysterically. 'It's madness,' I told James, 'to make people start on a climb in the middle of the night when it's so cold.' He looked down taciturnly, knowing what I ought to have known – that it would have been worse had we waited until the scree thawed during the day.

One of my gloves slipped off, and the hand became a frozen claw. At the end of a fruitless struggle to get it back on again, despair swamped me. James asked me what I intended to do. I did not reply, but tried to struggle on. After another bout of panting, something snapped. My mind started shrieking. I could no longer breathe. 'I can't go on,' I said. The body had won.

We slithered down the scree, past an American party humping their way up in the half-light like a huddled gang of zombies. James announced my defeat, but I no longer cared. All I wanted was breath, warmth and a smoke. Crouching in the Peters Cave, it took five minutes to unstiffen my fingers sufficiently to operate the lighter. Then, as I leaned back to suck the blessed smoke, the sun cascaded over Mawenzi's battlements. The North Pare Mountains assumed the shape of a great black bull in an early-morning meadow, Jipe a sliver of platinum at his feet. To the north, beyond the hump-backed Chyulu Hills, stretched the Yatta Plateau, a massive slab of Kenya studded with twinkling breakfast fires.

'I can't understand you,' James said reprovingly, handing me a cup of coffee at the Kibo Hut. 'You were less than 150 feet from Gillman's Point.'

Back at the Mandara Hut, the porters chaffed and took my cigarettes. James wanted to stay the night, but I was a routed soldier, anxious to retreat from the battlefield as rapidly as possible. He and Moses had a conference. I could not understand the proceedings, but their sly looks told me they had decided to run this damned European off his feet. This they immediately proceeded to do; but, no longer having to contend with altitude, I stood the pace.

On the final stretch to the hotel, James and Moses collected their girlfriends. We celebrated my defeat with a crate of beer and danced to music from the radio. Desmond's pale and peaky face swam through the doorway. He curtly declined to join us.

I do not remember how the party ended. At breakfast Desmond was visibly grumpy. 'I hope we didn't make too much noise,' I said conciliatingly.

'You were not celebrating,' he said, his face like Mawenzi; 'it was an orgy. I saw you. You were as drunk as an animal. How could you so demean yourself? And besides, how did you know they wouldn't make off with your money during the night?'

Having failed miserably on Kilimanjaro, I now had to endure a paternal lecture on my consolatory 'orgy' and I scanned the horizon for relief. From the west Mount Meru beckoned. I jumped on my bicycle and sped away, determined not to fail again.

Teleki and von Hoehnel had made only 6,000 of Mount Meru's height of 14,978 feet, having been plagued by heavy rain and aggressive tribesmen. Hopefully I would have no such problems. The rains were late, and the mountain was now encapsulated in a National Park.

A few days later we were encamped at Momella Lodge near some rondavels. Their broken windows and cobwebby bathrooms equipped with expensive plumbing whispered that the hurly-burly tourist days had ended long ago. An American film company had built the rondavels as scenery for John Wayne's *Hatari*. The lodge itself was once the home of a German elephant huntress named Trappe. It languished now, white and empty amid deserted lawns, a rattling old borassus palm keeping it awake.

The skyline was Meru, a stupendous fist thrust into the cloud-smudged heavens. 'Take it step by step,' Desmond advised. 'Rest when you are tired, and eventually you will get to the top.'

'Of every three who succeed on Kilimanjaro, two fail on Meru,' said my guide Simon, who had climbed Kibo, Mawenzi, Kenya, Elgon – and Meru eight times.

Through the binoculars the slope looked even steeper than Kibo's.

I followed Simon along a winding path into the high-altitude forest of evergreen cedar-like podo and white-flowering nuxia, whose heavy trunks were well buttressed against the wind by wedges of aerial roots. The air was redolent with a yew-like smell mixed with the sweetness of decaying leaves and bark. Nothing stirred except the tramping of our feet. Whenever we briefly stopped, the silence was absolute. But as we stepped out of the forest's gloom into the abrupt sunlight of an unexpected glade, a branch broke like the report of a rifle. Simon froze, and I barged into the back of him. He snatched my wrist. Across the open space, close by where the trees began again, an elephant and her calf stood concrete-grey against the luminous green foliage, hardly twenty yards off. The wind was behind us, so they had our scent. We both knew that bull elephants tend to make aggressive forays to frighten away intruders, but once a cow has laid back her ears to charge, she rarely relents until she has killed.

Very slowly we backed out of sight and stood rooted to the ground for five tense minutes. When we edged forward again, the glade was empty.

The tree heather zone which next we reached was underlaid with a spongy carpet of pink-blossoming heather. Mauve ground orchids and orange gladioli peeped like coloured lights out of the undergrowth. Butterflies speckled blue and yellow danced among them like miniature birds of paradise. The path was red and sometimes black. Its surface had been churned by hundreds of hoofs, and the rank smell of buffalo sweat lingered in the yard-high grass. There was no question of applying Desmond's 'step and rest' method; it was essential to leave the forest belt before the buffalo started moving in the late afternoon.

Viewed from the promontory of the mountain's lesser peak, Little Meru, the lakes of Momella appeared as little slabs of polished quartz laid out on the mottled violet and ivy-green brocade of forest swaddling Meru's feet. Kilimanjaro ploughed a sea of royal purple like the biggest ship in the world. As the sun began to set, a stiff breeze swept Kibo free of cloud, setting it briefly afire. The clouds – black, ochre, yellow and grey – scudded westwards towards the barrier of Meru's summits, standing in their way like the erect fin of a Nile perch, aglow now, first like the pale gold of Wales, then darkening to the cinnamon of India's. The next few seconds washed away all colour, leaving Meru satanically black and transforming Kilimanjaro into a gigantic beast asleep upon the plain, also black, but somehow as benign as Meru seemed threatening.

The hut was empty but for a few loose planks. Bottles, tins and paper littered the floor, conveniently providing us with candlesticks and cups, and helping us to light a fire. As we crouched over it, Simon told of how he had been with the Tanzanian army and gone with it as far as Arua in the remote north-west of Uganda. 'That's where our job was to capture Amin's soldiers after the fighting was finished. We would watch how the men walked and arrest any who kept in step. But I wouldn't go back to soldiering if they paid me 2,000 shillings a day.'

He showed me the visitors' book kept in the hut. A Danish girl had written: 'Anyone who climbs mountains must be an idiot.'

In the sepulchral hour which precedes dawn, we were already pushing through the tangled tree heather, Simon climbing like an ibex. A rough slope brought us quickly to the crater's edge. Although the sun had not yet cracked the horizon, there was light enough to make out the ash cone and its black striated lava-skirted sub-crater crouching in the vast shattered lap of its mother. Behind it rose the 2,000 foot almost vertical wall of what remained of the original mountain. The other side of the wall was a slope which fell steeply away towards the foothills. It ended in a jumble of dark brown rocks lying where they had fallen after the eruption which tore the mountain apart.

'Only fifteen minutes now,' said Simon. Adrenalin shot into my blood, lightening my feet. Then we were sitting under the party flag flying over the 'Socialist Peak'. From that pinnacle of the east-facing precipice the ash cone assumed the shape of a frightened sea anemone which had sucked in its tentacles. I felt like a tick on an elephant's head and childishly triumphant. Reaching the top of a mountain may be idiotic, but it is a moment as precious as anything else that is rare.

We could not sign the book because neither of us had brought a pen. Simon said it didn't matter. He would make sure I got a certificate. I picked up a chip of rock shaped vaguely like Meru. 'I'll take this instead as the proof that I've been to the top,' I said. Simon laughed.

The Ruins of *Ujima*

Tanzania is a land of fighting peasants. The Arabs, Germans and British all tried to take from them what they were unwilling to give. The sigh of relief which followed independence, however, was soon replaced by dismay. No one had ever tried to take from them what Nyerere now importunately demanded.

The Arabs had wanted slaves. The Germans wanted labour for cash crops. The British wanted order and, in the cause of 'the dignity of labour', they populated the land with European settlers, saying the peasants were lazy and in need of supervision. But Nyerere wanted the peasant's soul. The peasant was to be the instrument to transform textbook socialism into a reality.

The means by which the peasant's soul was to be captured was an existing tradition known as *ujima*. This was work done with the help of neighbours when circumstances dictated. There was no reward for such work. It was done in a spirit of pure communality.

Nyerere grafted upon *ujima* an alien element of his own philosophy – that of communal ownership. A catalysis ensued in the form of *ujamaa*, literally 'familyhood'. The aim was to bring more land under cultivation by persuading the peasants to work on communal land in addition to their private plots. To enable them to do so, they would be collectivised in villages and provided with inputs, machinery and services. Nyerere believed they would work harder and production would increase.

He announced his intentions in the Arusha Declaration on 5 February 1967. In it he detailed how the peasant's obligation to help his neighbour had been transferred to the state. The peasant's individuality was, at a stroke, nationalised.

The task of supervising observance of the rules of this new game was handed out to Nyerere's protégés, the bureaucrats, who ran headlong into every corner of the land with as little idea of how the new game was to be played as they had of the old. They had been told what to do, but not how to do it. So, to get the new game going, they used the old methods: authoritarian persuasion and bribery.

At least five million peasants did not obey Nyerere. They suspected that if they did they would be the losers. A government survey proved that they had been wise to stay put. It revealed that in the 1971–2 season the private farms produced an average 869 kilos of maize per hectare, while the communal farms produced 595 kilos, in spite of access to tractors and fertilisers which the private farms lacked. The effects of the trend were reflected in the imports of staples, which rose from 20,000 tonnes in 1967 to over 400,000 tonnes in 1974.

Nyerere reacted exactly like his German and British precursors. He accused the peasants of being lazy and ungrateful. Not only that, but to neutralise the embarrassing performance of the private farms, he commanded all peasants who had not yet moved to collective villages to do so by the end of 1976.

The army went into action. Families all over the country woke to the sound of roofs being torn off and front doors being smashed in. When they reached their allotted villages, as often as not they found themselves sitting under trees with their possessions piled up around them.

This was at the time the greatest (and most unnecessary) resettlement exercise ever embarked upon in Africa. Driven by an extreme form of ideological obsession, Nyerere imposed hardships on the peasants resulting in chaos and further falls in productivity from which the country has never recovered.

Held firmly in the grip of intellectual vanity and blind to the destruction he had already wreaked, Nyerere then dealt the peasants another ruthless blow. He closed down all the country's private shops and ordered them to be replaced by communal shops. No preparations had been made. The brain-child was born with a full set of teeth, but it could not walk. Once again the in-and-out-tray experts were stampeded from their desks to dash around the countryside like headless chickens. How Nyerere failed to foresee the explosion of shortages this hasty decision detonated can only be attributed to a stunted imagination, but it was so shattering that a month later he had to eat his words. He ordered that private shopkeepers be given their trading licences back.

The magnitude of his mistakes, however, did not persuade him to change his course of replacing the market-place with mechanisms operated by an incompetent bureaucracy, always to the detriment of both the rural and urban populations. Nor did he cease his rantings about laziness and the need for greater discipline, rantings which unfailingly received worldwide publicity.

Tanzania became the most food-aid-dependent country in Africa. But whenever its reserves ran out, Western donor agencies leapfrogged over one another to fill the gap, their governments terrified lest

Nyerere fulfil his frequently made threat of turning for help to the Communist bloc.

Inevitably, then, a marriage was celebrated in Nyerere's cloud-cuckoo-land. The bride was the ruined economy and the groom the foreign aid donor. A child was born. It was named *choromchoro*. By the time I reached Tanzania, the child had grown up. It was competing for power with Nyerere's child, *ujamaa*.

How did Nyerere get his reputation of a great and wise African statesman? Perhaps it is his reward for single-minded devotion to an ideal, a devotion which outshines the essential wrong-headedness of the ideal itself, and the irreparable damage and misery its application inflicted on millions. And perhaps it was that reputation coupled with the respect that goes with it that has rendered the patient and tolerant Tanzanians incapable of recognising Nyerere as the source of their poverty and stagnation. They go on calling him '*mwalimu*', their teacher.

As I wound my way through this north-eastern corner of Tanzania, exposed daily to Nyerere's system of generalised misery, I often wondered why no one had tried to overthrow him. It was, I concluded, probably attributable to the fact that, in spite of his many short-comings, he had succeeded in bonding society with the medium of the Swahili language through an authoritarian form of education inherited from the Germans. The greatest stumbling block to African nationalism is tribalism, and the outstanding factor dividing the tribes is language. That is why the speeches of African leaders are punctuated with calls for national unity.

Tribal disputes are more readily solved if each tribe is mutually intelligible to the other. Tanzania embraces at least 110 tribes; all of them can now speak Swahili. Developing and maintaining them as one nation must be conceded to Nyerere as a success.

Hansen and several other Europeans in Tanzania assured me that the government was hated. No one I talked with expressed such a feeling, though many were openly critical. 'Nyerere wants the best for us, but most of the people working for him are inefficient or corrupt,' was a view I often heard. The fact that all those people referred to were Nyerere's personal appointees was hardly understood at all. But hatred, no.

On 27 February 1982, for example, as I had been on my way to Same, a man flagged me down at Makuyuni and handed me a note from Desmond saying where he could next be found. As I was reading it, two other men came up to ask me if I knew anything about a Tanzanian passenger aircraft which had been hijacked the previous day. I got out my radio, and there and then we heard the BBC reporting that the aircraft was at Stansted, and the hijackers, who were Tanzanians, were threatening to blow it up unless Nyerere resigned.

None of the audience had heard of the organisation the hijackers were claiming to represent, and all agreed that the threat was shameful. Surely there was a lot wrong with the government, they said, but this was no way of trying to bring about a change. Had they not seen what Amin had done once he had brought himself to power by violence?

In this way they reflected what I felt was the general mood in the country at the time: critical but opposed to violence. I believed that for as long as life's essentials were available at prices within the reach of all, Tanzania would remain, albeit discontented, basically peaceful.

As for those 'life's essentials', I found that the shortages of things other than food had spawned a squalor which had gnawed into every corner of life. The town of Korogwe lay languid and run-down under a pall of dung-permeated dust. People were wandering around in a state of comatose confusion. An Indian shopkeeper, a sallow young man with long, greasy hair, sold me a bar of yellow soap. It was from his own personal stock and therefore a gesture of mercy.

He no longer liked Korogwe, where he had lived all his life, he said. 'The government has imposed so many restrictions that I can't run my business properly any more. Just last week I was told that from now on I must tie a price tag to each and every article. That means if I have a gross of combs for sale at five shillings each, every one of them has to have its own label. That is crazy and if they go on like this I will emigrate to India.'

A schoolmaster, Joshua, who put me up for the night on my way to Lake Jipe, said bitterly that his family of five were rationed to half a kilo of sugar a month. 'We are two hundred families here at Butu. Between us we are allowed just one hundred bars of soap a month. How can we be expected to keep ourselves clean? Toothpaste? Julius says we used to brush our teeth before we even heard of toothpaste – with a twig. Why can't we brush our teeth in that way now, he asks us. I have to teach the children hygiene, but they can't even put the first principle of it into practice. And there is nothing to indicate that things are going to get better. The junior government officials get so little pay that the only way they can keep going is by playing *choromchoro* and then there is no time left for them to do the work they are supposed to do. Nyerere keeps telling us that we are in this mess because we don't work hard enough. But we do work hard. Very hard. Why can't he understand that?'

On the day I came down from Meru, the Momella Lodge was milling with visitors, all men, except for two girls who had come up from Arusha on the lodge's Land-Rover together with a load of food, drink and cigarettes. Desmond said the men were government officials who had been collected here for a seminar on ways to improve efficiency.

We shared the same dining hall and bar, but beyond returning polite greetings with equal politeness, the officials remained aloof. Had they been trained as a breed apart to be so different from the men and women whose affairs they directed – all those so avid for contact and full of questions about the outside world? It seemed to me a case of the besuited leading the bedraggled towards equality, but in the meantime there could be no equality except between the equally rich – or poor.

The two girls, Ann and Agnes, whose darting eyes, ready smiles and swinging hips suggested a role out of context with that of the serious conferees, were soon confidently mingling with them. Drinking at the bar with the head waiter, quaintly yet aptly named Action ('I am from the Mara Region, where the President of Tanzania, Mwalimu J. K. Nyerere, comes from'), and the two part-time washers-up, I speculated on the part the girls would play.

The evening wore on with the conferees keeping to their own side of the bar. Gradually they began drifting off in ones and twos until only the hard drinkers were left. Ann and Agnes, apparently deserted, sidled over to us. Ann, the prettier of the two, laid her hand on my arm. 'Are you coming to Arusha?' she asked, her head aslant. Suddenly her face froze. The hand was snatched away. I followed the direction of her eyes. A tall man, fiercely mustachioed and burdened by a tight round paunch, stood in the doorway, feet apart. He was looking straight at Ann. 'Come,' he commanded and snapped his fingers. She rose like a marionette and faded into the night. When I looked back towards my companions, I noticed that Agnes too had disappeared.

I turned my eyes on Action. He inclined his head first to one side and then the other. Then he raised his eyes in the direction of the ceiling and lowered them again. Finally he leaned his elbows on the arms of his chair, joined the ends of his thumbs and successively the tips of each finger, gazing the while into my eyes.

We had just had a discussion on Tanzanian socialism.

But action had not been shocked by the official's morals or by his treatment of Ann, only by the high-handed way he had deprived us of her company. According to Bantu custom, woman is inferior to man for two reasons. First, she has an 'evil' which man does not. The 'evil' is the menstrual blood. Second, woman is a mere receptacle, a garden for the man. Man is procreator and cultivator – roles which the woman, even if she is better educated than the man, is physically incapable of performing. With such attitudes prevailing in Tanzanian society, women still take second place.

The acceptance of status typified by Ann's instant obedience was brought home to me even more forcefully at a guesthouse in Moshi. Sitting in the courtyard, I watched a pretty teenage girl emerge from the room opposite, followed by a lorry driver. She left him standing in the doorway, talking to the landlady, to whom he explained that he was half-caste, saying the word in English.

Aged about forty, he had black curly hair and a beard down to his collar bone. His eyes were dark and very piercing, surmounted by bushy eyebrows. Thick fleshy lips made me think of him as Bluebeard. He was dressed in nothing but a pair of striped shorts reaching down to his knees. Protruding over his waistband was a hairy belly, which he kept caressing with both hands. Sweat trickled from under his beard down the channel between his fat, almost feminine breasts. A little while later he went out, but returned within minutes, this time with two girls, both slight and even younger than the first. One went to his room and sat down on the bed. Then he entered and closed the door, leaving the other girl leaning against the landlady's old banger. I could see her moving her hips to the music from Bluebeard's radio. Ten minutes later, the door opened, and the first girl walked out. The second went in and closed the door.

The landlady caught my eye and leered. 'That fellow is strong,' she said admiringly.

The contrast between the lives of the bureaucracy and the rest in Tanzania is, if anything, more sharply delineated than that between the status of men and women.

Leaving Moshi in the direction of Arusha, the road takes one past rows of luxury villas for bigwigs and middlewigs, Mercedes and Peugeots parked gleaming in every trimly hedged driveway. Nearby, a huge block of party offices, an ugly cross between a supermarket and the Lubyanka, bristled like an apotheosis of *ujamaa* over the crumbling hovels at its feet. A few miles on sprawled Majengo Kwa Sadala, a dry and slummy market village. Women with lined faces carried plastic buckets from a communal tap. Their sarongs were faded and frayed, and their blouses blossomed with holes. Boys stood barefoot, hands thrust into the pockets of split-seamed trousers. Two others sat at a table in a restaurant, resting their faces on their forearms in a posture of inertia which seemed to conform with the soporific mood of the whole village. While I sat, sweat dripping from my elbows to the earth floor, another boy switched on a scratchy record player sending flamboyant rhythms cascading round the dirty tables. The other two boys did not lift their heads. As I absorbed the misery of that sordid room, the pretentious party building became for me a symbol of the communalism whose promises over fifteen years had produced nothing.

The Sanya Plain was a barren, rocky dereliction. Empty mud houses stood on both sides of the road, some incomplete, others already falling down. People had once been settled here. They had built, ploughed, sown, waited and starved. Then they had abandoned their wasted efforts as monuments to the addled thinking that had sent them there in the first place. Sanya village comprised a dilapidated petrol station slumped in the centre of a conglomeration of sagging huts and a few brightly painted bars, where people sat drinking maize beer out of plastic mugs. There seemed to be nothing else for them to do.

Then a sign bearing the words 'Tanzanite Hotel' led me into an exotic enclave concealed behind a screen of enormous and impenetrable hedges. It was a large white building surrounded by neat bedroom huts, all curtained and spotless. There was a spacious campsite with clear brooks soughing through damp lawns. I strode through an immaculately disposed dining hall to a row of tables on a veranda, where cold beer was brought for me in a few seconds.

Next to me two plump African girls giggled to each other in high-pitched Swahili. Their eyes told me that the object of their mirth was my scurrilous appearance. At the next table, two African boys and a Japanese man ate ice cream. They wore tee shirts inscribed: 'I have climbed Mount Kilimanjaro in Tanzania. Have you?' An elderly Indian padded paunchily past, followed by a middle-aged woman, whose wrists were heavy with gold. Her white trousers encased thighs so fat that each had to circumvent the other with every step. The couple swayed towards an artificial lake in a garden thronged with water buck, oryx, hares, wood ibis, ostrich, crested cranes, cattle egrets and hadada ibis. Followed by a sniffing eland, a uniformed keeper emptied a sack of feed by a tree, and the animals pressed in around him.

Two ample-waisted young husbands, each carrying a blond round-eyed little son and trailed by a wife weighed down with carrier bags, headed for a swimming pool where others like them were already splashing. The Indian pair waddled back, looking just as bored as when they had set out. Behind them came a pear-shaped German couple loaded with camera equipment in black shoulder bags. The woman posed by a pillar and issued instructions on how the picture was to be taken.

Although I was lusting for more cold beer, high-protein food and a soft bed, I did not stay at the Tanzanite Hotel. It was perhaps, in hindsight, a masochistic decision; but after pedalling through so vast a plain of dejection, I balked at taking refuge in that Indo-European zoo. Yet, as I rode away, I realised that my escape could detach me only evanescently from the world of relative affluence of which I remained a component. What I was doing was no more than an attempt to appease my conscience.

As I pressed on, I found there was no way of knowing how far I was from my destination, because all the milestones had been vandalised. A goatherd of whom I enquired the reason replied, 'They are no use to anyone except the owners of cars. Those are the people who don't care about us, so why should we worry about them?' He spoke in the same sneering tone in which the Pangani fish merchant had explained *choromchoro*.

An hour later saw me resting under a rock. A well-dressed man riding a brand-new Suzuki motor cycle, which still smelt of burning paint, stopped out of curiosity. Having satisfied it, he told me he was a farmer. From an envelope he drew several lumps of purplish crystal, which he put in my hand. 'Tanzanite,' he said conspiratorially. 'I know where to find it. Want to buy some?' The price of the biggest piece was 70,000 shillings, which was over £4,000. He smiled. 'You go back to Nairobi and have a look in the shops. Then you'll know I was right.'

I could almost hear Nyerere's voice: *honesty is the cornerstone of social consciousness, and social consciousness coupled with hard work is the key to the way out of our economic difficulties*. Quite true, but everything I had seen so far indicated that in Tanzania honesty coupled with hard work led nowhere.

That farmer must have been one of the lucky illicit tanzanite dealers; the middle-aged Chagga woman who ran the Mwangaza Guesthouse at Moshi was not. Snout-faced and bursting at the seams with fat, she answered to the improbable name of Grace. But in defiance to her appearance, she lavished me with kindness.

When I made to write my diary on the patio, she was sitting with a friendly drunk. A beer appeared for me, so I consigned the diary to the land of procrastination. The drunk asked me about my route as an excuse to lecture me on it. Suddenly he stopped in mid-sentence. A stern man in an immaculate safari suit was shaking hands with a very deferential Grace. Addressing the drunk, he said, 'I am a policeman, so I know the area thoroughly. I operate in it. The Samanga shown on the map is correct. There is a good road to Arusha Chini and from there one can cycle to Kahe and the main road.'

He turned to me. 'I am very happy to meet you, Mr Tom. My name is Joseph Mizrai and I am the Moshi district police commander. I have to leave now, but I shall be returning later.'

A second bottle stood before me. 'Mr Mizrai has bought you a beer,' Grace explained, 'but he only gave me a pound.' I concluded that he had paid her the proper price and that by giving her the extra five shillings he would have condoned her overcharging. But his generosity had made me feel expansive, so as well as meeting the deficit, I bought another round.

Just as I was going to bed, Grace breathlessly informed me that the police had arrived. The courtyard was alive with grey figures and the steely glint of submachine guns. My mind jumped back to Mizrai's promise; he had not returned personally, but had sent his representatives. One of them beckoned, and three more followed me into my room. They emptied the contents of my rucksack on the floor and turned it inside out. Every pocket was searched, nor did the saddle bag escape their attention. Careful scrutiny of my documents followed, but in the end they seemed satisfied that whatever they were looking for was not in my possession.

In the morning, the atmosphere was glum. Cecilia, the mouse-like maid, told me that Grace had been taken to the police station. 'They found my auntie with tanzanite.'

It seemed a final and calculated piece of cruelty. Once again Nyerere's eloquence floated into my inner ear. *We are beginning to have capitalists in our midst. If you allow people to build themselves by acquiring wealth, then you should realise that you are on a disaster course. We have uncovered some of these in Tanzania. Some of them are our own children, others are our uncles and aunts. They are stealing our country's wealth and sabotaging it.* In the eyes of Nyerere's men, Grace, who was feebly trying to make a few extra pennies, hoping to sell a piece of illicit gemstone to a tourist, was a saboteur. Nyerere's socialism, on the other hand, was leading where? Towards the wretchedness that was Majengo Kwa Sadala and the unbridgeable gap between it and the Tanzanite Hotel?

I rode off with a picture in my mind of a dejected Grace slumped in a dark cell. It seemed at the time to sum up the state of the whole country, which suddenly I began looking forward to leaving. That day was my last ride there. I could almost smell the spicy fleshpots of Kenya.

From Kahe the path followed the railway line through humid

banana plantations. Natural forest followed, where I could hear monkeys crashing through the foliage overhead. Then *nyika* and no path. In fear of punctures I walked along the railway, bumping from sleeper to sleeper until I reached a terrace of brick huts. 'Come over, welcome!' a voice rang out. 'Plenty of cool water here.' I propped the bicycle up on the track. 'Take it easy, bwana,' said a young woman cradling a robust baby which was sucking vigorously from a generous breast. Her dress was torn and grey, but her smile resembled a toothpaste advertisement. 'You rest with us a while and cool down,' she said.

An older woman holding a hoe told her to ask me my business. 'Ask him yourself,' she retorted. 'You can see he speaks Swahili.' I supplied my standard explanation – that I was following Teleki's trail to see for myself how life had changed since his day. 'I think it's a really good idea,' said the young woman, 'and it's always the same: if you want something, you have to sweat for it.'

I felt unsure if the gallons of sweat I had shed would come to anything, but was happy not to be told I was crazy.

Above an open doorway someone had scrawled in chalk 'Profesa Ojuku'. Through it I could see a blackened kettle on a table and a charcoal brazier on the floor. A young man with intense eyes and round cheeks brought me my third basin of water. His forearms were thick, his bare feet broadened by much walking. 'We are railway maintenance workers,' he told me. 'We keep the line in running order so that, when they open the border again, it will be ready straight away.'

'And when do you think that will be?'

'God knows.'

'What about the rains?'

'Coming very soon,' he said confidently.

'I'm surprised to hear you say that. Most people I ask that question of reply "God knows".'

'That's because I don't know anything about politics. I'm just an expert on rain.'

'Is that why you call yourself professor?'

The young woman burst into laughter so lusty that the nipple of her breast popped out of the baby's mouth. Suddenly they were all laughing, there on the bare concrete floor of the veranda in their ragged clothes, freed for a moment from their world of shortages and stagnation.

I found the main road, but by the time I reached Himo it was dark except for a brazier of opal clouds still glowing over Kibo. On the last lap to the Marangu Hotel, where Desmond was waiting for me, the hill became so steep that I could no longer ride, and a pain between my shoulder blades felt like a dagger. I took off the rucksack and balanced it on the saddle and handlebars, which relieved the strain but not the pain. Boys offered to carry it, but by then I was perversely determined to end the journey as I had begun it even though it meant pushing the damned machine.

The darkness became so intense that I kept bumbling off the road. 'Five more kilometres,' a schoolboy said. I would have collapsed into a ditch for the night, but my thirst was so intense that when I concentrated my mind on a bottle of beer my pace miraculously quickened. At last I stood in the ill-lit lounge, where I found Desmond. The waiter, Jonathan, performed a little dance of welcome. '*Habari* – what's your news?' he wanted to know.

'The news, Jonathan, is that I need a very cold beer brought to me extremely rapidly.' It was done, just as the journey was done. And that night it rained hard, just as Professor Ojuku had predicted.

Paradise

Von Hoehnel's 'paradise called Taveta' is seventeen miles from Marangu, and he walked there in a day. But in his day there was no border between the two. Now Taveta lies just inside Kenya. My papers dictated departure from Tanzania at the point of entry, Namanga; so to get to Taveta that way meant a journey of over 600 miles, first to Nairobi and then a great loop to the south again.

Arriving from socialist Tanzania in capitalist Kenya is like stepping out of Albania into Greece. There is no transitional, grey area in between. On one side of the line lies a land of sapped energies and respectful greetings; on the other you crash into a Hogarthian tide of men and women seething all around you, shouldering one another out of the way, vying to sell you meat pies, lemonade, biscuits, bead necklaces, carvings and walking sticks. This is Kenya, where life is precarious, and men are judged not by what they are but by what they have – Kenya, where everyone wants his shilling and he wants it right now. They tell a story about a man who visits his father in hospital. The son is sad to find him on the point of death. 'Father, Father,' he says, distraught, 'is there anything I can get for you?' The father speaks his last word, 'Shilling.'

We reached Nairobi at dusk. The pavements were already almost empty except for droves of uniformed watchmen hurrying, club in hand, to guard the affluent from the indigent.

At Sam's Inn, I dropped off Desmond by his camper. In spite of our incompatibility, he had tried his best to fulfil what I had asked of him, and I was grateful for that. Thus we parted amicably amid feelings of mutual relief, he to return to Uganda and I to go by train to Taveta to pick up Teleki's trail again.

Nairobi station still closely resembled its English country counterparts of the thirties. Porters rolled steel-wheeled trolleys, and there were notices to show passengers their compartment allocations: first-, second- and third-class carriages. Jim Fish, a BBC colleague who had decided to travel with me, entrusted our bicycles to the guard's van. Then, in response to a high-pitched whistle, the engine blared forth a trumpet call and clicked us slowly down the line.

A white-coated steward took names for dinner. It was served on tables covered with starchy cloths, each polished plate guarded by a phalanx of cutlery. In that train the Second World War had changed nothing; all was a delectable anachronism which had side-stepped the fifties flood of haste and lukewarm tea slopping out of squashy plastic beakers over small slices of junk cake. My bottle of beer was cold; the waiter apologised and returned with the warm one I had ordered.

The train stopped at every station. At Darajani, the platform was thronged with people holding up hurricane lamps. It was after midnight, and they were celebrating St Patrick's Day, all singing hymns with that syncopated lilt which dominates every musical expression in Africa. I leaned out of the window and moved my arm in time with the tambourines. The singers responded by raising the volume of their voices. Individuals stepped forward to take my hand, which in the space of a few brief minutes was pressed by a dozen well-wishers. Then, as the train jolted forward, they surged to keep pace with it, still singing and swinging their lanterns. I felt a sense of loss as the voices faded out of earshot and we plunged again into the darkness.

We reached Voi in the small hours. The platform was crowded with mostly women and children, but there were only three benches. We had a four-hour wait for the train to Taveta, so I spread my sleeping bag on the concrete. Next to me a young mother was breast-feeding her baby, watched by two older children. A two-inch dung beetle buzzed into the light and clonked to the ground between the little boy and girl, there to lie upside down like Kafka's cockroach, its legs jiggering in futile efforts to right itself. The children screeched with excitement. Gingerly the boy stretched out his toe and gave it a little kick. The beetle slithered, still upside down, towards the girl, who shrank away with a sharp indrawn breath. The mother smiled indulgently as the girl, not to be outdone by her brother, edged forward and tapped it back to him. He stared at the struggling insect. Now he would stamp on it, I thought, to show his sister how he would deal with enemies when he grew up. But no, he just gave it a slightly harder kick. This time the beetle hit a protuberance and righted itself. The boy ran after it to watch it unfold its wings, only to fly into a lamp post and fall again. But he had lost interest; he walked back to his mother and snuggled up to her. She put her arm round him and pressed him gently to her side.

I woke at dawn. Jim was talking with a man whose smart apparel, iron-grey hair and deep-set eyes suggested authority. At his instructions we bought two brown tags, which were inscribed with our names and tied to our bicycles. But when we made to wheel them to the train, we were ordered back to the office. 'These bicycles,' our mentor said stiffly, 'are now the responsibility of the railways and you will not see them again until they are delivered to you in Taveta.'

We had second-class tickets but got into a first-class compartment, as the train was nearly empty. A plaque at the base of the gangway giving access to it stated that the carriage had been made in 1926 by the Metropolitan Carriage, Wagon and Finance Company of Saltley, Birmingham. The whole interior of the carriage was in various shades of Baker Street brown. A notice over the emergency cord threatened that the penalty for unlawful use would by a fine and/or imprisonment, without specifying how much or how long. The compartment contained a basin, but my wish to shave was frustrated by the absence of water.

We were joined by the man who had helped us at Voi. He now introduced himself as Ogola, the railways inspector. I was still holding my shaving brush. 'They have forgotten to fill water,' he explained. It was the old British 'they' on whom all things that go wrong are blamed.

Two hours later the train slowly clanked to a halt. 'See you at the Safari Lodge,' said Ogola, handing us down our bicycles. 'You are going there, isn't it?' We had not known where we were going, but now we did. It proved to be the most luxurious hostelry in town. The front entrance led first into a narrow veranda, beyond which in a spacious bar-cum-ballroom white-overalled barmaids of substantial proportions were serving beer. A mural signed by Johnny Murai and covering the whole of one wall depicted a rosy-cheeked, ample-bosomed lady sitting opposite a sleek, besuited, Poirot-goateed gentleman, a bottle-laden table between them. He was shown as telling her: 'Ponda mali na utalipa' (Demolish the money now and then you'll pay for it). Delicately holding a glass between thumb and index finger, she smilingly replied: 'Usijali, bwana' (Don't you worry, sir). Yes, she meant, just you drink up, and then we shall see who will be the loser. Another mural by the same artist on the opposite wall lent emphasis to the threat implicit in the first. From it an enormous lioness looked longingly down at the patrons, while out of the corner of her eye she kept watch over a round-rumped zebra innocently nibbling grass under a tree.

Taabu, a young woman shaped like one of Rubens's models, guided us through a courtyard embracing a kitchen hut and a corner cosy bar, where men sat chaffing the barmaids while a young man wearing a baseball hat roasted meat for them on a brazier. Beyond it, on either side of a dark corridor, were two rows of bedrooms with ochre-red floors, bile-yellow walls and bright blue doors. Each contained a single bed and a small table. No chair, but nails to hang clothes from.

We ordered a kilo of goat meat and went to the dining room to wait for it. Ogola was already there, no longer dour but possessed of a newly found loquacity, indicating that the bottle in front of him was not his first. Beside him sat a woman even bigger than Taabu, whose long pigtails protruded from under her headscarf. 'This is Cecilia,' Ogola said in a singsong voice, patting my arm as he spoke. 'Now, she is a really fine girl. I met her three years ago when I first started this round and I was wanting to find a nice girl, you know, not the sort you will pay and then she doesn't give, you know what I mean, so that you feel you have paid your money for nothing, but a nice good girl that makes you feel OK and happy to give your money to. Well, I found Cecilia and since then I have been seeing her every Wednesday and Saturday when I come here. Now, Cecilia, you listen to me. You see these two young men, Jim and Tom, well I want you to make sure that they – well, you know they are here as strangers and need to have a good time – you make sure you get them really good girls who will make them happy, not cheating girls.' He paused to draw breath and accept the beer Jim had ordered for him. Cecilia nodded and smiled.

Ogola sank back in his chair, and now it was her turn for a monologue. Brought up by missionaries, as she told us, her English was nearly perfect. She had worked as a receptionist at a hotel in Malindi. 'The manager – he is English like you – liked me very much. Whenever he had a drink he would let me take a sip out of his glass and joke with me. But his wife, you know how it is, she got very jealous and in the end I had to leave. Then I got the same kind of job with the Shelly Beach Hotel in Mombasa. There was a really nice boss there too and in those days I really used to know how to drink – twenty-eight bottles a day. That used to make me go to sleep, but that boss, whenever he found me asleep at the reception, he would just wake me up and say: Cecilia, you book these guests into room ten or whatever. I would write their names down in the book, hand over the keys and go back to sleep. Yes, that was a really nice boss. And also I had a very nice German boyfriend – very tall he is – and he is the father of one of my children, so now I have a Mkamba, a German and a Mtaita. But, my God, I really had to stop drinking – because of my weight, you know. Usually I weigh 88 kilos, but when I get pregnant I go up to 102.' And so it went on. Her parents had insisted she gave up her job, so she had returned to Taveta, where she now lived with her children and always had to be home by seven p.m. 'so that my parents know I am being very good'.

Ogola did not stay to hear her out. His train was due to leave for Voi in two minutes. Would it go without him? Of course not, but he had to be careful not to overstretch his privileges.

We too decided to fade away, but before we reached the corridor, Cecilia had caught up with us. She leaned her bulk on my shoulder and whispered huskily, 'Tom, the nice girls that Ogola was talking about, well, one of them is me. So how about it?'

I grunted perfunctorily and walked on, knowing that there would be no further restraint. Taabu was hard on her heels. Cecilia obtruded a nether lip in her direction. 'And that,' she stated, 'is the other one.' They were in for the kill.

'Look, Cecilia,' I said in my schoolmaster voice, 'I have not come here to look for women. Besides, as I have already told you, all I have to live on while I'm on this safari is about 1,000 shillings a month, so really you are wasting your time.'

'Well, I can see that's not much, but what about Jim?'

'I haven't got much either,' he said. I noticed that his face was drawn with exhaustion.

Cecilia muttered a few words of Kitaita to Taabu, then turned back to us. 'OK then, you have a rest now and I'll see you at six for a drink.'

Both lumbered off, but Taabu was back almost at once. 'Take no notice of that woman,' she hissed. 'I have returned to tell you to feel relaxed here. Don't worry about anything. No one is going to disturb you and no one is going to steal anything. And if you need anything, you just call me.' She pressed my arm reassuringly before swaying away with a swoosh, swoosh, swoosh of her flipflops.

I soon learned that discipline indeed reigned at the Safari Lodge. As I emerged from the corridor on my way to the showers, I heard shouts and crashes. A gargantuan woman strode past me in advance of a posse of four waiters carrying a man. As he weakly struggled, face down, a waiter dashed up to give him repeated slaps on the buttocks. The grotesque cavalcade disappeared round the corner, soon to return without their burden, laughing and gesticulating. One of the waiters sidled up to me. 'That man very drunk, saying very bad things to that mama, so we have fixed him.'

The victim lay asprawl on the concrete floor in front of the urinal, his head resting on his forearm, his features soft in the innocence of sleep. He was still there six hours later. He had been 'fixed' and accordingly forgotten by all.

Taveta was established towards the end of the eighteenth century, probably by refugee Wakamba, who settled in the thick woods by the Lumi River. At the time of Teleki's visit they were surrounded by 'impenetrable vegetation', with only three narrow paths leading to the huts of the inhabitants, 'which were hidden among the shady trees like the nests of birds'.

No longer. Now its few remaining trees cringed with dusty leaves on broken branches as scraggy as the dogs sniffing the refuse beneath them. The buildings were disjointed in layout, their iron-sheeted roofs flaking under the hard sun. We walked over the railway line towards a vegetable market and a few shops. Opposite there was a newly built post office as starkly incongruous as a new car in a breaker's yard. Behind it we found a war cemetery of about a hundred white grave-stones in rows under the frangipani trees. All but the two inscribed 'Ein Deutscher Soldat' belonged to British, South African and Rhodesian soldiers and civilians, and nearly all were dated 1916.

That was the year the British forces in East Africa suffered their heaviest losses. There were in particular two battles fought near Taveta that year, one in February and one in March; most of the occupants of the cemetery died in one or the other. At the time, General Tighe was based in Voi in command of two divisions of Empire troops, mostly South African whites. They faced at Taveta a few hundred German and African *Schutztruppen* under Colonel Paul von Lettow-Vorbeck.

Tighe believed that with such overwhelming force at his disposal he could easily rout von Lettow and go on to seize an otherwise un-defended German East Africa. Von Lettow was dug in on Salaita Hill, thus blocking the gap between Kilimanjaro and the North Pares through which Tighe aimed to pass. On 12 February, Tighe threw against him two largely South African brigades, confident that they would win by sheer weight of numbers. The massed infantry assault of the attackers met a counter-attack so fierce that they were lucky to escape annihilation.

Eleven days later, command of the Empire forces was transferred to Jan Christiaan Smuts, who split them into two forces, sending one to attack the Germans in the gap and the other round the eastern base of Kilimanjaro to cut them off at Moshi.

Von Lettow was short of artillery shells. So when he heard about the pincer movement, he withdrew from Salaita Hill to high ground between the Reata and Latema Hills five miles west of Taveta, leaving the British to take Salaita and the town without firing a shot.

On 11 March, Tighe led the 3rd King's African Rifles, the 2nd Rhodesians and the 130th Baluchis in an attack on von Lettow's new stronghold. Again they met stiff resistance. During the assault, as he was crawling up the slope, Lieutenant-Colonel Bertrand Robert

Graham, the commander of the KAR regiment, heard his name being shouted. He stood up to get a better view and fell dead with a bullet in the throat, fired by the German officer who had called him. There were many other casualties, and the attack got bogged down to the extent that Smuts had to bolster it up with three South African battalions.

During the night of 12 March, the Germans slipped away, having suffered minimal losses. The British had won the territory, but lost the battle.

Jim and I crossed the bridge over the dark brown Lumi River and headed south to pick up Teleki's trail at the end of Lake Jipe. A few miles through fields of drooping sisal brought us in sight of a solitary white mansion perched on a low hill rising out of the plain. As we drew nearer, it became clear that it was empty and deserted. Wrecks of cars dating back thirty years and more lay at the foot of the hill as if the owner had pushed them off the top when he had tired of them.

The road seemed to be leading away from the lake, and I felt that we ought to turn right. Near a likely looking junction I questioned an elderly passer-by. 'No,' he replied, 'that is Grogan Road and it leads to the house of a European named Grogan. He left it many years ago and now he is dead.' We resolved to take that road and look over the house on the way back.

A transient shower had cooled the *nyika* into which we rode. Every acacia wore velvet leaves among its thorns, and the air was awash with a hawthorn-like fragrance. The red soil beneath had sprouted a feathery green studded with blue, orange, pink and white flowers. The bush reverberated with birds excitedly calling for more rain. I distinguished the rasping whistles of bru-brus, the clarion choruses of red and yellow barbets, the feverish chattering of superb starlings and the harsh squawks of white-headed buffalo weavers. When a flock of golden-breasted starlings flashed across the path I called out to Jim, but the beautiful phantoms vanished before he could catch a glimpse of them. The shimmering blade of Jipe laid against Ugweno sprang into sight as we emerged into a treeless plain patchy with trodden elephant dung and fresh hyena tracks.

The southern end of the lake lay lost in a vast reed bed. Of the rivers feeding it, the Mala, Mavraini and Mzukune, nothing could be seen, and its shores were bare of the acacia described by von Hoehnel. On a sward bordering the clear water we watched a pair of crowned cranes performing a mating dance. Wings spread and necks arched forward towards each other, they jumped up and down alternately in silence. For them we did not exist.

From the doorway of a hovel on Grogan Road, an old man shouted to us to come back. He was Onyango, guardian of Grogan's property for twenty years.

He told us to leave our bicycles. His daughter would take us up. Omondi, a slender and delicate-featured twenty-year-old, was just back from visiting Nairobi, where her efforts to find work had failed. Our help and advice were requested, but like her father we could only shake our heads. 'I really don't know what I'm going to do or where I'm going to go,' she told us in her schoolgirl English. 'My father is poor. He has paid for all those years to get me through secondary school, and now that the time has come for me to help him, all I can do is eat the food he cannot really afford to give me.' Her dilemma was that of millions, so many of them equally alert, able and articulate. What was there for her? No books, no games, no activities. She was at a standstill, spending her days sitting on a wooden stool to gaze over a desert of broken sisal spikes barring her from a world which had no need of her. What would we all do, I wondered, when that world became fully automated? Probably make bombs to blow up the computers.

A broad flight of stairs led to an elliptical portico entrance to an Italian garden around a fountain, with well-watered beds of oleander bushes and pink frangipani, still well looked after. The octagonal mansion was all arches, high ceilings, panoramic windows and verandas. In the east wing, each superimposed upon the other, were three identical rooms with bay windows facing east and north. Running through the centre of all was a great painted pillar, providing a pivot in each for a circular bar. Thus, I imagined, Grogan in his day could have held three separate parties at one go, each in its own room and with its distinctive form of carousal.

Omondi showed us the master bedroom. His grand double bed was still imprisoned in its wire-mesh mosquito cage. There was a drinks cabinet the size of a sitting room in an average British semi-detached house. The whole mansion seemed to be a monument to pretentiousness and self-obsession, and Grogan himself a replica of Citizen Kane, yet its siting provided views among the finest one could ever hope to see. Mawenzi's craggy summit clawing at a turquoise sky through the black rainstorm lashing its slopes; beyond it Meru, a tiny wedge in the distance; to the south, the North Pares; and to the east, the Taita Hills and Kasigau: all were spread out before the windows. I looked down upon a marsh harrier being mobbed by a flock of swallows. It was the first time I had witnessed such a happening from above.

This was the erstwhile palace of Ewart Grogan, the legendary

Grogan, who had walked from the Cape to Cairo to prove to his prospective father-in-law that he was man enough to marry his daughter. To build the house, hundreds of labourers had dragged up that hill thousands of tons of stone and cement. The great man had lived here in style, and the house had nourished his vanity, but what was it now? A useless pyramid. When Omondi brought me the visitors' book, I wrote in it, quoting Fitzgerald: 'The lion and the lizard keep the courts where Jamshid gloried and drank deep.'

Much later I was to learn how wrong I had been. Far from being a thick-booted colonialist, Grogan had been visionary and an obsessively inventive builder for the future. He had built the castle not for himself, but as an agricultural college to train Africans. What I had taken to be circular bars Grogan had designed as shelves for newspapers and magazines for the students. 'Grogan's Castle', as it came to be known, lay in the middle of three extensive estates comprising sisal plantations and hundreds of acres under citrus, pineapple and avocado. There were herds of cattle, fish farms and thousands of miles of irrigation channels, as well as three sisal processing plants, a brick and tile works, workshops, labour lines, staff houses, stores, schools and clinics. The students would have had access to many forms of agriculture, while housed under conditions nothing less than luxurious.

But when, as soon as the building was completed, Grogan offered it as a college, the Governor, Sir Philip Mitchell, did not even reply to his letter. It was probably meant as a snub to counter Grogan's well-known contempt for those in authority. Grogan's reaction was to move into the house himself, which was equally probably a gesture, because he had as little time for luxury as he had for the pomposities of government.

Nor, I learned, had Grogan gone on his famous walk to impress anyone. 'No, it wasn't because of a girl at all,' the eighty-year-old Grogan told Sandy Gall (*Don't Worry about the Money Now*) in 1955. 'I was asked to do it by the British Secret Service. At that time the French were showing a keen interest in getting their hands on as much of Africa as possible and I was asked by the British to travel from the Cape to Cairo to find out just what was going on in all these places. That was the real reason, but we had to make up the story about the girl to put the French off the scent.'

During our stay in Taveta we also visited Chala, Kilimanjaro's only crater lake. The missionary Charles New, who was the first European to visit it, was told in the summer of 1871 by his Chagga guides to listen for the lowing of cattle, the crowing of cocks, the thudding of pestles and mortars and the grinding of flour mills. These were the sounds emanating from a people, they said, who lived in crystal caves at the bottom of the lake.

'Long ago, there was no lake at all,' a Masai policeman told me on the train to Taveta. 'It was just a meadow. One day a Masai clan gathered in it for a feast of meat. When they had eaten their fill, one of the women remembered a sick grandmother lying in her hut who had been inadvertently forgotten. All that was left by then was a small piece of intestine, which so enraged the old woman that she willed a chasm to open up under the whole clan and that its members be inundated with water for ever. That is why the lake is called Chala, which in the Masai language means "rubbish dump".

'And if you go there, remember it is dangerous to bathe. The people at the bottom are feeling lonely and they hunger for news of the world they are cut off from, so they make whirlpools that can suck a man down into the depths. A man I know personally went for a swim in Chala. He was sucked under and swept into a cave, where he broke the surface and found air. Then a channel of water carried him for many days and many miles until it discharged him into the sea at Mombasa. He is still there – in Mombasa – but he will never tell anyone what he saw in that cave.'

We took the route followed by von Hoehnel between the base of the mountain and the Lumi River. Deep puddles everywhere showed that the previous night's rain had been heavy. The ground beneath the acacias was spotted white with clusters of the hyacinth-like chlorophytum lily. As I knelt to test their scent, a youth riding a bicycle halted by me. 'They don't have a good smell,' he said. He told me his father owned two hundred cows at Chala village and that it was his job to take two containers of milk to Taveta hospital every day. He did not believe the stories about Chala, he said; they were just old superstitious stuff. Nor did he believe what New had been told, that the lake had no outlet. He pointed to a clump of wild fig trees a few hundred yards from the road, where, he said, a spring from the lake formed a stream which flowed into the Lumi.

We now approached a long pointed hill which sloped gently down towards the east. At the top of it, the boy said, we would find the lake. There was no sign of it from the road, nor anything at all to suggest its existence. We trundled up the rough slope. One moment there was just a brownish fuzz of foliage, the next, a two-mile expanse of blue-black water sprang into view, a sapphire in a cushion of green velvet. It was surrounded by a precipitous wall of between 150 and 300 feet high. The shore was edged with white stones, behind them bushes and many old trees. All was spread before us just as nature had created it, the only man-made object visible being a steel-girdered jetty.

No sounds of cattle or cocks, but voices and laughter of men drifted up. The path leading down was too steep for the bicycles, but a ragged man appeared and took charge of them. Bicycles are expensive in Kenya, and he could have taken them deep into the bush never to be found again; such a thought did not occur to us, and we did not even bother to lock them.

We found men resting on rocks and in small caves, where they were camping as their cooking utensils indicated. Boys were swimming and splashing among the fishing boats, all but one of which were crude craft about 12 feet long and hewn out of tree trunks. I scooped up a mouthful of the clear water and found it as New had, 'as sweet as the sweetest spring'. We peeled off our sweaty clothes and immersed ourselves in the cool balm. I asked the boys about crocodiles. 'There are plenty,' they shouted, 'but they are not vicious.' The lake was full of tilapia and tiger fish, so the crocodiles were too well fed to bother with long pig.

Several men descended to the largest boat, on which we were sitting. All carried handlines and tins of earthworms. Where did they fish? 'Oh, we go over to the Tanzania side, that's where most of the fish are.'

'So, you're stealing Nyerere's fish!' I remarked.

'No,' they replied. 'The fish don't belong to Nyerere, only his side of the lake.'

They said they could catch up to fifty fish a man in an evening. Eight of them got into the boat and paddled away, etching the pellucid surface of the water with the angled ridges of their wake.

We returned to Taveta in a thunderstorm. Sticky mud soon clogged up the wheels of my bicycle and brought me to a halt. Only by dismantling the mudguards was I able to go on. Jim's machine, being Chinese, was built for such conditions. The gap between its tyres and mudguards was wide enough to enable him to keep his wheels free with an occasional poke from a twig. Mud was yet another contingency I had failed to account for when planning the journey through Masailand.

It was with regret that we prepared to leave Taveta next day. Although we had spent only a few days at the lodge, we had become so familiar with its ways that we felt as if we had been there for weeks. It was a cloudy morning with a southerly wind threatening more rain. We ate as large a breakfast as possible, for we had no idea where we would next be able to buy food. Our emergency rations comprised a few oranges, two small tins of mackerel and four chapatis.

Masailand begins just a few miles north of Lake Chala, and once you enter it shops become as rare as water holes in the desert. Living mainly on milk and blood, it is only intermittently that the Masai feel the need to obtain shop goods like maize meal, cooking fat, *shukas* or beads, and when they do they are prepared to walk long distances to obtain them. Items useful to ourselves such as bread, tins of baked beans or corned beef would almost certainly be unobtainable.

Rucksacks on our backs, we wheeled our bicycles out of the lodge. The plan was to cycle around the south-eastern edge of the base of Kilimanjaro via Rombo and Loitokitok and then to follow our explorers to Ngong, which in Teleki's day marked the border between the Masai and the Wakikuyu. Taabu, the elephantine cook, the thin waiter and two of the beefy barmaids stood in a smiling row to wave us goodbye. 'You'll never make it to Rombo,' Taabu predicted. 'You'll get stuck in the mud and die of cold or get eaten by lions during the night. Better to stay right here where there's food and beer and beds.'

None of her warnings was outside the bounds of possibility, I reflected soberly as we rode off, but soon found comfort in the memory of having heard such things before.

Ndindi's Problem

Towards the end of the nineteenth century, the most feared of all the East African tribes were the Masai. By the time Teleki stood on their doorstep at Taveta, their reputation as ruthless, psychopathic killers was already of long standing. They were known to have raided as far south as Lake Nyasa, and their attacks on Mombasa were still fresh in the memories of its inhabitants.

The Masai were at the height of their power when the first two European expeditions, those of Doctor G. A. Fischer in 1882 and Joseph Thomson in 1883, passed through their territories. The accounts of these two could not have inspired Teleki, the leader of the third expedition, with anything but trepidation. To his surprise, however, encounters with these 'dreaded inhabitants' turned out to be remarkable only for their lack of drama.

The first Masai the explorers met, on their way to Mount Meru, showed them a good camping ground, made them a present of goats without asking for anything in return and guided them to their next camp. Commenting, von Hoehnel says: 'Travellers are often falsely informed, partly unintentionally, as there are often many stories about the approaching of the dreaded Masai, and partly intentionally, the caravan people deceiving them in the hope of preventing them from going further.' His and Teleki's experience of the Masai was still sufficient to warrant excessive optimism, yet they pressed on undeterred.

Only twice did the Masai try to halt the expedition, each time complaining that some of the cattle accompanying it were diseased. Having been permitted to slaughter the suspect beasts, the Masai then allowed the explorers to proceed, eventually to reach Ngong after a 42-day march during which hardly a Masai shadow had darkened their path.

Masai fear of cattle disease was well founded. Disaster already loomed. Cattle brought into Ethiopia by the Italian army carried rinderpest. It spread to the Masai in 1891 and wiped out nearly all their cattle. Up to three quarters of the entire Masai people are estimated to have consequently died of starvation. Traditional enemies then mercilessly raided the survivors, turning them into fugitives in their own lands.

What almost certainly saved them from extinction was colonialism. That is why the Masai have been friendly towards Europeans ever since. Colonialism restrained the Masai from raiding, yet allowed them to preserve their way of life while protecting them from the depredations of other tribes.

The Masai regrouped and grew rich. Insulated from change-inducing stimuli, they turned their backs on their neighbours whom colonialism was stampeding into the twentieth century. The Masai preserved their traditions, including the taboo on breaking the soil for cultivation. They hardly noticed the departure of colonialism, for its successors, too, left them largely alone. They have yet to notice that the population explosion which followed independence now threatens them with the land hunger of its overspill.

Beyond Chala village we passed banana groves and rice fields, with fat cattle grazing under trees. Houses were well built and prosperous looking. At Chumvani we found a teeming market around a group of corky-trunked fig trees in an open space bounded by tin-roofed huts. We had not yet reached Masailand. The Masai thronging the market were there to trade. Wakamba and Wakikuyu offered baskets, maize, mangoes, tomatoes, bangles, rings, necklaces, tyre-rubber sandals and cresset lamps made of discarded tins. Masai had brought cattle, goats and calabashes of curds, every man, woman and child of them swathed in blood-red cloaks and sparkling with ornaments in sharp contrast with the monochrome, European-type clothes of all the others. The Masai men leaned on their sticks with clubs clamped between crossed thighs. The shaven women, all weighed down with brass, copper, steel and beads, sat on the ground, legs stretched out straight as decency demands, calabashes and baskets piled around them. Even in a continent renowned for exuberant decoration the Masai stand out. One young woman was encased in iron and brass bracelets from ankle to knee, wrist to elbow and elbow to armpit, her neck swathed in bead necklaces from chin to collar bone. Each ear carried two sets of rings; large brass hoops hung from the helix and copper pendants from the lobes. A band of brass encircled her head, and rings encased every finger. The sheer weight of the metal must have made it hard for her to walk.

At a teahouse we sat next to a spindly Masai girl, but when she turned she revealed a prematurely aged face and a baby on her lap. A Kamba man sat down opposite after leaning a serviceable bow and quiver against the wall. Three stout girls, eyebrows plucked and cheeks shining with health, served out bowls of meat stew, chapatis and cups of tea. Each had suspended round her neck a little cloth bag into which she popped the takings. They worked as a team and no one was kept waiting.

The humdrum bustle was suddenly immobilised by a jarring voice. Everyone turned in its direction. An idiot was roughly pushing aside two Masai men, his dribbling mouth half open, eyes red-rimmed and staring. 'Bring tea!' he shouted to one of the girls.

'Pay first,' she replied. He held up his hands, the palms upturned.

'Get out, then,' a Masai said acidly.

The idiot backed off. 'Dog!' he hissed. 'Dirty Masai dog!'

The Masai turned to his neighbour and laughed. The intruder was forgotten before he reached the door, but to me it occurred that idiots, like drunks, are apt to blurt out what they really feel.

Two men began firing questions at us like trained interrogators. What was it like in England? How dear were transport and accommodation? Were food and commodities available? How many children had I? Why only two? Attempting to emulate Charles New, I replied that it was not our custom to have many, but that did not satisfy them. 'Well,' I said, 'do you get a state pension when you are old? In England we do, so we don't need a lot of children to support us after we retire.' The reply may not have satisfied, but it served to change the subject.

As we were talking an old Masai woman walked through to the kitchen carrying a basket. She was tall and straight-backed, with a face wearing a look of haughty disapproval reminiscent of George V's Queen Mary. She emerged holding a banknote. 'Bring more meat,' a voice called out after her. 'No,' she replied grimly without turning her head.

'What about those Masai? How do they fit in with you?' I asked my interrogators.

They laughed. 'Masai? Nobody can change them. They will change when they want to change and until then they will sell us meat and we will sell them whatever we have that they want. But Masai?' They clicked their tongues with scorn.

We cycled off, heading north in the general direction of Rombo, little knowing that by next morning we would fully understand why some Masai abandon life in the bush for the greater comforts of the town. The ordnance map showed no path to Rombo north of the Lumi ford; but a map drawn by Hans Meyer in 1889, which I had seen in Marangu, registers what he describes on it as 'a non-dangerous route from Lake Chala to Rombo'. What we did not know was whether such a path still existed.

Beyond the Lumi River, cultivated land gave way to very green *nyika*, where the tinkling of bells accompanied the trilling of birds and cicadas. Masai boys in miniature red togas stood gazing at their animals with the raptness of pure love. They hardly spared us a glance, for we were an evanescent phenomenon, to be greeted and forgotten. The cattle were contentedly munching, and every udder was turgid; that was all that mattered.

The sky had cleared, but clouds still hid Mawenzi. Deep patches of mud forced us to ride along bumpy ridges. Had it rained the previous night we would not have been riding at all; were it to rain that day we would not reach Rombo. As we sat resting in the long scented grass, flock after flock of black-faced sandgrouse whistled overhead like arrows shot at the mountains.

Here we had our first face-to-face meeting with a Masai spearman, who tapped us for a cigarette. I reminded Jim that, on his first encounter with a Masai, Teleki had handed out 66 lb of wire, ten lengths of cotton cloth and a quantity of beads as *hongo*,* the customary tax imposed for droit de passage.

'*Hongo*'s no longer what it used to be,' said Jim as he gave the spearman a single crumpled cigarette.

Soon we lost our way and started going in circles. The gathering dusk pointed to a night in the open, when suddenly the same Masai stood before us again. He said his name was Leboo and that his home would be ours for the night. He led us to a patch of grass, where, sitting on a stone, was the elder of his *manyata*, or clan village.

Regal with large eyes and a long straight nose, the elder was dressed in a pink blanket, with a green trilby perched incongruously on his head. Brass ear rings weighed down his two-inch lobes almost to the shoulders. Shyly struggling to cover her nakedness with a piece of his blanket was a three-year-old girl, whom he fondled as he switched flies

---

* *Hongo* used to be imposed on travellers by chiefs in return for permission to pass through their territories. The first time Teleki paid *hongo* was to Sultan Semboja of the Usambara kingdom, one of Kimweri's unruly sons. The tribute consisted of 120 yards of white calico, 60 yards of indigo calico, several coloured *kitenges* (see p. 262), two brown caftans, two cases of gin, 15lb of fine gunpowder, a bottle of Eno's Fruit Salts, a few picture books and an empty metal flask. But, far from being pleased by these gifts, Semboja charged one of Teleki's men to transmit the following message: 'Tell your master that I am a great Sultan, and I want money, lots of money, hunting weapons, and medicine, and not all that rubbish.' What I call 'back-handed *hongo*' survives into the present day. The day before writing this note I gave a well-dressed middle-aged man a brief lift in the direction of Nairobi. At the end of it he demanded five shillings to finance the remaining part of his journey!

off her with a giraffe-tail whisk. Yes, we were welcome to stay the night. Leboo advised that a gift was expected. Before or after? Before was best. Using both hands I presented a twenty-shilling note, which was accepted with a satisfied smile. Cool water was brought from a nearby stream.

During the years I had lived in Kenya I must have driven past hundreds of *manyatas*, but I had never entered one. Indeed, it never occurred to me to do so. I now believe that our subconscious calculates constantly and cynically to steer us away from experiences of pure and unadulterated misery, such as the one we were about to have.

Flies gathered among us in divisional strength. They tumbled over one another to get into the tin mug from which we had been drinking. When I took off my hat, they dived into my hair like Afghan rebels under air attack. My fly whisk suddenly became a vital piece of equipment. I suggested making coffee, but this was not to be, because we would be getting tea later, said Leboo, who had by now become our director of operations.

We watched the homecoming of the cattle. A dozen women with children down to toddlers sprang among them like cheetahs, snatching out of their midst the calves, which had been released from the corral to induce their mothers to lactate. The calves were then held together in a group, each woman and child holding a leg or two, while the girls wound their way among the cows, milking every udder into tins and calabashes.

The *manyata* comprised about twenty loaf-shaped huts made of sticks, mud and cow dung and arranged around the inside of a circular wall of acacia thorn. Each faced an arena of trodden dung into which both the cattle and we were led.

The entrance to a Masai home is like that of snail's except that the passage ceases to wind after about three yards. Crouching, one then reaches an open space. The part beyond the inner wall of the passage is the kitchen, which adjoins the wife's sitting place of smoothed-out mud. Next to them is the sleeping compartment, about a foot above the floor. The bed is about the size of a double mattress and consists of several uncured cowhides, one on top of the other. The foot end of the bed is a repository for calabashes. Pots and utensils are kept in the kitchen, the stove being an oblong hole between two upended flat stones with a couple of old *panga* (machete) blades placed over them to support cooking pots.

As we entered, a young girl was grinding snuff between two stones in the sitting space. Embers in the fireplace were brought to life by the elder's chief wife, a slender, small-breasted woman, whose face was set in an expression of patrician disdain. This was her hut, and it was here that we were to sleep.

The plastic beads of her necklace were the only objects to be seen which were exclusively identifiable with the twentieth century. They were also the only objects which did not serve a purely practical purpose. Everything in that hut could be picked up at a moment's notice and carried away on the family's backs. They were semi-settled now, these Masai, but all their possessions reflected the harsh disciplines of their past nomadic life. Crouching there with them on a low and excruciatingly uncomfortable wooden stool, I began to understand why so many of them abandoned home and took up jobs as watchmen in the towns.

I realised also for the first time why it is so hard for African governments to persuade migrants in towns to return to the countryside. My mind went back to 1969 when my fellow teacher, Sam Mursoi, a Kipsigis by tribe and therefore akin to the Masai, used to extol the pure simplicity of sleeping on a cowhide in his father's mud hut. At the end of the summer term he asked me to give him a lift to Kericho, where he wanted to visit his parents. I agreed, secretly hoping that I would not be invited to spend the night on a cowhide, and to guard against this exigency I packed my sleeping bag. But when Sam brought his luggage to be loaded on the Land-Rover, I was astonished to see that he had brought his bed and bedding. We reached Sam's homestead in the pouring rain. To my even greater surprise then Sam, instead of alighting, sounded the horn. Only when the blanket-clad figures of his father and mother swayed drunkenly out of their doorway did he deign to brave the elements to greet them. He would not enter their hut even for a moment of politeness. Instead he hastily handed out a few shillings to them and to a line of shivering younger brothers and sisters, most of whose names he could not recall. Even more hastily he bade them all farewell. Then we drove off, back to Kericho town to stay with his civil servant friend – back to concrete floors, taps and electric lights. Huts and cowhide beds were over for my friend Sam for ever.

In our hut now, a pot of milk was put on the fire. We provided tea and sugar. More and more people pressed in until the entrance passage was jammed. No oxygen could get in, and what little remained was being consumed by the fire, the smoke from which in no way deterred the flies. We gulped down our tea and stumbled out like a pair of tear-gas victims, tripping over feet. It was better, we decided, to eat outside the compound so as to spare our hosts any feelings of obligation they may have had towards us.

Leboo soon ordered us back in, because the entrance to the *manyata* was about to be blocked. The press inside the hut had thinned out, but the fire was still roaring. The senior wife poured milk from calabashes into the pot and added maize meal for milk *ugali*, a sort of porridge. After handing us each a cup of milk, the Swahili-speaking daughter informed me that mama needed money for tobacco (which at the time cost 20 shillings a kilo). I handed over a ten-shilling note, which she examined in the firelight. 'It is not enough,' the daughter said. 'She needs another one like that.'

I promised further action in the morning, after which they began their meal, all dipping their hands into the communal pot. We were not invited to participate, which to the Bantu tribes would have been a breach of etiquette.

Besides ourselves and our hostess, the hut now contained her twelve-year-old son, two teenage daughters, six younger children, three kids and a newly born calf. There was an unending turmoil of entering, leaving and making way for one another, for milk was being boiled in every household, with an emissary from each coming to collect handfuls of our tea and sugar. A man pointed to his naked girl child and said he needed a dress for her. Told we were not carrying such things, he said money would do. I affected exhaustion and closed my eyes, hoping to inspire boredom resulting in the replacement of bodies by oxygen. Not so; I was being prodded. The man had brought me a head-rest, and the boy, smacking his lips, was saying, 'Lete seremende.' Not knowing what *seremende* was, I tried ignoring the boy, but he knew what he wanted and kept repeating the words. 'Perhaps he means sweets,' Jim suggested, and being right cost him nearly the whole of his supply. After everyone in the hut had been served, every other man, woman and child in the *manyata*, including the elder himself, pushed their way in for their share.

Once the last *seremende* had been handed out, we were left just with the senior wife curled up in her sitting space, the calf, the kids and, last but by no means least, the flies. The fire continued to crackle, the calf snuffled, the kids belched and whimpered. The still air smelt of fresh dung, damp rawhide, smoke, curdled milk and sweat. Not until the fire had declined to dormancy and made the darkness absolute were the flies lulled into rest.

Drumming feet and voices raised in alarm breached the midnight stillness. Mama lithely uncoiled to fling chips of dry wood into the fireplace. Flames lit up the hut as she sprang out of the entrance. Soon she was back, dropping a smoking cudgel into the fireplace. A leopard had trespassed into the *boma*, and she had put it to flight by banging it on the head with her firebrand.

The flies woke before dawn and breakfasted in our hair. The elder and all his household gathered to see us off. The daughter reminded me of my promise. I was able to find only a five-shilling note. Mama looked at it as if I had just put chickenshit into her hand and turned huffily away. I felt guilty, as she had given up her bed for us, even though I would have preferred sleeping in the open, leopards and all. But the elder smiled his approval.

Leboo's reward was more substantial. He smiled as he led us back to the Meyer path. Two hours later we reached Rombo and, to our pleasure, its Catholic mission.

On the path leading through a compound hedging in half a dozen modern houses with flower gardens and citrus trees we found a European talking with a young African, who rewarded our handshake with unhesitating hospitality. Brother Albin, a shabbily dressed and tiny man with a Pinocchio nose from that little triangle of Italy tucked between Austria's Oetztal and Switzerland's Engadin, led us to a small building containing the luxuries of bunks, shower and flush toilet. Then he brought us fresh milk from his pedigree Jerseys, very large eggs laid by his Leghorns and grapefruits from the trees he had grown from seed, and left us with his companion, Jonathan Leparan.

Jonathan was only a little taller than Albin. That combined with an aquiline nose and long-lashed eyes with very dark irises on very white eyeballs led me to think he was a Mchagga, but I was wrong. He was Masai from both his parents' sides. Visitors to Rombo, he said, were very rare. His need to communicate was extreme.

The site on which the mission was built, he told us, had only been conceded after years of resistance from the Masai. The resistance had arisen not out of fear of the white man as such, but from the knowledge that these particular white men were missionaries intent on persuading the Masai to abandon their religion in favour of Catholic Christianity and ultimately also to abandon their customs and traditions in favour of alien ones. Such a process, it was feared, could bring the wrath of God down upon the Masai. Accordingly, when in 1960 the Masai eventually agreed to allot a site for the mission, they chose it very carefully indeed. It was a triangle, the apex of which was formed by the confluence of the Engare Len and one of its tributaries, both fast-flowing perennial streams and difficult to cross at the time. However, as one of their first tasks, the missionaries built a bridge over the Engare Len. Thus their influence soon became more than the Masai had bargained for, but not enough for Jonathan's liking.

'Here, as in most other parts, the Masai use vast tracts of arable land to perpetuate their cattle economy,' he explained, 'but now more and more of the land is being sold to immigrants of other tribes, and if the process continues at its present rate, the Masai way of life will die out. The Masai sense the danger, but fail to understand that they can survive only by abandoning their mystical belief that any occupation other than herding cattle not only demeans the individual but insults God. I believe that only by converting to Christianity will they find a way of overcoming their abhorrence of breaking the ground to grow crops.'

I said, 'Don't you think that then they would throw away their weapons, change their style of dress and learn to prefer houses with metal roofs, thus losing a great part of their distinctive culture?'

'Those are superficialities. It does not matter if the Masai come to look like everyone else. That is happening everywhere. It is the Masai language which must be preserved, for so long as it survives, the Masai will survive. The motto of the Masai today must be: cultivate or die. At this stage the only way which holds out hope of persuading them to adopt that motto is through compromise. They will not bend to open rebellion by young educated people like myself. We are too few and lack the necessary social clout. We have to go in for a sort of semi-rebellion. For example, I have been through my age-set initiation, but I refused to have my ears pierced or to wear ornaments. I wear Western clothes but still live in my *manyata*. I do not carry weapons, but I always go around with a walking stick by way of apology. Thus I have remained within my clan and strategically well placed to influence its members.

'There are Masai here in Rombo who are gravitating towards another form of compromise. Instead of selling, they are leasing their land to outsiders, who are then permitted to erect temporary homes and sell their produce. The outsiders arrive penniless, but then they work hard and in time save up enough to make the Masai an attractive offer for his land. To sell out thus to the lessees is a constant temptation, so the Masai have begun forming societies for communal landholding called group ranches. These act as a brake on land sales, but are not fully effective because they cannot stop members from disposing of privately owned plots. There is only one foolproof way: the Masai must cultivate the land themselves.'

Jonathan was on fire. It was already late, but he would not stop, so sharp was his hunger for converts. 'Now the trouble is,' he went on, 'that the Masai conservatives hate education. The average man must have at least two wives to cope with his stock. Education tends to render the individual receptive towards Christianity, which, by insisting on monogamy, curbs his ability to increase his wealth. An educated girl, on the other hand, is reluctant to marry an uneducated man and submit to the menial tasks he would expect her to perform. The uneducated man is equally reluctant to marry such a girl, knowing that she would only want to marry an educated man and live in a house with a concrete floor, piped water and electric light. He will not hand over the customary fifteen cows to her father, who comes to learn that not only has he lost on paying school fees but in the end his daughter is worth less on the market for having done so. As one conservative put it to me: An educated girl is of no use to anyone but her husband.'

'But why should men be so greedy?' I put in. 'What is this obsession with the constant need to increase one's wealth?'

'It is not greed. Traditionally, it is the responsibility of an eldest son to support his father's widows and all their children. A man is accordingly motivated to accumulate sufficient wealth to enable his son to perform this duty. But these days there is a growing tendency for an eldest son to favour his own mother and her children, while the other widows slide into destitution, with social consequences such as the birth of illegitimate children. And then, as tradition also entitles the eldest son to receive bride price for his sisters and half-sisters, he will tend to keep them illiterate. A junior widow, however, tends to do the opposite. Neglected and aware that her daughter will be sold to no benefit to herself, thereafter to devote herself to her husband to the exclusion of her mother, such a widow will try to educate her daughter in the hope of finding her an educated husband, who will not discourage her from helping her mother.'

I told Jonathan about Sialo, a Masai I had known in Ongata Rongai. At independence Sialo had fifty acres, which he proceeded to sell piece by piece while spending the money on drink. He went on like that until he had just four acres left, which he sold to a Kikuyu living near Ngong. The Kikuyu allowed Sialo to go on living in his wooden shack and to grow a few beans to feed himself. Then the land price went up, and the Kikuyu sold. Sialo had to move into lodgings in the village and thereafter worked as a day labourer for the new owner of the plot, digging and weeding the land that had once been his own.

Jonathan was not impressed. 'That was alcohol,' he said. 'We are not all like that.'

Outside Jonathan's *manyata* next morning, a girl of about nine walked up to him and bent down her head to receive the hand laid upon it as a child's traditional greeting from an adult. She was dressed in a red smock and was festooned with plastic beads and ornaments.

When she looked up to speak to Jonathan, I noticed that her eyes were grave and her voice unsteady. 'This is Ndindi,' he said, 'a victim of our ways. Her father is dead and she is asking me to help her get educated. She already knows that it would be useless to approach her eldest brother, so she is asking me because I am well in with the missionaries. I have told her I will try, but there are so many like her that I don't really think I shall be able to do anything.'

Jim photographed her as she stood pensively on a stone, gazing towards a horizon of gently waving trees along the river as if she knew they would hem her in until her dying day unless Jonathan helped her now. Otherwise the best she could look forward to was to be sold like a heifer to an illiterate steeped in a tradition of inapplicable belligerency, thereafter to live in institutionalised bondage.

'Come back to Rombo,' Jonathan told me in his farewells. 'I'll give you ten acres and you can live on them till you die.' Jim, he stated, needed a wife. If he was still unmarried when he returned, there would be one waiting for him.

All over Africa people want the traveller to stay. They want him to live in their houses and tell them everything he knows. They want to feed him and give him their daughters as wives. If he says he wants to go, they will be happy to fill him with drink until he goes to sleep so as to delay him even for just another day.

We left Rombo at noon. Both Mawenzi and Kibo leaned over us now, Kibo streaked with fresh snow. The road was rough, mostly steep uphill slopes with long mires of black cotton soil which drove us to the grassy verges. Increasingly the land we passed through was cultivated, and the numbers of Masai declined.

One last long gruelling hill flushed us into Loitokitok, 'the place of the bubbling springs', a higgledy-piggledy proliferation of single- and two-storeyed houses and shops scattered over the east-facing slope of a Kilimanjaro foothill veined with rutted dirt tracks. Like Taveta, it had the atmosphere of a frontier town – as indeed, for a different reason, it was.

Asleep after Reveille

Loitokitok was a town built and owned by the Kikuyu. The only Masai to be seen were lounging against the walls of buildings which did not belong to them. A helpful fellow-cyclist led us to Mwalimu's Day and Night Club and Lodgings. Loitokitok, he told us, was now Masai only in name. 'There are five bars and hotels here and four of them belong to Kikuyu. My brother runs one of them. This is a town for uneducated Kikuyu like me. We don't have a chance in our home areas any more. The land is too expensive and there are too many educated people competing for jobs, so we others have to come to places like this to make money and buy land – and even here it now costs 6,000 shillings an acre.'

'What about the Masai?' Jim asked.

'We want their land to grow food on and if they won't sell it to us we are going to push them out and take it by force.' I believed him.

The bald statement of intent clothed all of Jonathan's predictions in hideous flesh. The Masai of 1891 could have taken no precautions against the scourges of rinderpest and smallpox, but this was no longer the case in 1982 when, for all to see, a new scourge was closing in on them. Why could they not visualise, as I did at that moment, the desperate hordes spilling out of the seething Kikuyu homelands, marching with hoes held high for the open rangelands of the Masai? Why were the Masai still as fast asleep as Rip van Winkle? It seemed suddenly inevitable that I would live to see the day when the whole of that beautiful, wild and spacious land would be hidden for ever under a patchwork quilt of beans, maize, potatoes and wheat. I felt an absurd impulse to run up to one of those lounging Masai of Loitokitok and shake him until he came to his senses.

To get out of town, we had to go through the customs post, a well-built and imposing symbol of starched khaki-drill authority over sweat-stained *shukas* and frayed trousers. 'Aren't you afraid of lions?' the official asked us.

From there we rolled at breakneck speed down the hill up which we had pushed so laboriously the previous day. I had not been on that road for eight years. There had been nothing but bush then, but now new mud-and-timber houses stood amid bean fields. Kimana was a brightly painted shopping centre adjoining a new secondary school. Unlike the Masai, the cultivators prized education as an effective component in the logistics of expansion.

At that point, Teleki turned west through Amboseli to Namanga. I had hoped to follow him through the game park, but the rangers said not even motor cycles were allowed in. We had to change course and make for Kajiado through remote country in which we would be lucky to find anything to eat. By the time we reached the bottom of the slope, the sun stood high. Beyond the Lolturesh and Kikarankot rivers, the trees gave way to open steppe, where a long uphill gradient awaited us. The road had been recently resurfaced with gypsum, which reflected the sun into our eyes. At the Lemepoiti turn-off, I blacked out and fell off my bicycle. Jim brewed tea. There was no sugar, but it gave me enough strength to reach Makutano's line of tin shacks at the top. Between them their stock of soft drinks was down to two bottles, which we bought from a tall Masai shopkeeper. Told we were British, he lamented our decline. 'There were days,' he said, 'when we used to believe that if the world was not behaving the way Britain wanted it to, she would just make a threat and everyone would stop and take notice. But now . . .' He shook his head and gazed at us empathetically. '. . . you're just like us Masai – anybody can push you around.'

We took the pipeline road into a steppe empty but for a few herds of goats tended by Masai children. Two buses, one travelling from Emali to Loitokitok and the other vice versa, drew up so close that we could not pass between them. Men tumbled out to urinate, all standing except for the Masai, who squatted like Arabs. I had often wondered how ordinary actions like squatting, sitting cross-legged or with legs stretched out, reaching the ground by bending from the waist or kneeling came to be determined regionally or racially. In Tanzania I had noticed that from Pangani as far as Muheza, all women worked squatting and sat on one side with their legs bent under them, while from Muheza to Kilimanjaro they worked bending from the waist and sat with legs stretched out straight. Why did Chagga women carry burdens on their heads, while Kikuyu women used their backs in combination with a headstrap? And why was it that only men had emerged from those two buses, while all the women had stayed aboard? That was the easiest question to answer: the men had drunk more beer.

The Kiboko was dry. Beyond it we came to Murueshi, a line of shop shacks and two government camps, one for road menders and the other for the rest – galvanised iron rondavels as hot as a ship's engine room in the Red Sea. The settlement stood in an eroded patch at the edge of a hummocky plain that extended without interruption all the way to Kilimanjaro and the brick-brown wedge of Meru. The flyblown air hung in an inertia of boredom. I felt sorry for the two dejected policemen who said they had to sleep under bushes until they were posted back to Loitokitok. I supposed that the arrangement was designed to help them keep awake at night.

They took us to the shack which was the '*hoteli*', or restaurant. Shelves behind the counter held crockery; a sack of flour, a charcoal brazier and a cast-iron chapati pan lay on the floor. Murueshi was very secure and populated exclusively by Masai, which they were themselves, the policemen informed us. No sooner had they closed their mouths than we learned that Rafael, the proprietor, was a Nyeri Kikuyu, who had been there for four years as a land adjudication officer. As lately he had not had much to do, he had opened the *hoteli* as a means of supplementing his salary. His tea was sweet and his chapatis crisp. Most of his customers were Masai, who also supplied him with milk.

I bought beer from a woman in the shop next door. It was well stocked but offered nothing we could usefully take into the unknown next day. The woman was a Kikuyu married to a Masai. 'Masai don't know how to run shops,' Rafael said smugly, 'so they marry Kikuyu women to do it for them.'

That was true only in so far as there were so few numerate Masai girls. It was also easier than admitting that bride price for Kikuyu girls was so much lower that Masai often married them as second wives – or even as first wives if they were hard up.

In the morning we headed west with a parcel of Rafael's chapatis through *nyika* full of hartebeeste and wildebeeste. These animals' placid observation of our passage was evidence that we had progressed beyond the area of Kamba penetration; for Masai, who did not eat the flesh of wild animals, rarely molested game. Gradually the country opened out again into savannah dotted with *manyatas*. Great herds of black, dun and white cattle gleamed in the billowing grass, the rounded volcanic hills of Soysambu and Kiasa standing behind them like sentinels.

Midday coffee finished our water. The Selengai River was a deep dry rift of white sand. Hidden among trees beyond it we came upon the game post, where the rangers gave us access to their rain-water tank. The place was neglected and forlorn, the gravel track leading through the broken gate overgrown with grass. Gone were those busy bloody days when hunting parties used to book into Block 65 and report on their way out what animals they had killed. 'What do you do now?' I asked the two bored rangers reclining on the cracked steps of the veranda.

'We protect the animals from poachers, who have steadily increased in number since the hunting stopped.'

'What animals do they kill?'

'Anything,' they replied. The behaviour of the plains game we had passed convinced me that the rangers were lying and that their excursions away from their compound probably took them no farther than the shops, of which we found one a mile or two on.

The owner, a florid Masai wearing clean Western clothes, asked where we intended spending the night. In the bush, we replied. 'If you are not afraid of lions,' he said, 'you ought to be.' We admitted that we were. 'Well, then, you'd better not camp here. They've been around here every night for weeks now, because it's by the only bit of water left in the river. There are six and they have some cubs.' What about staying in the game post compound? 'You can do that if you like,' the shopkeeper said, 'but those lions have even broken into there a couple of times. Don't forget you're going to be outside and the rangers are going to be locked in their rooms. And then if the lions come and you start shouting for help, those fellows are not going to come out and save you.'

So we rode out of the thick bush and camped at the foot of Kiasa Hill. No roaring of lions there, only the barking of a distant fox. But at midnight heavy rain drove me into sharing Jim's tiny tent.

Dawn unveiled an African tableau. A black-striped orange-and-white herd of Thomson's gazelle was grazing within a hundred yards. Twitching their tails, they watched us crawl into the open, then lowered their heads back to the grass. A pair of Kori bustards strode through the long grass, tall grey necks upthrust, but started running for a ponderous take-off as soon as they spotted us. Beyond them, close to the Mashuru shopping centre, a pair of wildebeeste grazed, while Masai herds ploughed like flotillas through the distant swell of undulating meadows.

The road snaked up through showers and thunderstorms to the Olengasaloi Hills. Every water hole had been mired by cattle, so we filled the container from a puddle in the road. A young man stopped to watch this bizarre procedure. He looked a townee right down to his platform shoes. Only a bead bracelet, sword and club remained to advertise his Masaidom. We opened our last packet of biscuits and offered him a handful.

He was Kalo, a cattle dealer. 'I have finished secondary school,' he said with pride. 'My father is a progressive and all my brothers and sisters are educated too. I had a job as a clerk until I found out I could make more money out of selling cattle to the Athi slaughterhouse. That's where I'm on my way back from now, heading for my land. I employ two Wakamba to grow beans, which I sell. Eat any myself? No, milk, blood and meat are enough for me. I can live on milk for a month and it's ninety per cent enough to feed me. We also believe that our babies can thrive only if they get plenty of milk and fat, so although I think we must change and become educated, still we must keep our cattle and our way of life. There are many of us who think like that now, but none of us want to stop being Masai.' Jim asked him what sort of changes he envisaged. 'What I mean is we must stop things like cutting ears and wearing *shukas*. We must get more money by renting out more of our land, which will also help people who don't own land themselves. And we must sell more of our cattle so that by going over to a more cash-centred economy we can reduce the need for polygamy and have something to spend on projects.'

I quoted him what Jonathan had said about the need for the Masai to cultivate their land themselves. 'No,' said Kalo with feeling, 'that is something we will never do.' The emphatic reply reflected the depth of even this educated man's abhorrence of taking the one fundamental step essential to the survival of his people as a cultural entity.

Kalo was hardly out of sight before a platoon of ochre-smeared teenage *morans* (warriors) trotted past, flashing the blades of their spears in our faces. They were undergoing the rites of the vigorous military training originally designed to enable the tribe to attack others and steal their livestock. The British put an end to such raiding, but the training had continued, supposedly to provide a corps of young men to protect cattle from predators. But where was its relevance now? Most of the predators had followed their prey into the game parks to the extent that school-age children and handicapped individuals sufficed to herd the cattle. Of the *morans* we had just seen, only those destined to become watchmen in the towns would benefit from their training. The rest would stay in the *manyatas* or hang about in hotel car parks as part-time photographic models.

In the last paragraph of his fanciful book, *The Masai Story* (1956), Oskar Koenig says: 'How should the Moran, with his traditions, exchange action for conference or the spear for the pen? He has not found it possible yet, and it will surely be many years before he does. Instead of this, a proud, lone man has walked back into his reserve, his own undisputed kingdom, taking good care to bolt the door firmly against all the revolutionary ideas of European "progress". And so the familiar picture remains, one that many of us find very heartening, rekindling our faith in human nature – the picture of the Masai warrior, his blanket around him, gazing towards the infinite horizon, guarding the cattle on his wind-swept highlands.'

Indeed a fine picture, but today's *moran* is brawling in the bars of Loitokitok or sleeping off his hangover in the *manyatas* of Narok. The door of his kingdom has fallen off its hinges, and the invader stands on the threshold. The time for the *moran* to get earth under his fingernails has come.

Next morning we took the old Nairobi road through the treeless Athi plains, startling zebra, Grant's gazelle and even a herd of eland.

The edge of a valley unfolded a dramatic change of scenery. The plain abruptly ended in a patchwork of homesteads. Kikuyu mud-and-thatch huts – both round and square – interspersed with modern tile-roofed houses surrounded an extensive Catholic mission with its church, classrooms and dormitory blocks. Acacia and dark-crowned acokanthera stood between the dappled fields. This was Kiserian, 'the place of peace', where the Masai *laibon* (spiritual leader), Lenana, was buried in 1911 after conceding the Laikipia Plateau to European settlement. 'Tell my people,' he is reputed to have said on his death-bed, 'to obey the government as they have done during my life. Tell the Laikipia Masai to move with their cattle to the Loita plains.' The Laikipia Masai did not like the idea, but the British moved them all the same. Kiserian became one of Kenya's many tribal melting pots, with Kikuyu married to Luo, Boran to Masai and Kamba to Kisii, a small corner into which diverse people came together to form what Oskar Koenig, typical of the European of his day, called 'the loud, decadent, rootless urban proletariat', who were now selling produce, working in shops, bars and restaurants, driving buses, taxis and lorries, repairing roads, making furniture and engaging in all the other activities of a settled society. It was also a picture of what all that remained of Masailand was likely to become.

We rode to Ngong over a series of ridges through closely cultivated fields at the foot of the hills, whose thicketed peaks still sheltered buffalo, eland and reedbuck. Ngong came into being early in the last century as a place for caravans to halt and rest on their way to the north. It then also marked the boundary between Masailand and the forests of the Wakikuyu. Teleki and von Hoehnel camped there for a fortnight. 'A very pretty neighbourhood,' von Hoehnel says, 'on the edge of a thick wood behind which dwelt the dreaded people of Kikuyu, while on the south stretched vast pastures tenanted by the great herds of cattle belonging to the Masai.'

Southern Kikuyuland

The Wakikuyu are Kenya's most numerous tribe. They settled in the area surrounding Mount Kenya and the Aberdare range between the twelfth and fourteenth centuries. During the nineteenth century, when the coastal slave and ivory traders were pushing ever farther northward, the Wakikuyu became one of the first tribes to produce a food surplus, which they sold to the passing caravans. They were also among the first to come into contact with the British colonisers, who violently plucked them out of the Iron Age and dragooned them into the twentieth century. With frenetic dynamism then, the Wakikuyu applied themselves to the new state of affairs. They extended their tentacles into every corner of the land and every activity undertaken in it. Today they are Kenya's industrial powerhouse, the omnipresent worker, bar owner, trader and bus driver.

However, despite their intelligence, adaptability, energy and success, a newcomer is still likely, not many days after his arrival, to hear from members of other tribes or from expatriates the warning, 'Never trust a Kikuyu.'

The horrors of Mau Mau have not been forgotten, but the events that led up to them largely have. Aversion towards the Wakikuyu existed long before Mau Mau. By the time they reached Ngong, Teleki and von Hoehnel had already heard many tales about this tribe's violence and treachery. A trading caravan, they were told, which had attempted to cross Kikuyu territory a few years earlier, had been totally destroyed, since when 'no traders had dared to venture within the range of their poisoned arrows'. Thus, as they now stood poised on the threshold of Kikuyuland, the explorers braced themselves for 'a time of trial and adventure'. They were unaware that Kikuyu resistance to foreign intrusion was fully justified.

Violence for its own sake belongs to the behaviour pattern of the mentally unstable. When the sane resort to violence there must be reasons. The reasons for Kikuyu violence were understood perfectly well by the coastal traders, but were too unsavoury for European ears. From their earliest contacts with the Wakikuyu, the traders had tended to evade payment for goods, to forage for food in gardens without the permission of the owners, to take sides in local affairs and even to resort to intimidation by using firearms.

Stories about the Wakikuyu were also told to Teleki and von Hoehnel as a deterrent. Their chief guide, a Swahili from the coast named Jumbe Kimemeta, was a professional ivory and slave trader. He had already crossed Kikuyuland, which no European had yet succeeded in doing. Kimemeta suspected that if he now helped the explorers to cross it, he would also be helping them to discover his ivory sources and become his trading rivals. Hence, at Ngong, it was he who spread rumours of impending Kikuyu attacks in order to undermine morale. Unbeknown to his employers, Kimemeta was also well known for his habit of kidnapping Wakikuyu and taking them away as slaves. Quite naturally then, the Wakikuyu feared Teleki and von Hoehnel by virtue of their association with this scoundrel and resolved to bar their passage.

But just as the explorers' prospects were beginning to look gloomy, a piece of luck came their way. Waiyaki, probably the most influential Kikuyu elder of his day, befriended them and led them from Ngong to his village. From there he did his best to smooth the way by introducing them to his peers and protecting them from xenophobic young warriors. Teleki's caravan was nevertheless forced to fight three relatively minor battles against the Wakikuyu. The tribesmen's abhorrence of intrusion made resistance inevitable, but Waiyaki's efforts went a long way towards ensuring that Teleki did not become involved in full-scale war. Had Waiyaki not made those efforts, that is what would have happened, and Teleki would never have got through.

Teleki's route during this part of the journey is not easy to reconstruct, mainly because few Wakikuyu were of a mind to enlighten him of his whereabouts during his stormy passage. However, from the available clues it is possible to plot a line running roughly north-north-east over more than thirty-six rivers, all flowing south-east from the slopes of the Aberdare Mountains. The line runs from Ngong to Mang'u and from there to the confluence of the Thuruthuru and North Mathioya rivers up to Kiganjo.

Jim and I set out on foot in an incandescent noon on 1 June 1982 to follow this route. The just-ended long rains had left puddles and soggy ruts. Trees and bushes glistened with moisture. Insects shrilled with incautious contentment as birds hunted them in the foliage. My rucksack had been packed with severe economy, yet its weight was almost intolerable. Jim's was a makeshift affair with his rolled sleeping bag tied to the top of it. We had no idea where we would spend the night, and our heads had been stuffed full of stories about gangs armed with *pangas*. Thus, a hundred years after Teleki, we were in exactly the same state of trepidation as he had been.

Dagoretti Road passes for its first three miles through Nairobi's posh suburb of Karen, named after the writer Karen Blixen. Here mansions nestled behind hedges so high that only wrought-iron gates betrayed the existence of habitation. Two decades earlier, land prices had so rocketed that people of modest means, mostly Europeans, found themselves suddenly gentrified. Now their children rode fine horses, accompanied by faithful syces. It was memsahib country, from which the white Mercedes swooshed the master silkily to town, and where the back seats of well-washed Peugeots were piled with shopping, their rear windows proclaiming their owners' philosophies: Save the Rhino; I'd rather be sailing; I love Kenya.

A lane led us into the Motoine valley. For years I had watched barefoot women and girls carrying bundles of firewood down that lane but, as an inhabitant of memsahib land myself, I had never bothered to explore their destination. After barely five minutes we were already in a land apart, almost in another age, passing among mud houses with roofs of flattened tin cans and doors made of packing cases. The water supply was the Motoine. A nine-year-old girl was dragging a plastic container to her shack during her lunch break. She would take it to a kitchen range of three stones on an earth floor and do her homework that night by the light of a paraffin cresset fashioned from a discarded tin.

Then we reached Dagoretti, in the valley of the Nairobi River, a huddle of timber shacks cheek by jowl, its market square a splatter of colour lined with barbers' shops, radio repair shops, timber and charcoal yards and many little bars and cafés. The stink of raw sewage hung in the air. Women in brilliantly white dresses were walking home from church, Sunday-best-clad children trailing them stiffly in unaccustomed shoes. It was Madaraka Day, the anniversary of Kenya's self-rule. The President's speech blared from every radio, and every bar was full.

Walking up the long steep hill towards the suburb of Kikuyu, a route I had often driven along but never touched with my feet, I felt the sensation of stepping into an unknown, where all the experience I had acquired since leaving Pangani would be irrelevant. 'You are not going to like it,' Rafael, the Kikuyu restaurant-keeper of Murueshi in Masailand had said, and his words had stuck in my mind. 'You're going to meet people very different from those you've come across so far. You're going to get rudeness and aggression, because people will take you for a hippie and treat you with contempt. They'll notice that you're old and seeing you walking with a sack on your back they will think you're a failure. So many of them have been taught by whites, told that whites have high standards they ought to copy, so when they see you they will think you have fallen below the standards of your fellow-whites, that you are a freak.' Suddenly my mind was awash with ominous visions.

At the top of a slope we reached an open pasture, beyond which a lone white mansion rose before us from the dusky greenery of a coffee grove. But it was incomplete and empty. Curtainless windows gazed into the distance with the despondency of a host whose visitors have failed to arrive. The house was almost as incongruously imposing as Grogan's Castle; would it, too, I wondered, one day become too expensive to run and be left to crumble into the bushes?

The coffee grove was bounded by a man-high hedge resplendent with spikes of indigo-coloured flowers. This was the muigoya (*Plectanthrus barbatus*) plant, traditionally used by the Wakikuyu to mark off the land boundaries which the British claimed never existed. Its velvety soft leaves were – and continue to be – used as toilet paper and handkerchiefs. Pushing our way through we startled a schoolboy, who was taking cuttings. Githika was his name, he said, a descendant of the famous Waiyaki, and he became the first of our many guides. It was, he added gravely, a Kikuyu tradition to put strangers on the right path. There and then Githika laid aside what he was doing and led us through a cluster of trees as old as his ancestor to the edge of a potato field. It was here, according to Githika's grandfather, that Teleki had camped in September 1887. Beyond it stood a modest house belonging to another descendant of Waiyaki's: Munyua, a one-time foreign minister. And the great mansion, Githika said, also belonged to an ex-foreign minister, Njoroge Mungai.

From Mbugici we walked into a suburb of impeccably built bungalows, all tile-roofed and standing in gardens enclosed by meticulously trimmed Kei apple hedges. Panelled doors and polished windows reflected the weight of their owners' bank accounts. Engraved brass plates fixed to the railings of gates bore the names of well-known Nairobi commuters, mostly Kikuyu. On this public holiday, members of this bourgeoisie could be seen pacing lawns, their wives and daughters smart in expensive blouses and flared slacks, dead-heading and watering carnations. 'Where are you heading?' a woman called out. 'Nyeri? Impossible. No one can walk to Nyeri!' What she meant was that it was unreasonable for anyone in his right mind to walk if he could afford to be transported.

At Muthure we were sold cokes by a strikingly beautiful woman, who smiled with large clear eyes, her skin as pale as milky coffee. Her shop was stocked with everything from chicken feed to chewing gum, and every item in it made in Kenya. She handed out sweets and cigarettes by the piece and weighed out on a Kenya-made pair of scales.

'You there!' someone shouted. A scraggy young man in a stained suit stood unsteadily before us, holding out half a pear in one hand and a penknife in the other. Precariously he cut us each a piece and watched as we ate his gift. 'You stay here and eat paw! Where are you going? Down the road, you say, down the road? Don't go there. You will meet cowboys – you know, like thugs, very bad. They see you carry bag, they take everything.' He staggered after us until we shook him off. 'Everything,' he wailed, 'you'll see!'

'Wouldn't it be humiliating,' I remarked to Jim, 'if our walk ended in disaster on the very first day.'

'The man was drunk and talking rubbish, so just stop worrying,' he said brusquely.

Wangige was an untidy village, sprouting on both sides of the road leading back to town, a stage with revving buses and taxis. Here too Madaraka Day was still in spate, with every other man swaying at some stage of intoxication. Suddenly I heard my name called out. From behind a derelict car emerged Kabuthia, burly and smiling, a man I had known for years. Anxiety evaporated. It was dusk, but now our fate was in his hands.

He shepherded us into a bar, where, he said, we would also be able to get a room for the night. By virtue of being in his company, we ceased to be curiosities and became honoured guests. A barmaid, dewlaps quivering with every step, brought our order on a tray steadied upon a cushion of bosom. Noticing an old man opposite struggling with a dud matchbox, I gave him a light. He rose and took my hand in both of his. 'Njoroge Mungai's father,' Kabuthia said. 'Circumcised on the same day as Kenyatta, so he's at least eighty-seven.' What was the secret of his longevity? A broad smile creased his thin, austere face, revealing a row of gleaming white teeth. He ostentatiously picked up his beer with one hand and waved his cigarette with the other.

Among the Wakikuyu around the time of Mungai's birth, beer drinking accompanied almost every social and ceremonial occasion. Intoxication was in those days a golden chariot drawn by foamy stallions for transcendental rides into the land of the departed spirits, there to rest for a while as close to God as the ancestors and then to be carried back suffused with divinely inspired wisdom and energy to apply to the mundane problems of the here and now. By the time that we sat in the bar in Wangige on that eighteenth anniversary of self-rule, the drinking accompanying the initiations of warriors and diviners, the ceremonies to save failing crops and the oblations to God existed only in the records of historians and anthropologists, but the social significance of beer had survived. When friends meet, business is transacted or a house built, after a birth, baptism or marriage, there must always be beer. 'Beer,' Kabuthia said, 'does not just mean that we are drinking, but that our hearts are coming together.'

It was clear that serious drinking was about to begin, for by now a dozen Kabuthia cousins were already lined up. One of them, Njau, was already extremely drunk. A middle-aged woman dug an elbow into him, throwing provocative glances in my direction. 'She wants to know,' Kabuthia explained, laughter shaking his heavy shoulders, 'if you have come here to fuck. You see, nobody would dream of spending the night in a place like this unless he was going to sleep with a woman. Of course, I know that you and Jim are not here for that, so I'll make sure you are left alone.'

But he had obviously not yet passed the word around. One of the pink-smocked barmaids, who had just flounced off with the grace of a beached dugong, was making explicit gestures to me from the door. When I shook my head she stuck out her tongue.

For the past half-hour Njau had been pouring his life story into my ear in a voice rendered inarticulate by drink. Leaning against me, he was becoming insufferable. 'Kabuthia,' I said with a wink, 'these girls in here are useless. Can't you send Njau to get us better ones?'

'Go, Njau,' Kabuthia told him, 'go and get women for our friends. Get spring chickens. They don't want old ones like these in here.'

Njau's face fell. 'At this time of night? Where shall I get women now?'

Kabuthia was relentless. He had seniority.

Njau staggered out. After a brief hiatus of sanity he was back. 'No women,' he muttered. 'All gone. Can't find.' But the night air had steadied him and curbed his verbosity.

The evening had edged towards incoherence. Boys in flat caps, high-stepping like gangsters, began floating in to see if anyone would buy them a drink. A woman fell asleep in her chair and knocked her glass over, but no one bothered to mop up. Kabuthia and Njau escorted us to our room. 'See you at seven tomorrow morning,' Njau promised. Like hell you will, I thought as I fell into bed.

But he was true to his word, standing at the door, fresh and bright in a smart grey suit. I was still half asleep, head ticking like a Chinese clock. 'I'm off to town,' Njau announced. 'Just wanted to make sure you guys are OK. Here's your *gitete*.' It was a dozen boiled eggs in a brown paper bag. The *gitete* is the bottle gourd every Kikuyu traveller used to carry for his host of the night to fill with gruel.

At the edge of the damp Mutundu valley, whose scrupulously cultivated fields lay fat under the sun's slanting rays, was Kirangari, a typical south Kiambu village with its square of shops, all high at the front and low at the back where a wall enclosed a courtyard with not a window facing outwards.

As we stopped to watch a smith welding an iron window-grille, children crept up to watch us. Surreptitiously they enclosed us in an ever tightening corral of expressionless faces with eyes the colour of roasted coffee beans rinsed in water. There was not a flicker of mischief in any, but every pair radiated an indecisive curiosity, the look of a hungry puppy encountering a stranger, hoping for a biscuit yet fearing a kick. As the children edged forward inch by inch, pushed forward by ranks of others behind them, they made no sound save the occasional awed whisper. It seemed to me that to them we were symbols of the unattainable luxury they had most often seen as bodiless heads flashing past behind the windows of cars; on foot we were more tangible and therefore rarer.

Noticing the growing press around him, the smith looked up and shooed the children away with sharp reprimands. 'They have never seen a white here before and some of them have never seen one anywhere,' he told us as if he thought we were entitled to an explanation of their behaviour. We were hardly ten miles from Nairobi, yet we were to learn that in rural Kenya the average black hardly ever meets a white at eye level.

That evening we booked in at what seemed an orderly lodging at Kiambaa. I was less sure that it would remain orderly when I found on the wall of my room a framed picture displaying a Japanese lady in high-heeled shoes wriggling out of a white sports car, naked. Jim's room had one of the same lady wearing nothing but a Father Christmas hat, kneeling on the floor decorating an aspidistra with candles and tinsel. However, apart from these scenes of Japanese high life, the lodging was a place of wiped bottles, formica-topped tables, sausage and chips, and a reassuring notice that said 'No Dancing'.

In the bar, we settled contentedly down beside a silent juke box to a day's-end beer. We spread out the map and began working out tomorrow's route. Suddenly the doors burst open. With a whirlwind leap a blue-clad figure flew across the floor and crashed against the bar beside us. To our surprise he was a European, very young, thickset with a head of curly light brown hair. Beetroot-faced and choking with exertion, he smelt strongly of hot sweat and carbolic soap. For a minute or two he was quite unable to speak. I called for a brandy, and he downed it in one long gulp. 'Christ!' he panted. 'Am I glad to see you blokes in here. I've never been so frightened the whole of my life. You see, I've only been in this country a week. I joined the Mountain Club and today I went climbing with a group at Lukenya. I wanted to get back to the Grange School at Tigoni where I've got a job as a teacher, but those people dropped me at Banana Hill, where, they said, I'd be able to get a taxi. It was nearly dark and I couldn't find anyone willing to take me. The drivers all said so many taxis had been hijacked that none of them dared move after dark. So I started walking. First one boy started walking with me, then two. Within ten minutes there were about fifteen of them, all telling me they would show me the short cuts. Well, everyone had already told me how easily one can get beaten up and robbed and so I was really scared. I kept telling the boys I didn't want to go along the short cuts, but the more I said so the more insistent they got. Look, there's one of them – he's over there sitting at the bar. Anyway, in the end I just started running and them with me. That's when I reached this place and just rushed in hoping to find protection.'

It had taken just a week for the foundations of fear to be laid in the mind of this young man, fresh from the Lake District of north-west England, in Africa for the first time in his life. We calmed him down and tried to convince him that the boys' intentions had probably been above board, but he went off to bed unconvinced. Von Hoehnel's image of the Wakikuyu as a 'dreaded people' was still alive and well.

For three more days Nairobi's silvery towers and the buffalo-black Ngong Hills remained visible beyond the pencil cedars which rose above the feathery eucalyptus and croton. Beyond the Riara River we rested by a hut in a bee-humming garden of pastel-coloured cosmos and heavy-scented sweet peas. A young man put down a bundle of tomato poles and stopped for a smoke. He said he was a landowner growing vegetables by the river and making a good living, with nearby Kiambu providing a ready market. His bare feet and tattered trousers made it hard to believe that even the poles were his property. Having enquired our destination, he said we had strayed. He led us a mile back to a high-hedged path which meandered into the bungalow outskirts of Ndumberi. Through a wrought-iron gate I glimpsed a white-gloved lady in a pink frock and high-heeled shoes pruning yellow roses. Only her face was a reminder that we were not in Surrey.

Ndumberi was on the brink of becoming a Nairobi suburb, with a bank, shoeshop and petrol station as its trappings. It even had a miniature golf course, famous throughout Kenya and carefully tended by a boy using a push-mower. Retired caddies with such a passion for the game that they could not bear the thought of giving it up had pooled their resources to buy the land. 'I have a handicap of eight,' a seventy-year-old man proudly told Jim. 'We even have our own club house – you can see it over there by the market – and we play matches with clubs all over Kenya. You can come and play here any time you like.'

Just as we were folding our map, a young man asked us where we were heading. He too was bound for Riuki. Ndung'u's broken shoes were indistinguishable from those worn by the hundreds of others like him we had passed, but within minutes he had asserted his individuality.

We climbed ridge after ridge until we rejoined the main road to Githunguri. A lonely cluster of shops perched on a knoll inspired thoughts of a cool drink, but on approach they proved to be shuttered, locked and bolted. A solitary shirt fluttering on a line was the only sign of life. 'They started in 1965,' Ndung'u explained, 'the Kiambu robber gangs. Whenever they noticed a centre like this being built, they would patiently watch and wait until the shops and bars flourished and got well stocked. Then they would drive up in cars and lorries and empty the lot. A butcher I know near Githiga was robbed three times. They even took his meat. In the end he gave up and bought a bus.'

Ngemwa, another raped trading centre had an air of desperate expectancy, while a smell of failure hung over the empty shells of the buildings, all stoutly built of stone but powerless none the less. 'When those fellows come,' said Ndung'u, 'they are in groups of twenty and thirty, fully organised like a military operation. They have guns, crowbars, wire cutters and pickaxes. No one can resist them. You will find Riuki the same. We used to have restaurants and lodgings there, but all but two of them have been forced to close.'

Ndung'u did not know that tribal discipline and the influence of elders would have made such raids impossible in the centuries before the coming of the white man. As it was, the spectacle of Ngemwa represented to me a sad illustration of police inability to protect the populace.

Ndung'u told us he had left school six years before when he was eighteen, but had never tried finding a job. 'I knew then as I know now that you will not get one unless you know someone important, so what I did was to find a lorry owner. We started taking green maize to Nairobi until the government banned it. Then we resorted to putting it in the middle of the lorry and covering it up with sacks of potatoes. But that was risky, because if you were caught, the owner would be fined and even have his lorry confiscated.

'In the end it got so hot we had to just stick to potatoes. These days I go to Narok. I buy them for 40 shillings a sack and pay the driver another 40 for each sack he carries. At the market we usually get 100, so I make 20 on each. But it's an uncertain business, because I can fail to find a lorry or, if I do, I can get to Narok to find that there are no potatoes.'

Why Narok in particular? 'It's because there are Kikuyu there who grow nothing else. What they lack is transport and that is why the potatoes are so cheap. But most of the land there is owned by Masai, who do nothing but sit while the money comes rolling in. How? Well, it's the breweries. They provide tractors, seed and labour. Then they harvest the barley and take it away, after which the Masai are paid in proportion with the amount harvested.'

Ndung'u's home was two unlined clapboard huts. One, divided by partitions, served as living room and bedrooms. The other was the kitchen. In the small courtyard between them, chickens scratched and a bushy dog slept. We sat on hard chairs round the living room table. A radio shrouded in a cloth stood on a sideboard. There were two wooden shuttered windows, and an old piece of carpeting on the floor. The walls were decorated with family photographs, one of them of Ndung'u's parents' white wedding displayed next to a certificate signed by a representative of the Pope. Ndung'u's father was over-weight and sad, in retirement due to heart trouble after working in Nairobi as a plumber. He now sold firewood and burned charcoal for a living. 'You shall return to supper,' he told us. 'There will be eggs.'

Apart from Ndung'u's efforts, the father's trade and a small piece of land, the family had no source of income. Ndung'u's three brothers were all unemployed. His sister Wangari, who looked as sad as her father, had taken a typing course, but there had been no work for her either.

That night we were gripped by hospitality until we could hardly stand. Finally, at the lodging, the head of a family of epileptics, whose only daughter had died in a fit with her head in a charcoal brazier, was determined to buy us a drink. He pushed us physically into the bar, from where, after attempting to hit Ndung'u, he was taken away by his friends.

A bright young man informed us in an American accent that he was 'a fan of the international pop scene', adding that he owned a very good record player and that he was our neighbour. I silently prayed he would spend the night elsewhere. We left him and made for our beds. His door opened and shut. Then came – at full volume – two hours of Zaire, Kikuyu, Swahili, reggae, soul, Beatles, German love songs and the dreary but beloved Jim Reeves. In the small hours my guts exploded. Repeatedly I had to stumble to the hole over its stinking pit, my wind bursting like grenades. I slept in fear of cholera.

At dawn the tap was dry, and we left rubbing grit out of our eyes. Ndung'u, who had planned to go to Narok that day, had been ordered by his father to escort us to the Catholic mission. We had chanced upon its priest along the road the previous day. In the course of a brief conversation, he had invited us to stop off for breakfast with him, the mission being on our course.

At his modest bungalow tucked away amid coffee fields, Father Brady welcomed us ecstatically. But as he extended his right arm to enfold us, his left was thrust out to exclude Ndung'u and his brother, Nderi. 'You two wait here in the garden while I talk to these two gentlemen,' he told them in a soothing Irish accent; then turning to us, 'They'll be all right out there.' We subsided into comfortable armchairs between a well-stocked book case and a plaster statue of the Virgin. But the priest's act of exclusion had made me feel distinctly uncomfortable and alienated.

Father Brady had spent forty years in Kenya. He spoke Kikuyu well enough to preach in it, which seemed a commendable achievement. 'Yes, well, round here I know almost every family,' he said. 'I visit their houses and they treat me as one of themselves. The father of those boys out there, Paul, is the chairman of my church committee. They are all such nice, friendly people, but my goodness, when you get to know them like that you find out things about them that others – people like yourselves – will never get to know of.'

'What about the population explosion?' Jim asked abruptly – out of context, his voice betraying a hint of Protestant fervour.

The priest reacted with trained equanimity. 'Well, you see, being of my persuasion,' he said in honeyed tones, 'I think that God in His wisdom will take care of all of them and find a place for each. God has His own way of taking care of problems of this sort and I am confident it will all work out satisfactorily in the end.'

As Jim fruitlessly pursued this topic, I speculated on how aware Father Brady – clearly a well-liked extrovert – was of the non-spiritual problems of his flock. Trusting in God does not always fill the belly, and if it remains empty for long enough there are limits to what one can do short of taking to theft. How long would Ndung'u and the multitudes like him tolerate the prospect of falling out of school straight into a social garbage pit?

Once out of the compound and having crossed in a step the border between Ireland and Kikuyuland, guilt caught up with my well-fed complaisance, and I voiced disapproval of Father Brady's repudiation of the boys.

'That's all right,' Ndung'u said calmly. 'I told you yesterday that the customs you whites have are different from ours. I understand that, but Nderi is shocked, because he's still young. If people are standing at the door of one of our houses, we cannot ask some of them in and leave others outside.'

Jim took Ndung'u's comments at face value, but I interpreted them as the outward dismissal of a bitterly felt resentment. Having lived in the country for so long and on such intimate terms with the people, the priest ought not to have behaved with such callousness. Jim argued that Father Brady, who had come here at the height of the colonial period, could not change his ways, could not come down from the pulpit to the congregation. Such men regarded their privacy as an essential refuge, he asserted. I disagreed. Certainly everyone had the right to privacy, but favouring two of his own race to the exclusion of two of another could only be an expression of apartheid – intellectual, racial, or both.

On the high ridge above the Ngewa River we told Ndung'u, who had shown no sign of wishing to part from us, that we could easily find Mang'u on our own. We gave him a hundred shillings, hoping it would go some way towards compensating him for his lost time. Beyond the river I became so weak that I could think of nothing but rest. I trailed Jim over three more ridges until we reached Kibichoi, a one-street village dominated by a two-storeyed building, grim and square like a south Arabian fort. When I spotted a board-and-lodging sign over its door, I confessed I could go no farther that day.

We climbed up a dark stairway to a courtyard, where our appearance generated bewilderment so extreme that everyone scattered, leaving us perplexed. Perhaps they took us to be a pair of white gangsters. A few minutes later a furtive-looking fellow enquired our needs and gave us a room each. Drinking water was brought in a plastic bottle that had originally contained engine oil. I laced it with chlorine tablets and spent the rest of the day drinking it. This was my time-tested treatment for diarrhoea.

Next day a boy who guided us to a short cut out of Kibichoi told us his family was landless, his father dead and he himself jobless since leaving school. He spoke without emotion, fully aware that he was not unique. His mother had work with accommodation on a coffee estate, and through her he was able to get picking jobs at three shillings a *debe*, or four-gallon tin. If he worked hard he could fill ten *debes* in a day, but outside the season there was nothing else. The future? What future? Life would go on and probably get worse. He made me feel paternal, wishing I could offer him a job and see his eyes light up. But when he had shown us the path, all I could do was press his hand in unhelpful gratitude. It was a familiar feeling, the same feeling that had overwhelmed me countless times when in this most hospitable of continents I saw the endless lines waiting resignedly for rare and overcrowded buses. Each time I felt myself wanting to help out, only to become bewildered in the face of such numbers and pass on in an empty car.

Gatundu was a larger and more affluent version of Ndumberi. At a spotless snack bar with tables bearing purpose-made salt cellars instead of the ubiquitous aspirin tins, the waiter told us Mang'u was only five miles off and we would find a good lodging there called the Leejam.

We followed the Ruabura valley for twelve miles, during which I rued believing the waiter. It was always the same: the greater the degree of fatigue noticed by an informant, the more irresistible the temptation to offer pleasing information. It was a long haul before we reached the tall trees of Mang'u. The Leejam was yet another fortress and the only double-storeyed building in the town. A heavy girl with a rippling walk, whom I described in my diary as a sweet-lipped tigress, brought us iced lemonade from behind an iron-grilled bar.

In the bathroom: no electricity, dry taps; several plastic basins in the bathtub, a drum of water in the corner; washbasin broken, mirror transferred elsewhere; no key in the door, handle broken. Why? I asked myself, remembering the countless times on which I had asked the same question of others. The response had consistently been a look of embarrassed surprise. That morning's young man at Kibichoi, not a shilling in his pocket, picking coffee, his head full of Eng Lang, Maths, Geog, Chem and Phys: what was it all for? Why had he not been trained to become an itinerant carpenter and plumber?

Waiting for supper in the veranda bar, we were joined by two men in their sixties. One was short and sharp-featured with eyes like an owl's and hands that never stopped moving. The tigress introduced him as Kamau, her uncle. The other, saddle-nosed and built like a wrestler, was Mburu, the local chief. The number of bottles on the table more than doubled within seconds.

Kamau picked up the book Jim had put on the table and riffled the pages. It was *The Myth of Mau Mau* (1970) by Rosberg and Nottingham. 'Yes,' said Kamau with a trace of pride, 'I knew this Captain Nottingham. Very good man. Never fired a shot during the whole of the emergency.'

In Kenya the word 'emergency' remains as evocative as 'Black-and-Tan' in Ireland. Directly it is mentioned, a discussion of Mau Mau becomes inevitable. Jim, investigative reporter by nature, hungrily took the bait. But in Kamau and Mburu, who soon proved themselves to be unusually erudite even by Kikuyu standards, he met his match.

'How is it that you fought the British then,' asked Jim, 'but now you're happy to sit and drink with us?'

The reply, which came from Mburu, did not surprise me. I had heard it before. 'We never fought the British. It was not the British we hated, but the settlers who were too greedy. The British we always liked and still do.'

'But most of the British who did the actual fighting were not the settlers and the same goes for those who tortured Mau Mau to "rehabilitate" them in the detention camps,' Jim argued.

'They were forced to do that. The settlers were too strong for them. They leaned on the government and the government people could not refuse. Left on their own, the government people would never have done such things. We never wanted to fight them. All we wanted was our land back and we wanted to get it peacefully. That is why most of us disagreed with the Mau Mau and even helped the British fight them. That is why thousands of us died but less than a hundred of your people.'

'Which side was Kenyatta on?' I asked.

'I'll answer that one,' Kamau put in. 'He was against Mau Mau from the beginning and in 1952 he made a very famous speech in which he said just that. He said everybody should search out Mau Mau and kill it and that Mau Mau should perish for ever. I was there myself in Kiambu when he said that.'

'Why then did the British put him in prison?'

'Ah, that is very easy to answer. We know that after that speech, one of the Mau Mau leaders went to Kenyatta and told him if he spoke against them again, they would kill him. Kenyatta knew they meant what they said, so from then on he had to be very careful. That is why the British began suspecting him. But as they had no proper evidence against him, they found a fellow called Rawson Macharia, one of Kenyatta's neighbours who bore him a grudge. They bribed this man to say he had seen Kenyatta administering a Mau Mau oath.'

'And that,' added Mburu, 'was how the British turned Kenyatta into a national leader. Before that he was supported mainly by those who were against fighting. But when he was punished for being on the side of the Mau Mau, even those people became his supporters. Those of the Mau Mau who knew the truth about Kenyatta's views were so few that all they could do was join the rest and keep quiet. That is why when Kenyatta preached reconciliation, everyone had to follow what he said.'

'But Ngugi Wa Thiong'o makes out that by agreeing to the principle of compensating the settlers, Kenyatta was effectively compensating gangsters,' Jim said. (Ngugi Wa Thiong'o is Kenya's best-known novelist and playwright, now living in exile in London.) 'He says making people pay for that land was like forcing them to buy back what thieves had stolen from them. And he also says that the only people who had the money to pay for the land were those who had earned it by helping the British fight the Mau Mau.'

'My goodness, here we go again!' Kamau chuckled gleefully before taking a long pull at his beer. 'The settlers didn't steal the land like gangsters. They bought it legally under a system we didn't think was fair to us. If we had tried to take it back by force, then we would have been behaving like gangsters and that was exactly what Kenyatta didn't want us to be. So, there was a compromise into which the British government put a lot of money and the people were helped to buy the land with loans. That was all very fair.'

'On whose behalf was Ngugi writing, then?' I asked.

'There are always some people who believe they have been unfairly treated. We Kikuyu learned very quickly that the British were too strong to resist. Instead we became Christians and sent our children to the mission schools. We changed and by working made ourselves rich. It was those rich, educated Christians who became the leaders of the people who didn't want to fight. They were on Kenyatta's side, because they did not want to risk losing what they already had and as Christians they deemed Mau Mau to be repugnant. The Mau Mau were mostly the pagan poor, who thought that by fighting they could get something for nothing. After Kenyatta went to prison, they were defeated. Those of them who had owned something had it confiscated and those who had nothing were the same as they were before.

'Then, over the years, the number of landless people increased. Ngugi is telling them to take by force what he believes ought to have been given to them. That is very wrong, because if fighting started, we who are rich would become poor and those who are poor now would become destitute. You only have to look at Ethiopia and Uganda to know what fighting did to those people.' ·

Jim would not have it. 'On the contrary,' he insisted, 'Ngugi is a passionate but true critic of society's selfishness, corruption and pitiless attitude towards the poor.'

'Not at all,' Kamau replied coolly. 'What he wants us to do is to destroy everything we have built on the European model. He wants us to knock down our factories and power plants, root up the railway and return to the old tribal customs. And there is no one in Kenya but he who wants to do that. We don't want tribes any more, but a modern people who will prosper in the modern world.'

The arrival of our food put an abrupt end to the conversation. Kamau and Mburu discreetly said it was time for them to go home. We were soon to regret their departure.

The portions of stew put in front of us were too small to satisfy, but when we called for more there was none to be had. Instead we ordered a large plate of chips. Its appearance coincided with the inception of a scene which was to bring a pleasant and instructive evening to an agonising conclusion. But what followed also illustrated that the rift which split the Wakikuyu during the Mau Mau times had survived in the form of a schizophrenia very near the surface of consciousness and never very far from the border with violence.

The noise level rose somewhat as the bar filled up, mostly with men whose well-pressed suits signalled prosperity and places near the top of the social ladder. The Falklands War – at its height that summer – dominated their quiet and well-mannered conversation. Britain is great again, was the theme; Britain can never be defeated. It was unlikely that any of them had read the *Sun*, but their opinions closely matched its attitudes.

The space opposite us had been taken by a lean elderly man, whose thick-lensed glasses hinted at intellectual leanings. He sat wedged between two very fat girls in da-glo-pink dresses who looked like identical twins. Together they made up a tableau of two well-fed wood pigeons on a branch either side of a sparrow.

The little enclave of silence in which we sat was broken by a creak of protest as a tall young man threw himself roughly into the chair beside me. I turned and met a pair of glassy eyes. There was no response to my nod acknowledging his presence other than an almost imperceptible narrowing of the lids. A reek of raw spirits reached me, and I turned away to spear some chips. Hardly a moment elapsed before he assailed us with three consecutive questions delivered like short bursts from a Sten-gun. 'What is this rubbish you are eating? Why don't you eat the food of men? Where do you come from?'

The last question was not an enquiry to establish the whereabouts of our starting point that day, but a way of demanding to know our tribal origins. As such, it was by local conventional standards considered to be even ruder than the two questions preceding it.

Taken aback by this blustering intrusion and lulled into a false sense of security by the decorum dominating the atmosphere in the bar, I embarked on a foolish attempt to defuse the man's anger. 'Are you from Kakamega?' I retorted, implying that he was a Luhya from western Kenya.

His eyes shot me a volley of poisoned arrows. The sparrow-man opposite leaned forward. 'Good question,' he said in an Oxford-accented voice. 'Very good question.'

Vainly I hoped he would also address the drunk to curb the rising temperature, but he said no more before edging back into his pneumatic bower.

The drunk now turned tack and launched at us a platitudinous lecture on education. Cambridge was the best university in Britain. He needed to go there for a degree in engineering, but also needed a sponsor. An index finger rose and travelled like an accusation to within an inch of my nose. 'This old man can pay,' he stated like a judge issuing a verdict of guilty. 'He is rich. I can see that he is rich.'

Jim came to the rescue by explaining that I was not, that I was on a journey I had saved up for. 'How can you expect me to save?' the drunk asked rhetorically, his tone suddenly plaintive. 'I hardly have enough to pay my children's school fees.'

Momentarily forgetting the state he was in, I pointed at his beer. 'By giving this up for a start.'

He threw me a look of hatred and stormed out of the bar.

'That was well done,' said the man opposite. 'And you played a clean game.'

I said I was glad it was over.

I was wrong. The drunk was back at the table. A bellow in my ear nearly flung me to the ground in fright. He pulled his chair so close to mine that our shoulders touched. Politely I asked him not to shout at me.

'This is Africa!' he roared. 'We can shout here any time we like. If you don't like it you can get out.' His voice rose to a crescendo. 'Who are you to give me orders?'

He looked away and addressed the company in general. 'Now this old man is becoming difficult.' My sleeve was being tugged as he redirected his attention to me. 'Why are you becoming difficult?'

'Difficult' in that context meant stiff-necked or arrogant. The term has racial overtones. The question was a declaration of war. I knew that any rejoinder would provoke his fist.

It was as if his voice had scooped up all the others. The hush that descended was that of an empty church. We were encircled by rows of eyes, but all were as expressionless as those of fish gazing out of an aquarium. Not a finger stirred, and not a shoe scraped. All I could hear was the agitated pumping of my own heart.

Escape was the only possible course. We rose like automatons from our chairs and made for the door. Silence pursued us, but when we reached the top of the stairs a tinkle of glass set off a bedlam of voices amid crashings of furniture. Out of the ferment repeatedly rose the words 'black', 'white' and 'brother'. To me they signified that the scar tissue which had grown over the wounds of the past was still very sensitive and that the slightest of scratches could be a sharp reminder of the pain once suffered, of old enmities only superficially reconciled.

A great deal of property was destroyed that night, but when we left the next morning there was not a policeman to be seen.

John Boyes's Kingdom

Haraka, haraka, haina baraka (there is no virtue in haste), the Swahili saying advises, but so obsessed were we to put distance between us and the schizophrenia of the previous night that we jogged out of Mang'u like a pair of light infantrymen. That madness even more turbulent lay ahead and that it was ubiquitous was something we were still happily unaware of.

Von Hoehnel says that on 22 September 1887 his party crossed a stream, which he does not name but describes as having been 5½ yards wide and 27 inches deep. On that day their guides told them that 'all the chiefs of Kikuyuland had entered into a league to take vengeance on us and prevent us from going any farther'. The vengeance was for the Wakikuyu whom the explorers and their men had killed the previous day at a place identifiable as Mang'u. L. S. B. Leakey, in *The Southern Kikuyu before 1903* (1977) recalls that Kabetu Wa Waweru, who claimed to have been present, said Teleki wanted to punish the Wakikuyu for some thefts 'and fought them without mercy, killing about 250'. Leakey says the 'stream' Teleki's party then crossed was the Chania. That river is the natural boundary between southern and northern Kikuyuland.

On the road parallel with its right bank, a boy aged about sixteen offered to help us find a ford. He seemed very self-possessed and spoke English with a remarkable precision. He was also so unusually well dressed for his age that I complimented him on it. 'It is my secret,' he said, smiling, 'but I will tell you. By the time I was in standard seven I had seen so many of the older boys failing to find a job that I decided going on to secondary school was a waste of time. Now Mang'u is the only place between Gatundu and Kandara with a vehicle-repair garage. I noticed that it was the welder who always had the most work. I made friends with him and started helping at weekends for a shilling a day. That year I left school and started working for him full time. Welding isn't difficult, but you have to know exactly what to do. After a few months of learning I started getting work in my own right. Then the welder inherited his father's farm and left to take it over. He sold me his tools and now I have his business. All welding to be done here comes to me. That's why I can buy everything I need without having to trouble my parents.'

He had other ambitious plans. Growing passion fruit and wattle trees would bring in enough to build himself a house before he was twenty. He was one of the hopefully growing number who were realising that a living need not be made by using one's brain or one's hands, each to the exclusion of the other, but could be made by using both.

He left us at the end of a path, which, he said, led down to the ford.

At a crowded restaurant in Kirwara, we ordered *irio*, the standard Kikuyu dish of mashed potatoes, peas and maize, which, taken in the middle of the day, renders supper superfluous. We were just finishing the last crumbs when, whooping, jangling and cavorting, a trio of madmen rolled in.

Their leader was very old. He was dressed from head to foot in a patchwork of gunny sacking, which hung from his frame like moss on a juniper. It was from this, I later learned, that he derived his nickname, Magunia ('Sacks'). A bunch of cock's tail feathers waggled from his hatband, and an insecticide spray canister protruded from his breast pocket. Strapped to his forearm with a band of beaded leather was a cow's horn. A dozen spoons dangled from his belt.

With staring eyes and twitching beard he bounded from customer to customer in a series of crouching leaps like one of the Zulu chieftain Shaka's witchdoctors smelling out an evildoer. Tea was what he wanted, but no one would oblige. His tatterdemalion companions meanwhile – the one bald and one-eyed, the other fox-faced and rheumy-eyed – gyrated in the centre of the floor, shouting with theatrical menace that they would do as they pleased 'in this free land of Kenya'.

There is only one mental hospital in Kenya. It is situated in the Mathare suburb of Nairobi and is always full to overflowing. The vast majority of insane people are outside it. They wander around like stray dogs, begging and scavenging to keep alive. Uneducated Kenyans – and even some of the educated – attribute insanity to evil spirits introduced through witchcraft. The insane know that they are not only pitied but also feared. Instinctively they use this knowledge to help them survive. When nothing is forthcoming by inspiring pity, fear comes readily to hand as an alternative. Only when one of them goes to the lengths of assault will the police intervene, but even then, only with great reluctance.

The waiters stood back helpless in the face of a manic invasion in such force, for madmen usually appear as isolated individuals, rarely in groups. The boldest waiter crept out from behind his counter and made a timid move to remonstrate. Magunia's face assumed a look of gargoyle ferocity. A stern finger pointed at the shrinking waiter's nose. 'You leave me alone!' Magunia roared in Swahili for the benefit of the representatives of all tribes who may have been present. 'This is a public place where I can do as I please!'

The waiter withdrew to his refuge, muttering. Jim, his face a shade paler than usual, slid away to the toilet, no doubt praying that the situation would resolve itself during his absence.

Trapped now in the fragile isolation of my whiteness, I pulled a book out of my satchel and tried to read, hoping to escape notice. But inevitably I had become a magnet. Before I was able to read a paragraph, the trio had settled in the empty chairs around my table like foul-smelling vultures descending on a wounded pig. 'I am a trained metal worker,' Magunia announced stridently, adding with the irrefutable logic of the insane, 'and therefore you are going to buy us tea.'

His companions sat opposite, gripping the edge of the table with knotted hands, their eyes fixed expectantly upon me. Had I been armed with the hindsight garnered from subsequent encounters with insane people, I would have given them money, called down upon them the blessings of God and politely asked them to leave me in peace. But on this first occasion, the intimate proximity of grimacing faces and putrid breath panicked me into the feeble strategy of white man's aloofness. 'I am reading and drinking my tea,' I said with haughty pomposity. 'I did not come here to buy tea for you.'

Magunia edged closer and added volume to his voice. 'You, *mzungu* (white man), I am talking to you, do you hear?'

Spittle sprayed my cheek. No voice other than Magunia's was audible. Nervously I threw a glance over my shoulder, only to find to my surprise that, unlike the previous evening, all eyes were turned away. Why? I asked myself. The answer came swiftly. The man at the Leejam had been drunk but not insane. The others at the bar had been watching and would have intervened had he turned violent. He could still have been persuaded to see reason. By contrast, the trio around me now were not only drunk but mad and, as such, feared. Eyes were averted in a silence of helpless embarrassment.

Except in the case of one elderly man. When suddenly the trio left the table, he deftly took Magunia's place, bringing with him a half-empty cup of tea. It was a deliberate act, fully in keeping with the old ruling that no Kikuyu could escape the wrath of God and the spirits if he allowed a peaceful stranger to be harmed.

He nudged me. 'Mad,' he said apologetically. But he was overheard. Magunia had pushed his shoulder between us from behind. 'Mad?

Who is mad? You are mad. You have taken my place. Now get out!' he roared.

My protector sipped his tea. Magunia sat down opposite and fixed upon us a pair of red traffic-light eyes. That proved too much for my kind neighbour. He got up and left. The madman swooped into his place and resumed his shouting. 'Fuck off,' I said, getting up to pay the bill. His companions loomed up to stand on either side of me. At that moment I felt a real fear of violence. Then, as I stood at the counter collecting my change, Jim returned. Once again, our exit coincided with the crash of a falling chair and a cacophony of voices. But this time people followed us hastily out.

In a trance-like state of shock we covered several miles before realising that we were heading south. A schoolmaster waiting at a bus stop put us right. An old woman who found us resting beside the Kiama River took us to the next short cut, where she handed us over to a schoolboy. He led us across the Thika and entrusted us into the care of an old man, who guided us as far as the bridge over the Ruchu River.

Weithaga, for which we were now heading, was the place John Boyes made his capital after founding a 'kingdom' in the area. Boyes, an adventurer from Yorkshire, set himself up in Kabete, near what was later to become Nairobi, as a trader. In June 1898 Kabete was struck by famine. The caravans and railway workers were in the habit of buying most of their food there. Boyes decided to make a fortune by bringing in supplies from Murang'a. He went there with his friend, Karuri Gakure, a seller of ochre and part-time herbalist. Boyes needed food to sell, and Karuri had enemies who could be robbed to get it. The adventurers recruited a private army of Kabete Kikuyu and Swahili riflemen and proceeded to raid and massacre, living like kings on the proceeds. In 1900 Boyes faced a charge of 'dacoity', but was acquitted. He next joined the government forces under Francis Hall and set about helping to restore the law and order he had himself disrupted. Later he returned to England and wrote an account of his career, *The Company of Adventurers* (1928).

The valleys broadened as we progressed farther north. Mango trees dotted the hillsides like dark balloons, and we saw tea fields for the first time since leaving Nairobi. Ahead now the Aberdares stood dark and forbidding, but to the south the whole of Kikuyuland was spread out like a brilliantly coloured carpet, a thousand ribbed ridges, all laced and filigreed by countless streams that flashed the sun towards the black clouds shrouding Mount Kenya.

Marching west along the ridge on the left bank of the Thika River, we came upon a group of noisy children filling jerrycans from a stream.

'*Ngai!*' shrieked a girl as her eyes registered us. She fled, with the others on her heels, dropping her container as she went. It clattered down the slope, and after it came to rest, there was no sound left but the sweep of the wind and the gurgle of water.

Why were these children so afraid of us? Here we were very near to Kihumbuini, where in 1902 the villagers – very probably victims of Boyes – caught a European settler and tied him spread-eagled on his back. They propped his mouth open with a stick, and every man and woman urinated into it until the victim died. Richard Meinertzhagen (*Kenya Diary – 1902–1906*, 1983), who was in charge of operations in the area, then issued the following order: 'Every living thing except children should be killed without mercy.' He goes on to state that 'every soul was either shot or bayoneted'. Perhaps one of the Kihumbuini children who witnessed the massacre had become the grandmother of one of those who fled from us that day, for 1902 was not too far in the past, and no survivor of Meinertzhagen's massacre would have been likely to omit the fable that whites are bogeymen who eat little children.

It was dusk, and the road lay wet under a steady drizzle by the time we reached Weithaga. At a bar we learned that there were no lodgings. We would have to go another four miles to Kangema. As we strode, then, through the gathering darkness, getting wetter and colder with every step, a drunken man we had seen at the bar ran up behind us, volubly asserting that he would see us safely to Kangema and a splendid lodging there. He got a surly response, for it was the first time we had ventured to move after dark, and all our subconscious fears had surged to the surface. What kind of a man was it who would leave a warm bar to lead a couple of strangers four bone-chilling miles through the rain? Altruist or footpad? Besides, I told myself, wasn't this the wet season, when the swishing patter of the rain blunts silence, dulls footfalls and disperses every scent, also the thieving season?

'Burn him off,' I said to Jim, and we lengthened our strides into what was turning into a heavy downpour.

'What's the matter with you fellows? What's this madness of walking during the night?' our unwanted friend kept protesting as he panted to keep up. 'Why don't we just wait under a tree till a taxi comes? I'm a bus conductor and everyone here knows me – why, I could even get you a free ride if you're broke.' Our object was to walk, we said, and he grudgingly reconciled himself to our insanity, becoming as indefatigable as we were pretending to be.

Walking ahead with Jim now, the drunk kept glancing back every few minutes. 'Yes, our old man is still all right,' he would say, before repeating how determined he was to keep faith with us. Who had cheated us during this walk? I began asking myself. No one. Ought we not then give our companion the benefit of the doubt? Ought we not cease grunting churlishly every time he addressed us? Numbed by weariness, I said nothing, but when I slipped and fell on my face, the man rushed back to help. He brushed the mud off me with the palm of his hand as one does to a child.

The night was inky-black under the shrouded sky, and visibility was hardly two paces. The only trace of Jim and the guide was the dull splosh-splosh of their footsteps in the teeming rain. Suddenly voices, loud and hoarse, floated ominously out of the darkness. My heart began pounding, and panic stiffened my limbs. Had I been Teleki, I would have cocked my rifle and slipped the safety catch. As it was, I unfolded the only weapon I had – my old Swiss penknife – and gripped the handle with the blade pointing up my sleeve.

Abruptly I collided with a shape. I pushed it violently away, reversing the knife at the same time, then stood back tautly, legs apart, ready – but for what I did not know.

'Sorry!' a voice called out with real regret.

'It's OK, thanks,' I replied.

Realisation of the absurdity of my reaction swept over me even as I spoke the words, and shame soon followed. Had that innocent passer-by who collided with me been ill intentioned, what could I have hoped to achieve against his sword or club with the pathetic weapon I still clutched in my hand? Surely it would have been far more sensible to have run away in search of refuge in the darkness. I could hear Teleki's ghost chuckling knowingly. As much as he had fought his way through Kikuyuland, the nearest I had got to violence had been the drunk at Mang'u and the madmen of Kirwara, and in neither instance had a finger been laid upon me. So why had I just assumed the worst? It was because, over the years, my mind had been poisoned. As I stumbled on along the muddy path to catch up with Jim, the thought sickened me.

We stepped at last into the lights of Kangema. Music boomed from bars, and the fragrance of charcoal smoke and sizzling goat meat wafted out of eating houses; the streets were full of people. Our guide took us straight to our host-to-be, Michael Ngugi, a heavy-jowled chain-smoker and proprietor of the Cave, who conducted us to a double room. 'Wait here,' he said, 'and I will send some food.'

A waiter brought beer. 'You see,' said the guide, palms up and fingers outstretched, 'told you it was a good place, didn't I?'

'What are you going to do now?' Jim asked.

'Finish my beer and walk back, of course.'

'Why walk?'

'No money, what else?' he grinned.

Jim gave him thirty bob, which he pocketed with a little flourish. 'See you,' he said and stepped back into the night.

I felt moved and strangely affectionate towards that man, who had not even told us his name nor asked ours. He had set himself a wearisome task and, after carrying it out, had been prepared to double it – without even expecting to be rewarded. He had nothing, but a mere meeting of eyes in that bar became a recognition which evolved into a sense of responsibility; our mere presence had made us his guests. He met our resistance with a determination to prove himself a good host, but from the moment he handed us on to Ngugi his mission was ended. I had no doubt then that, had we been attacked that night, he would have defended us with his life. And, by the same token, so would all our other guides who had passed us from hand to hand like sticks in a relay race.

When we tried to pay for our plates of steaming rice and meat, the waiter told us they had been cooked by Ngugi's wife and were therefore on the house. Down in the well-stocked bar, we offered Ngugi a drink as he sat gloomily on his high stool, but all he would take was tomato juice.

Ngugi was a businessman, for besides owning the Cave, he ran a tyre shop in Nairobi and had a couple of acres under coffee. By Kangema standards he was rich. His suit was well cut, and he had a Datsun parked outside. Most businessmen are mean with their employees. They work them as hard as they can for as little money as possible, and God help anyone who complains or falls short, because for every one who does there are platoons of replacements waiting in the streets. Ngugi employed only men, because, he asserted, women could be loyal only to the men they slept with, so when they got pregnant, they tended to filch from the till and run away with their men. Either that or they sold themselves on the side and earned their employer a bad name by distributing gonorrhoea or providing a motive for fisticuffs.

If Ngugi, too, limited his generosity to those he could benefit from, then he must have made exceptions of us; for, from the moment we crossed his threshold, he treated us like house guests. I woke to the sound of a child's voice talking about the '*muthungo*' – the Kikuyu version of the Swahili *mzungu*. It came from the passage, where what appeared to be the child's mother was teaching it to say 'good morning' in English. The words were repeated over and over again. Then there was a knock on the door, and our host's five-year-old daughter, Njambi, presented me with a mug of cocoa and a plate of bread and margarine in conjunction with her newly learned 'good morning'. Her skin was so pale, the brown of her eyes so light, that Jim jumped to the conclusion that she was half-European.

Ngugi did not have to ask us what we wanted to eat or how we wished to spend our day. He was the host and could not, therefore, fail to arrive at impeccable conclusions. He drove us across the broad valley of the Mukungai River to the Weithaga McGregor Bible School in its hilltop setting of old trees. On the wall of a simple one-roomed building made of stone held together by laterite and roofed with tin, someone had scrawled in chalk: 'The first church in Kenya built in 1902'. Another building, similarly constructed, had been, Ngugi said, the first hospital, and was now used as a sports store. The house that McGregor had built himself in Scottish-cottage style was intact and inhabited. 'This is where I went to school,' Ngugi said. 'My father was one of McGregor's first converts and that is why he made me have a Christian education. But I am sorry to say that, although I am still a Christian, I am a polygamist. I have an older wife, who has borne me eleven children, and now I also have this one who lives with me at the Cave and this child, Njambi.'

I should have asked him more about his father. He must have been a contemporary of Boyes, who at the time of his arrest in 1900 already had three Kikuyu wives. It did not seem unlikely that there had been children, and, if so, could Njambi have inherited her hazel eyes from one of them? Another quest for the future, I decided.

Next morning Ngugi gave us breakfast and set us on the path for Gakuyu. Our destination that day could be anywhere we found lodgings, but first we would detour to Mukuruwe wa Gathanga, the legendary home of Gikuyu and his wife, Mumbi, and the birthplace of their nine daughters, Wanjiru, Wambui, Njeri, Wanjiku, Nyambura, Wairimu, Waithera, Wangari and Wangui, to whom the nine clans of the Kikuyu trace their ancestry. Mukuruwe is the Kikuyu name for the mimosa *Albizia gummifera*, a flat-topped, high-altitude forest tree, which can grow as high as 100 feet. Gikuyu's name means 'a very large mukuyu tree' (*Ficus capensis* or *sycamorus*), while Mumbi means 'the creator'. When Teleki crossed the North Mathioya River, he was within five miles of Mukuruwe wa Gathanga, but no one had told him about it. Nor is it marked on the 1981 Survey of Kenya map, but we knew it was at a place called Gakuyu.

We found a row of shops strung along a commanding height. Tea in an almost clinically clean restaurant was served by a young man, who said he was an air force cadet on leave. It was he who led us to

Mukuruwe, which was on a hillock at the western edge of the village. It consisted of a circular garden hedged by the blue spikes of maigoya, pillar-box-red muhuti (*Erythrea abyssinica*) and the off-white inflorescences of the musarisari (*Dracaena afromontana*). Towering over all were two gigantic trees, one a mugumo (*Ficus natalensis*) and the other a muringa (*Cordia africana*), their branches extending so far out that nearly everything lay in their shade.

In Kikuyu lore, both the mukuyu and the mugumo were potentially sacred, the former more so due to its association with the tribe's male ancestor. When their shade came to be used for prayer meetings, they became sacred and protected from damage. Such sacredness had, however, to be determined by elders, who 'appointed' individual trees as such. Others of the same species could be felled and put to use, usually for making beehives or footstools.

In the garden also stood two thatched round huts representing the homes of Gikuyu and Mumbi. Formerly their walls had been of mud, but people had tired of rebuilding them so that finally they resorted to concrete.

During the Mau Mau uprising, the British used the site as an observation point and dug a trench around it. What inspired them after half a century's experience to countenance such a desecration, which could have served only to stir up hostility far outweighing the tactical advantages gained thereby? No one had bothered to fill in the trench, which had gradually transformed itself into a grassy depression.

We rested with our backs against the thick grey aerial roots of the mugumo. I felt absorbed by the tranquil timelessness of the place, which rendered plausibility to the idea that Ngai (the Kikuyu God) had seen fit to give it to Gikuyu as a home close to his own among the white-horned summits of Mount Kenya. Here, I thought, the grass would always grow; if the trees fell dead, others would be planted, and the red, white and blue flowers of the hedge would remain as a mute reminder of the boots which had briefly trampled the garden of Mumbi.

At Kirimacharia village we reached a vantage point from which we could see the confluence of the Thuruthuru and North Mathioya rivers and the triangular meadow between, on which Teleki camped on 29 September 1887. From there the party ascended the Thuruthuru valley and climbed a hill, from the top of which they could see the wood marking the northern frontier of Kikuyuland. The hill was Kamacharia, and from it a company of warriors descended to harass them. Feeling provoked beyond the limit, Teleki allowed his men to retaliate. They burned several villages, capturing 19 prisoners, 90 cows and 1,300 sheep. Von Hoehnel wrote: 'Of course, we greatly regretted the burning of the villages, but it could not be undone now, and Jumbe Kimemeta declared that it was the very best thing that could have happened, the only thing, in fact, which could have saved us from a general attack.'

Six years later, J. W. Gregory, who was travelling in the area, was told by an elder that he could not go on, because 'some white men came some few harvests back to our friends there at Karthuri, they stormed the villages, they seized what food they wanted, and then burnt the rest. When the elders asked for payment, they were shot, while the young men were taken away as slaves in the land of the Masai, and we have heard of them no more' (*The Great Rift Valley*, 1896). This was perhaps only partly true; von Hoehnel says all the captives were later released. The livestock, however, was retained, for he subsequently refers to action being taken against the Wakikuyu 'to stop their attempts to steal our sheep'! The accounts vary, but it is certain that the Teleki expedition made its own particular contribution towards arousing Kikuyu xenophobia.

What is equally certain is that Teleki's contribution was personal. He treated the journey through Kikuyuland as a military expedition, of which he was the commander-in-chief. He always marched at the head of the column to 'cleave his way through the natives, who always gathered in force at streams'. Teleki weighed 17 stone. One of the engravings in von Hoehnel's book depicts him at such a crossing, firing at close range into a crowd of Kikuyu warriors. He towers over them and his own men like a giant. Von Hoehnel tells how on several occasions he witnessed Teleki firing in self-defence, but there were others when Teleki led punitive expeditions, leaving von Hoehnel behind. Killings took place during such raids, and Teleki's role in them could only have been offensive. There is also a strong indication that Teleki was a cold-blooded killer. Von Hoehnel describes how, towards the end of their journey through Kikuyuland, one of their men was lost. At the time the man was so sick that 'more than once he had crept into the bush, as he expressed it, to die in peace'. Then, 'as we were hunting for him we saw a number of warriors gathered together some 400 paces off, one of whom was mockingly holding up a bloodstained shirt towards us. A shot from us avenged his death.' Turn the page and the next provides an etching to illustrate the incident. The shooter is Teleki. There had been no hostilities in this area, so how did he know that the warriors were hostile? How did he know that the shirt was being held up as a gesture of triumphant mockery? And is it possible to identify bloodstains on a shirt at 400 paces? There is no mention of using binoculars or a telescope. To assume that Teleki was trigger-happy would be fair, and there is ample evidence of this all the way through the book.

Throughout our journey through Kikuyuland, Mount Kenya was theoretically visible, but not once had it drawn aside its veil. It was from the roof of an Othaya hotel that we saw for the first time Mount Kenya's gleaming peaks protruding out of a blanket of cloud, the sparkle of their snows bringing to mind the mountain's Kikuyu name: Kirinyaga, the Dazzling Mountain, home of the almighty Ngai, who was otherwise known as Mwene Nyaga, the Dazzling One. And there, over to the left, the Aberdares hunched black and baleful up against a streaky sky – Thimbara, place of mist and gloom, and Ngai's alternative residence. Perhaps, I thought, he moved there when his mood grew bleak, to ponder down upon his unruly creations.

Teleki reached an altitude of 15,355 feet on Mount Kenya. It was my intention at least to equal this. Teleki made his ascent during the rains, in October, and the fact that he got as far as he did is testimony of his toughness. I reached the mountain in July, the middle of the dry season, and looked forward to a walk-over. What it turned out to be, however, was a shameful rout.

Jim was to have returned to Nairobi to fetch our warm clothes, but the plan was scrapped because his leave had been cut short. From that moment haste and ill-preparedness began to dominate the journey, beginning with a bus trip to Naro Moru, which in Masai means 'place of the donkey dung' – an apt name, for it was a dusty little shambles of shacks put together from packing cases, cardboard and old tins.

We were now 20 miles from the park gate and another 10 from the meteorological station, which marked the start of a seven-hour climb to the Teleki Valley. Jim wanted to walk from the gate. So did a young Frenchman we had met, who wanted to go with us. I did not, because the road was notorious for buffalo. I told them how some years earlier I had accompanied a hunter friend as gunbearer. He wounded a buffalo which charged us twice before he killed it. For my friend it was a record trophy – 45 inches. To me it became a resolution to keep as far away as possible from buffalo for the rest of my life.

After hearing me out, they both laughed, and Jim called me a coward. 'OK,' I said, 'we'll walk from the gate and to hell with it.' I was so angry that I found myself wishing we would meet buffalo. I wanted to see the pair of them up a tree pissing into their shorts.

There were no lifts to the park gate, so we started walking. A roadside board advertised a 'Mount Kenya Safari Lodge'. Perhaps, I

127

suggested, climbing arrangements could be made from it. A track through desiccated bean fields led to a ramshackle bungalow in a vandalised garden, which showed signs of erstwhile splendour, but was now full of scruffy chickens and flea-bitten dogs. On the grass stood an elderly white Peugeot saloon. As the dogs withdrew to a safe distance to yap, a man followed by a slatternly woman appeared on the veranda and asked what we wanted. No, there were no such facilities. 'But isn't this a lodge?' I asked.

'Yes it is,' he said.

'Well, then, can you make us some breakfast?'

'No breakfast.'

'Then why do you call yourselves a lodge?'

'It is. You come in and look.'

In the days of dauntless settlers it had probably been a country club. The walls were lined with caricatures of Europeans dressed in the fashions of the thirties, frames all askew. Broken furniture pointed in all directions, and filthy cushions lay on the floor in a debris of dust and bottle tops. Next to the bar a door led into a room containing a double bed heaped with grey pillows and crumpled old blankets. 'You see,' said the man, 'it is a lodge.'

I asked if we could hire the car. The owner was brought, a man in his early twenties, sharp and dodgy looking. Mwangi. We bargained him down to 400 shillings for the return trip. But there was a problem: no petrol. Mwangi ran off with a small container to Naro Moru. Again I pleaded for breakfast. Couldn't they even fix us a cup of tea? No milk. OK, *turungi* – the Kikuyu name for tea without milk. The woman, who was reclining on a heap of scrap iron, smoking, laughed. The kitchen door had fallen off its hinges. She got hold of a panga and started chopping pieces off it. Smoke soon billowed, and we each got a cup of *turungi*.

It was well past two by the time we had driven to Naro Moru to fuel the car. The park road was rough and muddy, very steep in some places. Mwangi kept changing to second gear instead of staying in first, so the car repeatedly stalled, and we had to push. When we reached the meteorological station, he promised to come for us again the following afternoon.

Crazy. Somehow I had thrown all good sense to the winds, driven now only by Jim's determination to reach the Teleki Hut that night even if we had to walk in the dark. We soon got to what is known as the vertical bog, an unrelenting slope overgrown with coarse grass and pitted with holes full of water. The Frenchman, Bernard, was over-weight, and I thought he would soon turn back. When he and Jim stopped to rest, I decided to press on, knowing I would be the slowest in the long run. Every fifty yards or so the route was marked by a white pole. As I passed more and more of them, my spirits began to rise. I was making better progress than expected, and my feet were still dry. The sky was overcast and the slope ahead shrouded in cloud, but it was neither too cold nor too hot. Maybe we could make the Teleki Hut after all.

A slight drizzle started, but I did not care because my woolly titfer was keeping it off my pate. I looked down. No sign of Jim or Bernard. Oh, well, better carry on, they're bound to catch up. But now my showerproof windcheater is tinkling somewhat, and a small heavy object strikes the tip of my nose. Blast! It's started to hail. No matter, just a passing shower. Crash! Really loud. The hail burgeons and crescendos. Crash! Crash! Crash! Lightning too now. This is getting serious; the bloody stuff is going down the back of my neck and freezing the spine. Must take cover until it stops. I cower under a sage bush by a rock, but the hail is still slashing my face. A group of well-clothed young British climbers pass me. They've been up a week, they tell me, and this is the first bit of bad weather they've had, 'but you've only got about another 200 feet to the top of the bog'. Then how much farther to the hut? About three hours. Good luck, they say and continue down.

A new gurgling noise has turned the trio of the wind, hail and thunder into an ominous quartet. The vertical bog has become a waterfall. Brown floods are cascading down, and every path is now a brook. Jim has caught up. We look at each other wordlessly. Below us Bernard stops, vainly shaking the water off his sleeves, his hair wild. A gripping cold has thrust a wet hand down my back as far as the waist. To go on in these clothes, I tell myself, is actually risking death.

'We've got to go back,' I say to Jim.

'I'm going down,' Bernard calls.

'He's right,' I say.

'You go down,' Jim replies obstinately. 'I'll go on by myself.'

I remember how determined he has been all along, but now the risk is not worth taking. He too is inadequately clothed. 'Let's think,' he insists.

'Well, I've made up my mind,' I shout against the wind. Everything is dark, savage and menacing now. A few steps down I look back. Jim is still standing there. 'Come on down,' I yell at the top of my voice.

'OK,' he says, and now we are all off, stumbling, slipping, falling – but down, away from this icy fury. I curse with every step, shouting abuse at the mountain, at my own luck, at the money I've spent just to get wet in this stinging wind.

The non-reappearance of Mwangi left us with no alternative to walking, but all we found of buffalo were tracks and droppings. We reached the junction with the main Naro Moru road just in time to spot a white Peugeot packed with passengers racing towards the forest station. Could it be Mwangi? Suddenly it came to a halt in a cloud of dust. It backed, fast – and straight into a murram stack, rising high on its backside and burying its exhaust. Mwangi and his fares tumbled out and rushed to the back of the car. We helped them lift it down to the road. 'I see we were just in time to give you another push,' I said to Mwangi.

'We were just coming to get you from the gate,' he lied. 'So what now?'

'Nothing now.'

We left them peering under the vehicle at where the exhaust had sprung its brackets.

Once again mountain climbing had proved a disaster. But now, just a hundred miles north-west of Mount Kenya, lay Lake Baringo. I could do that stretch in a few easy bicycle rides. Beyond it I would step into the domains of cattle raiders and the endless red deserts where Teleki nearly died of thirst.

An Explosive Interlude

Two unrelated events prevented me from reaching Baringo as planned. The first was that hardly an hour out of Naro Moru I fell off my bicycle and broke two ribs. This put paid to cycling for six weeks, so I returned to my wooden shack near Ngong to rest up.

The second event took place a week later. It was the coup attempt of 1 August 1982. That morning I woke to the sound of animated conversation outside, which at that early hour of ten to seven was unusual. I kept hearing the words 'government' and 'Moi'. These indicated politics – a topic I had never heard broached on that rustic little patch of land. Outside the front door my neighbours, Mama Kamindo and John Njoroge, were sitting on the grass with a transistor radio between them. 'The government has been overthrown,' said John, breathless with excitement. 'The radio says Moi is out and the military are in.'

The Voice of Kenya was playing reggae, soon to be interrupted by an announcement saying the 'corrupt government' had been overthrown, political prisoners released and the country taken over by the armed forces. All ministers and MPs were to report to their local military commanders, and the police had been reduced to civilian status. My heart sank. Kenya was in the hands of soldiers. Was Kenya now about to follow the footsteps of Uganda into disorder and mayhem? Who was going to be this new military ruler? How much hatred was now, at that very moment, poised to spill and over whom?

The radio had gone as silent as the skies. My shack lay directly under the flight path of the big jets, but already they had been diverted. Ground traffic too seemed to have come to a halt. The familiar shouts of the bus touts, laughter of market women and crying of babies dwindled to faint murmurings.

Suddenly the Voice of Kenya came back on the air. No announcement, but curiously a Swahili song in praise of Moi and the one called 'Hakuna Matata' ('All is well') which exhorts foreigners to relax in ever trouble-free Kenya. Then an announcement that a coup attempt had been crushed. Air force rebels had been defeated by the army, navy and police. Afternoon came, and Moi told the nation that order had been restored. All was back to normal, he said, and the remnants of the rebels were being pursued.

It was a silent night, that one. Even the dogs kept quiet.

Not until a month later was I able to assemble a sequence of events. On the last day of July, a large part of the army, which had ended a period of manoeuvres in Turkanaland under the command of Brigadier Mahmud Muhammad, assembled to return to barracks. During the afternoon of the same day, an air force convoy set out for Nairobi from its Nanyuki base. In the small hours of the next day, a group of uniformed airmen walked into Nairobi's Imani night club and ordered the barman to supply everyone with beer to celebrate the revolution. At about the same time, others seized the radio station, the Eastleigh and Embakasi air bases, the main post office and a number of other key points. All very precise and well-organised it seemed.

A rot, however, set in from the very inception of the action, and that rot was drink. The rebels began celebrating their victory before winning it. Meanwhile, people from the poorer parts of the city began converging on the centre. There they found air force Land-Rovers tearing off shop-front grilles and airmen shooting off locks. They watched airmen driving along the streets shouting 'Power!' with arms raised in clenched-fist salutes. 'Take the wealth of the Indians!' they commanded the crowds, who instantly and enthusiastically obeyed.

Brigadier Muhammad had reached his home in the middle of the previous night so tired that he fell asleep on his sofa. He was woken up by a phone call from GHQ telling him that the coup attempt was in progress, but he was too exhausted to register the significance of the message. He went back to sleep with the receiver in his hand, thus rendering himself incommunicado. It took several hours before he could be reached again.

Muhammad then sprang into action. He pulled together what he could of the army and the paramilitary General Service Unit police. A unit of the latter, led by their British-born commander, stormed and recaptured the Embakasi air base. The Eastleigh air base was bombed by helicopters. Muhammad took a group of soldiers and attacked the radio station, in the process killing some seventy airmen, all of whom were reportedly drunk. Elsewhere the airmen scattered.

The city became a battlefield. The crowds marching towards the centre found themselves under direct fire from the army. Looters were shot on sight.

And then it was all over. In the afternoon the President made his broadcast, and a curfew was imposed.

Was there an *éminence grise* behind the coupists? Probably not. Had it been a matter of a member of the ruling group seeking to dislodge such of his peers with whom he disagreed over policy, he would not have used the air force as a cudgel, because he would have wished to seize as intact a country as possible; he would have ensured that weapons were used only to the degree required for the realisation of that objective. Had a foreign power been involved, it would have abided by the same principles in embarking on a process of tipping the scales to the point at which its puppets could be safely installed. Nor was the rebellion an attempt by any ethnic grouping or clan to impose itself upon the others, for an analysis of the names of those subsequently arrested and found guilty of involvement revealed that every tribe was represented among them almost exactly in conformity with the ratio of the preponderance of those tribes throughout the country.

But there was a new, non-ethnic tribe, the tribe of the detribalised intellectuals, whose common language was English. Its members were installed in all sectors of society – parliament, the universities, the hospitals, the economy, journalism, the arts; and its echelons extended deep into the ranks of the unemployed, the unions and, significantly, the air force. The members of this new tribe could be heard in streets, offices, bars, shops and restaurants, vociferously communicating. The message was that they were ahead of everyone else. As such, they believed themselves to be the country's most efficient intake valve for ideas and the best qualified to apply those ideas to the evaluation of the dominant social imbalances and ways of rectifying them. They expressed their ideas with mounting stridency. Inevitably, the ruling group, the older élite and their conservative advisers, came under criticism. For a while, the old guard remained tolerant, but when the voices of its detractors began to reach a crescendo, it came to the conclusion that the new tribe was a threat to stability and said so. The new tribe reacted with strikes, demonstrations and pamphleteering. The old guard resorted to repression.

What was it that the new tribe wanted so badly that it then decided to reach for the gun? In general terms, it demanded a reformed land policy to ease the hardships of the landless. It called for a reappraisal of the economy in the interests of those at the bottom of the social heap. It wished to see an end to corruption and nepotism.

Militants of the new tribe turned to their peers in the air force, which of the three services embraced the greatest number of intellectuals. A naïve and loosely conceived plot was hatched, according to which the air force would seize a number of strategic points in the capital and announce the overthrow of the government from the radio station. The plotters innocently expected that such a course of action would suffice to spark off a general uprising, in which the masses would, French Revolution style, establish a 'people's government'.

The plan was doomed even before the first step was taken to implement it, because the would-be coupists misassessed their own potential and the psychology both of the masses and the other arms of the services. The crowds which responded to the drunken exhortations of the airmen did not do so as revolutionaries, but as hungry looters given licence to indulge in the forbidden. When the rebels drove round shouting 'Power!' their audience translated the word into a fleeting assertion of will by the have-nots over the haves. What then started with smash and grab rapidly became grab and smash: smash what you can't grab, teach them a lesson.

The army soldiers, far from joining the mob, sprayed it with bullets. They did not join the rebels, but routed them. The old guard resurfaced and the masses applauded.

Why? Because in Kenya the intellectual was still viewed by the masses as a surrogate foreigner whose ideas were not readily under-standable, someone who had set himself apart and was therefore suspect, unreliable and probably rash. He was influenced by books written by motivated aliens, which only he and his ilk had read. Moreover, no one could be looked upon as a leader until he had earned standing within his local community, proved his ability by becoming a man of property and possessing the visible accoutrements of power-wielding. Until he had done so, the intellectual remained a nonentity like any other. The rebels failed to realise that, far from being influenced by their intellectual ideas, the masses and the majority of the less well-educated soldiers in the other services were actually far more in sympathy with the thinking of the existing leaders. Mis-understanding that attitude was the fundamental mistake the rebels made.

Fortunately for the Kenyan people, the ineptitude of the would-be coupists secured the survival of one of the most emancipated forms of parliamentary democracy in Africa.

First Steps into No Man's Land

Lake Baringo lay smooth as olive oil in the pale light of dawn, and the air was still cool. A phalanx of pelicans filtered through the few remaining wisps of mist, dipping their fish-trap bills in rhythmic unison. Fish eagles jeered overhead, while hippos honked from their beds of reeds in the shallows. A string of flamingoes flew jerkily past, a pink scribble on a backcloth of purple hills. The skyline to the west was dominated by the couchant lion mass of Mount Mosop. Not far north of it protruded that serrated peak below which I had lived and worked as a schoolteacher for two years.

I shaved using the mirror of my compass balanced on the gunwale of a little boat woven from papyrus stalks, which was lying on the beach. It was my fifty-fourth birthday, and I could think of nowhere more pleasant to spend it than by the side of this idyllic lake.

To get there I had cycled through Rumuruti and to the Laikipia Plateau. The slope of the escarpment leading down to the lake had been such a tangle of scree and rock that there had been no question of riding. On being wheeled, however, the bicycle assumed the temperament of a refractory beast, repeatedly dragging me to my knees. That day ended in a prolonged thunderstorm and a wretched night spent huddled under a bush. I was relieved to have that stretch behind me. But now I thought about what lay ahead and compared it with the prospect Teleki had faced.

He had reached the same point at the southern end of Lake Baringo on 7 December 1887. From it he planned to head north into the unmapped wilderness never before penetrated by Europeans, hoping to find two legendary lakes known in the language of the Masai as Empaso Narok and Empaso Naibor (respectively the Black Lake and the White Lake), which Teleki was to name Rudolf and Stefanie in honour of the melancholic Crown Prince of Austria and his unloved consort.

The explorers' efforts to obtain information proved frustrating. No one they encountered had ever seen either of the lakes, so all was hearsay. Was there only one lake or were there two? How large? How far away? No answers were found to these questions. Estimates of how long it would take to march round one of the lakes varied from two months to a year.

On one point only was there consensus: there were three possible routes. The first ran due north, but could only be attempted during the rainy season because there was no ground water – and the short rains were already over. The second was a westerly course, passing through inhabited areas where food would be available. The third lay to the north-east; no food would be available there.

By the beginning of February 1888 the explorers had amassed food sufficient to last thirty-five days. They decided to follow the north-easterly route, hoping that their supplies would last them long enough to march round the lake to the inhabited areas to the west of it, where they expected to replenish their larder.

The party left Baringo on 10 February. Their route to what Teleki was to name Von Hoehnel's Bay at the southern end of Lake Turkana (Rudolf) led through Barsaloi and Suiyian, then across the El Barta steppe to Baragoi and the Tum area around the western base of Mount Ng'iro. Finally they climbed the Likaiu barrier, from whose summit they first caught sight of the panoramic view of the lake I was now so anxious to reach.

That section of the journey took them twenty-six days. They arrived at Von Hoehnel's Bay with nine days' worth of food left and no other to be had but game and fish. Jim and I set out with food and equipment which were, for reasons beyond our control, minimal.

To give an idea of what lay ahead, it is necessary to describe briefly the human environment through which we would be passing. If you pinpoint Lake Baringo on a map, draw one line from it to the north-facing slopes of Mount Elgon to the west-north-west and another line running east-south-east to the border with Somalia. The whole of the area bounded by these lines and spilling over the borders into Uganda, Sudan, Ethiopia and Somalia was for millennia and even today remains the home of nomadic or transhumant pastoralist or semi-pastoralist tribes. During colonial times it was known as the 'Northern Frontier District', or 'NFD', and there are some who still nostalgically call it by that name.

In Teleki's day the law in that land was the law of the spear, and so it remained during the colonial period. The British did little more than attempt to police the NFD, largely with a view to ensuring that other areas of greater economic interest were not interfered with by its inhabitants. That remained the case in 1982; except for administrative centres such as Maralal and Lodwar, the countryside in between was still known as a *tanganyika* – a term not to be confused with what used to be known as Tanganyika Territory but one denoting to all the inhabitants of northern Kenya a wild and lawless territory, an empty quarter where violence is king.

Most of the tribes of this region remained mutually hostile, notably the Turkana and the Pokot. The Turkana are reputed to be the world's toughest people. They have to be, for they eke out their living in one of the world's most daunting environments – the desert plains and bone-dry hills within the triangle delineated by the southern end of Lake Turkana in the east, the base of the Karasuk Hills in the west and the border with Sudan in the north.

About two hundred years ago, the Turkana broke away from their Karamojong-speaking grouping living on the Dodoth escarpment in Uganda and moved south. Little is known about why they made the move, but in doing so they came up against other tribes, notably the Pokot, whom they pushed into the surrounding hills and whose livestock they ruthlessly pillaged. The Pokot retaliated, and the two tribes have been in a state of war ever since.

The Pokot are members of the Kalenjin-speaking grouping of Kenya. Their language is as different from Turkana as Russian is from English; but in their ways, economic pursuits, dress and outlook, there is little to distinguish them from their Turkana neighbours.

Not long before Teleki's arrival upon the scene there had been another development, which also affected the tribal pattern. In the eighteenth century there were two main Masai groupings: the Iloikop in the north and the Purko in the south. In the third quarter of the nineteenth century a war broke out between them. The Purko, led by the famous Mbatian, routed the Iloikop and captured all their cattle.

One of the Iloikop clans, the Njamus, whose original name was Il-tiamus, known to von Hoehnel as Njemps, took refuge at the southern end of Lake Baringo. They gradually built up their herds again, supplementing their pastoralism with agriculture and fishing. Von Hoehnel mistakenly concluded that the Njamus were Bantu and remarked that their character was 'inferior' to that of the Masai, who, by defeating them, had done 'a good thing for the cause of progress'. He went on to comment: 'The people of Njemps are quite spoiled by the constant and long visits they receive from caravans.' An experience I was fated to have seemed to militate in favour of that observation.

Living to the north of the Njamus on and around the Loroghi plateau, but separated from them by the eastern Pokot, was another branch of fugitive Iloikop Masai, the Samburu. Von Hoehnel described them as 'a wretched tribe' called the Burkeneji. This name is a contraction of what they still call themselves, Il-oo-ibor-kineji – the

people of the white goats. After their defeat they took refuge with
other tribes, who scornfully nicknamed them after the baskets –
i-sampurri – their destitute women carried on food-begging missions.
Samburu is a mispronunciation of that name.

If the Samburu were 'wretched' in Teleki's day, this was certainly no
longer the case by the time I met them. Now, with their enormous
cattle wealth carefully accumulated since the long-gone day of their
humiliation, they had assumed the aristocratic arrogance of a minor
master race. Yet it never ceased to surprise me how often, after
encountering one of these immaculately clad, painted, beaded and
braided warriors, the word 'shilling' would creep into the conversation, and an upturned palm would slide forth from beneath the
snowy-white *shuka* as if to confirm the aptness of his tribe's nickname.

All these tribes continued to share a tenet that ownership of all the
cattle in the world was their particular God-given right. Thus each
tribe had licence to seize the cattle of others. Stealing cattle and killing
their owners had become not only a way of life but an industry.

Until the relatively recent past, the arms used in such raids were
mostly spears, swords and bows and arrows. However, the 1972 peace
accord reached between the Sudanese rebels and their government, the
defeat of the royalists in Ethiopia after 1974 and the end of the Ogaden
war in 1978 all produced surpluses of firearms, some of which reached
the tribes of northern Kenya. In 1979, after the fall of Idi Amin in
Uganda, the Karamojong looted the Moroto barracks armoury. This
had the same result, while soldiers of the defeated Ugandan army also
exchanged their rifles for cattle.

The tribesmen who acquired the weapons wasted no time before
using them in raids. Such raiders fell into two categories. Those who
stormed into settlements or set upon travellers were known as *shifta*,
the Amharic word for bandit or robber, which has become part of East
Africa's lingua franca. The other category were the *ng'oroko* – cattle
rustlers and killers of men, women and children. Derived from the
Masai *a-ng'orokino*, the word means 'hunt'.

The aboriginals the Turkana and Masai displaced were the hunter-
gatherer Wandorobo, who fled into the forests. The Turkana and
Masai believed that people hunted only because they possessed no
cattle and, as such, despised the Wandorobo as destitutes. In modern
Turkana *ng'oroko* denotes a man who has tied a band of cloth or
leather round his head as an insignia to advertise that he possesses
nothing else. It also advertises his readiness to take whatever he finds
and kill anyone who resists.

I heard two conflicting accounts of the ethnic identity of the *ng'oroko*. One was that they were Turkana. The other maintained they were deserters from the armed forces and escaped criminals of various tribes. Whoever they were, they made themselves universally feared. In 1978 they swarmed into the area around the southern end of Lake Turkana and the Loriyu Hills to the west. Everywhere they attacked the Turkana and Samburu, burning *manyatas* and driving out the inhabitants, naked and dispossessed, to seek refuge in Loyiangalani, Tum, Baragoi, South Horr, Rumuruti and even as far south as Mogotio near Nakuru, where most of them were reduced to begging or working as labourers.

Attempts to dislodge the *ng'oroko* failed; their empire was too remote and barren, too full of hiding places. Richard Leakey told me that in 1981 he climbed from Lake Turkana to the summit of the Loriyu Hills and made camp with the intention of going on to the Kerio River. That evening he was visited by armed men, who brusquely told him that if he and his party had not returned to the lake by next day they would all be killed.

Teleki stepped out from Baringo with 225 men, 19 donkeys, 21 head of cattle and 50 sheep and goats. To face a rabble of spearmen who had never seen firearms, he had what amounted to a company of infantry. Jim and I faced the descendants of those same spearmen, armed now with sophisticated weapons. We supplemented our armoury of penknives with a Masai sword – for chopping wood – and came to the conclusion that our best means of defence lay in the paucity of our possessions and our lack of tribal affiliation as evidenced by the colour of our skins.

Precisely as in Teleki's day, our chief problem was food. We could not rely on buying anything before reaching Maralal, the administrative centre of the Samburu. Maralal lay about seventy miles to the north-east as the crow flies, but a lot farther as the man stumbles. What we needed was donkeys. What we got instead was a first lesson that things were going to be different in the north.

Before arriving at Baringo, I had arranged for my friend Hakim Khan to buy three donkeys complete with packs. He said all would be ready in advance. Hakim was a Pathan born in Tangulbaye in East Pokot, where his father had set up as a trader in the twenties. Married to a half-Pathan half-Masai, Hakim remained in Tangulbaye until the beginning of 1982, when he lost 180 cattle to *ng'oroko* and his Land-Rover was hit by rifle bullets. The setback impelled him to move south to Mukutan, leaving his premises to a relative married to a Pokot woman. In July, just as Hakim was preparing for bed, a gang of Pokot *shifta* broke into his shop. Holding a pistol to his head, they robbed him of all his cash and stock. On that day Hakim decided he had had enough of the Pokot. He moved to Marigat at the southern end of Lake Baringo, where he established a restaurant and started growing peppers and maize.

A brave and resourceful man, hook-nosed and hawk-eyed like his warrior ancestors, we found him at a fund-raising meeting. While speeches were in progress we waited by a cluster of spears stuck in the ground. Their bored Njamus owners, who were resting under the trees, were unpainted, but wore brass pendant ear rings, bead necklaces, finger rings and metal bracelets just like their Masai cousins.

'Hello, how are you?' said a broad-faced man, whose eyes shone with sincerity. 'I am Andrew, a Njamus from here, and I work with the Ministry of Livestock Development.'

What a piece of luck to meet him, for Hakim had forgotten all about our arrangement. He slapped Andrew's back and called him a rogue, so I knew that all would be well. Andrew brought a Njamus and a Samburu who would guide us all the way to Maralal. They looked a shifty pair, but what did that matter so long as Hakim and Andrew recommended them? Another Njamus, called Tiren, came up on a bicycle, all straight talk and no nonsense. He had three good donkeys, all trained, and we would do a deal tomorrow. I was euphoric. 'See what it's like, Jim? Everything simple – guides arranged, donkeys arranged – all in a couple of hours. You wait, bet we'll be off by noon tomorrow, day ahead of schedule.'

Early next morning we were drawn up in front of Andrew's *manyata*, which comprised a crescent of five mud-walled huts with conical papyrus-thatched roofs and two cattle corrals fenced with acacia thorn. Tiren parted with his donkeys for 450 shillings each. The guides came, but on being offered twenty shillings a day plus rations they laughed. They wanted 1,500 shillings each for the whole trip. I laughed back, and they walked away, chins up. An elderly Njamus offered to go with us for 30 shillings a day, to which I agreed, as we could not manage the donkeys on our own.

Tiren had no spare packs. No problem, said Hakim. In the veranda of a shop, he helped to have them made of gunny sacks, two per pack, open ends sewn together, closed ends folded up halfway and sewn up at the sides. Simple, but it was mid-afternoon before they were finished. 'Never mind,' I told Jim soothingly, 'you'll see, we'll still get away ahead of schedule. All we've got to do now is load the donkeys.'

Hakim left us. 'You'll be able to look after yourselves now,' he said.

The donkeys were standing in the shop garden, ears attentively erect. As soon as the first pack touched the mare's back, she reared as if she had felt a branding iron. Andrew held her by the muzzle with one hand and twisted an ear with the other. Another helper got her by the tail and leaned back, while a third wound his arm round her neck. A fourth began to strap the pack on the immobilised but still struggling beast. Donkey number two required even more muscle power but he too was eventually laden. Deep transverse identity cuts had been made in the ears of the youngest; the central sinew having been severed, the pinnae hung down, giving him the look of a misshapen Scottish deerhound. Superhuman efforts by six men to load him ended in failure. He broke free and galloped braying out of the garden.

That was the signal his mother and brother had been waiting for. They too dashed off, scattering their loads and high-kicking to rid themselves of all vestiges of encumbrance. 'How's your schedule looking now?' said Jim dourly as we watched the backsides of the mutineers receding into the distance.

Next came the humiliation of retrieving our belongings from the dust. Then, as we trudged heavily laden and sweating in the afternoon sun, bemused passers-by burst into hoots of laughter on hearing the explanation of our companions.

At Andrew's *manyata*, the donkeys were intercepted and driven into a corral. Andrew led up a tall, muscular man in a red *shuka*, saying, 'Don't worry. This is a donkey expert who will train your donkeys in just a few hours. By tomorrow morning they will be perfectly behaved.'

I believed him because I wanted to believe and in doing so forgot to ask Tiren why he had said they were already trained. Disaster induces straw-clutching. The tongue tends to leave the cheek and cleave instead to the roof of the mouth.

The donkeys stared at the trainer with knowing insolence. He ordered three holes to be dug in the trodden dung, each about nine inches in diameter and a foot and a half deep. With a single leopard leap he captured donkey number three, whom I had named Mephisto. Using a combination of impressive strength, stroking and gentle pats, the trainer persuaded the fiend to stand still while he knotted a rope round his neck. Andrew doubled up the other end of the rope, dropped it into one of the holes, covered it with dung and trampled it down. The trainer released Mephisto, who, after standing still for a second, made a dash for the exit – only to get to the end of the rope first. Astonished, he turned his head in the direction of the hole and put himself into reverse gear. Nothing gave. He leaned back and strained. Unconvinced, he wheeled round and tried again from the opposite side.

This final effort gave him, as von Hoehnel put it after firing ten rounds of a .577 express rifle into a wounded buffalo, 'his quietus'.

I was amazed that the beast had been unable to dislodge the rope, but Andrew assured me that even a bull could be restrained in this way. The other donkeys got the same treatment, after which each was loaded with two 20 litre jerrycans of water and released. The idea, said the trainer, was for them to get used to the weight; by morning they would be docile and obedient.

That was a bad day, and the next was worse, for the training only hardened the donkeys' determination never to have anything put on their backs again. When the jerrycans were removed, they pranced and reared, brayed and shrugged; nothing the trainer, Andrew or their several helpers tried could break the resolve of those three devils.

Tiren's timing was perfect. He came upon the scene even before the armistice had been declared, having known all along that we would never leave in the company of his donkeys. A tirade from me left him unmoved. 'My donkeys are trained,' he insisted calmly, 'but they are unaccustomed to the sort of packs you are using. As a result, your men have been ill-treating them and now they are spoiled.' He was prepared to buy them back, but by now the money had been taken to his uncle at Maji Ndege, which was a long way off. And 400 shillings would be deducted for the 'damage' done to the animals. I called him a liar and would have said more, but Andrew restrained me because he did not want a brawl in his *manyata*. It was the sweat running down Andrew's face that held at bay the doubts I should have had in the part he himself was playing in the transaction. Tiren being his neighbour, Andrew would have known the truth about the donkeys, but instead of trying to persuade Tiren to decrease the penalty, he urged me to pay it.

I did not know it then, but the deal was for Tiren to get his donkeys back and split the money with Andrew. I never saw a penny of it again.

The now urgent need to get away and a newly conceived abhorrence of donkeys persuaded me to agree to Tiren's terms. Hastily then, we divested ourselves of food, tents, jerrycans, fishing gear, spare shoes and clothing, lamp, paraffin, gas stove and – most unwisely of all – the cooking pot. The little that remained we hoisted on our backs and even that was heavy enough. The Njamus guide we had engaged could not be found, so we trudged off on our own.

All in a hand's turn, the prospect of the journey ahead changed from an idyllic sauntering alongside obliging donkeys to that of a gruelling route march. Walking with rucksack straps biting into collar bones was pure exertion obscuring all thought other than that of destination.

As the sun climbed, it became impossible to persevere for more than twenty minutes at a time. Even Jim, whose exhaustion threshold was much higher than mine, complained that the weight of our loads had degraded us to participants in a commando endurance exercise. We agreed that the walk would become a dull drudgery unless we could get help.

As we descended into the Kalabata valley, a young Pokot fell in with us. He volunteered to carry part of our load. We put it into a makeshift sack fashioned from the tarpaulin, one of the essentials we had not abandoned. Lost morale returned with the unburdening.

Our porter's name was Buga, and he was as spindly as a stick insect. His pock-scarred face was lighter than the norm; his lips were thin, his eyes narrow. 'The Turkana are wicked people,' he informed me, 'of whom we Pokot live in constant fear. They are all *ng'oroko* and when they come, they come in hundreds. These days they have many guns, good ones, better than those of the police, and when they attack they kill as many of us as they can before making off with our stock.'

Several times as we continued northward through uninteresting scrubland we were stopped by Pokot, each of whom asked Buga the same questions: why weren't these Europeans travelling by car, and had they got any sugar? Told we were writing about the country and carried sugar only sufficient for ourselves satisfied every questioner. They were without exception most friendly, yet there was something indefinably sinister about them as they receded into the distance, black *shukas* flapping in the wind. 'We are people of the night,' said Buga, 'and if we have to flee we can melt into the darkness.'

I felt a twinge of malaise, remembering that von Hoehnel's first attempt to move out of Baringo on 9 February 1888 had been frustrated by rumours that the Pokot were coming. So feared were they that the porters had refused to proceed. It was only on the following day, after it had been confirmed that the Pokot had been driven back by the Tugen, that he had been able to set out again. And now, here we were, after being warned by Hakim and the Njamus, right in the thick of them.

We were joined by two Pokot women in their thirties, who walked with the same long easy strides as Buga, their frames as spare and athletic as his. During a rest under a tree, where Buga said he had once been confronted by a lion, the younger and prettier one asked me for a cigarette. Then she sat, legs delicately crossed, smoking with her little finger pointing away from her. Her gestures perfectly matched a once popular portrait of Marlene Dietrich – until she was convulsed in a fit of coughing and, choking, confessed she had never smoked before.

143

Later she relieved me of my rucksack, leaving me feeling ridiculous with nothing to carry but Buga's spear. Buga told every passer-by that the government had now decided to send in Europeans with spears to protect them from the *ng'oroko* and that we were the vanguard. People kept grabbing my arm, then falling back doubled up with laughter.

Nearing Tangulbaye, we met increasing numbers of people, all Pokot and all asking the same questions as before. The shopping centre was animated by a commotion. Crow-like beaded women and men with ostrich feathers waving from blue caps thronged the open space in front of the only hoteli, all faces turned in the direction of the police post across the road. There in the forecourt two men in battledress were hammering each other with their fists. Others attempting to intervene were successively thrown to the ground by the combatants. The onlookers said the men had arrived from Kabarnet that morning as reinforcements, information having been received that *ng'oroko* were on the move towards Tangulbaye from Pakka. Directly the policemen's feet had touched ground, they had trooped off to drink at the very shebeens they were supposed to eradicate.

We turned away into the hoteli for tea and chapatis served by a young Pokot woman in full regalia, fourth wife of Loteka Areyot, an elderly retired police sergeant, who sat on a sack of beans in the corner, supervising. It was relaxingly cool in there as Mrs Loteka bustled in and out. Glasses clinked to a background of hushed conversation until the door crashed open to the blustering entry of three burly policemen led by a corporal bigger and drunker than the others. 'You shut up,' the corporal told my neighbour, who had been talking to me in English. 'When I'm here, it's me that does the talking.'

I attempted to engage the corporal's attention, but he was already deaf to all voices but his own. 'I'm from Kisii,' he announced. 'Do you know where Kisii is? Good place, Kisii, not *shenzi* (primitive) like this place.'

As Mrs Loteka placed a cup of tea in front of him, he dropped a heavy hand on her shoulder and forced her down beside him. A rough forefinger stabbed into her bead necklaces. 'Why do you wear all this junk and this filthy leather dress? Why don't you get yourself properly dressed like a civilised woman?' he asked her roughly in crude Swahili.

Mrs Loteka raised her nose an inch. 'These are the clothes we wear around here,' she said, unruffled. 'We don't have money to buy other clothes. Can you give me some money? If so, I'll get some better clothes.'

He turned to Loteka. 'Why don't you get her some decent clothes?'

'The clothes my wife wears are none of your business,' replied Loteka without getting off his sack.

The policeman began shouting aggressively, and too incoherently for me to understand. It was time to leave. The other patrons, including the other two policemen, had already slipped out. We too withdrew, leaving Loteka alone with his boorish protector.

I asked Loteka to accompany us as far as the Amayo River, which divides the land of the Pokot from that of the Samburu, and he eagerly agreed. We reached it after a strenuous but uneventful seven-hour march only to find that the shelves of the only village shop (Kikuyu-owned) were all but bare.

Our food supply had shrunk down to a cooked chicken, ten boiled eggs and eight of Mrs Loteka's chapatis. Maralal, 36 miles away now, would therefore have to be reached in a single march. Loteka was persuaded to accompany us, but Buga would not cross the river. Why? Because he was just as afraid of the Samburu as he was of the Turkana. To replace him we hired a spivvy-looking Samburu called Lolenguya, a trader in *miraa* (the sprigs of the privet-like *Catha edulis* shrub, chewed for its mildly narcotic effect).

The track led north-east through a vast tree-covered plateau, which sloped up towards thickly wooded hills in the east. The farther we went, the fewer the trees and the thicker the grass. But in all those miles of rich pasture there was not one head of cattle. Fear of the *ng'oroko* had delivered up the land to eland, buffalo, Grant's and Thomson's gazelle, Grevy's zebra and hartebeeste. Only the pads of lions and hyenas overprinted their hoof marks on the path. This was the first of several intertribal territories through which I was to hasten, frequently looking over my shoulder and scanning the horizon for signs of the enemy – man.

Once we had passed the tiny settlement of Lolmulok, we reached the edge of a vast plateau thickly carpeted with turgid grass and smudged red, white and black with herds of cattle and goats. It was like stepping into a new country. I remembered having the same vision of antithesis before the Second World War when reaching the manicured *Ordnung* of East Prussia after motoring through the poverty-stricken squalor of the Polish Corridor.

A lone tin roof at the edge of the tree-line bounding the plateau was the Maralal game post. Lolenguya said, 'When we reach those trees, we're going to see a lot of Samburu *moran*. Be careful of them, because they can be very aggressive. A few weeks ago they speared a European tourist who had come out of his tent at night to urinate. That man had to be taken to hospital in Nairobi, so when we pass these young men, don't greet them and don't look at them. Greet them only if they greet you.'

A year earlier, walking down Oxford Street with Jackie, I had seen for the first time the punks with their coxcomb crests of dyed hair and their 'chicks' with safety pins poked through their ear lobes. I had looked at them in curiosity only to be hissed at by Jackie. Did I want to get smashed up, behaving like that? The behavioural tendencies of these Samburu punks would not be very far removed, it seemed, so I walked on, mentally prepared.

Suddenly we were in a forest as thick as Arden. Ancient trunks reared up high towards dark canopies of turgid leaves, which rustled above ochre-banked rivers and grassy glades patched purple by clumps of wild petunia. And there, on the raised bank of the Loragai River, stood the first *moran*, their foreheads shining persimmon red, *shukas* white as clean paper, brass armlets flashing back the rays of the setting sun. Demurely flanking them were their glittering *nditos*, whose shaven little heads were crowned high with intricately beaded pagoda-like ornaments tinkling with tinsel. They were to the ragged black-cloaked Pokot of Tangulbaye as the golden-breasted starling is to the scavenger crow, but over their painted splendour hung more than a hint of menace. The message of their eyes was: you are a pack of dogs rolling in your own excrement. We want nothing from you and will give you nothing. We will tolerate your intrusion, but get out of our world and back into your own as soon as possible. Quickly I averted my eyes, and we passed on in silence.

Was Jim married? Lolenguya wanted to know. 'No, but actually he would like to marry an educated Samburu girl,' I replied mischievously on his behalf.

'Oh, that could easily be arranged,' Lolenguya said truthfully.

'How old would she be?' asked Jim.

'Like those you've just seen. Eleven or twelve – in the first efflorescence of womanhood, that's the right age,' said Lolenguya.

'Far too young for me. In our custom we never marry girls younger than sixteen.'

'But those would be regarded as old women here. You'd better take one of the right age.'

Loteka turned to me. 'What about you? Are you married?'

'Yes.'

'How many?'

'One.'

'What, only one? Why, that's like having only one eye. If she dies, you'll be left a blind man. Me, well you know I've got four, which makes me a staff sergeant to your lance-corporal. But the oldest one, she's so bent with age that these days when people ask me who she is, I tell them she's my grandmother. But tell you what, why don't you take one of my daughters? I've got about eight. Just come to Tangulbaye and take your pick. Go on, promote yourself to full corporal, no trouble. All you need to do is bring me a sack of beans and a couple of sacks of maize so that I can get that hoteli going properly.'

Lolenguya pointed to a spur three or four miles ahead. 'Maralal is just the other side of that,' he said comfortingly, noticing my exhaustion. Maralal. That was all I could think of – 'the place of the pearls', as the Samburu had named it after the tin roofs reflecting the sun from their setting in the greenery.

When the lights sparkled only a few hundred yards ahead, I was suddenly overcome by a sense of total defeat and lay down on my back in the middle of the path. Only the sight of Jim striding ruthlessly away into the darkness brought me to my feet again. We reached the main square, and there, just beyond the familiar petrol station, stood the Buffalo Hotel. Loteka helped me to a table. I felt so cold that he made me take four tablets of quinine. When the beer arrived I could hardly guide the glass to my lips. Loteka, a decade older than I, had carried my rucksack all day, yet he was still full of energy and jokes; he said he needed just two beers to get the tiredness out of him. Lolenguya settled for a lemonade, his first drink of the day since his morning tea.

North to the Lake

Why Teleki did the march from Baringo to Lake Rudolf during the dry season is a mystery. Had he waited until the arrival of the rains, a great deal of severe hardship would have been averted. As it was, the party lost its way in the thirsty lands north of Maralal. But for one of the men finding, quite by chance, a store of subterranean water in the dry bed of the Barsaloi River, the whole party might well have died of thirst.

By 8 March 1888 Teleki's party had marched from Von Hoehnel's Bay some thirty miles northwards along the south-eastern shore of Lake Rudolf. That day they halted early due to the difficulty of finding firewood. Fierce heat and an incessant gale had pursued them relentlessly all the way. The brackish lake water had been all that was available and it failed to quench their thirst. Their cattle were so weakened by the scarcity of fodder that many had to be slaughtered. The men's morale had sunk to a level approaching despair. Even to the explorers 'there appeared to be no way out of the monotonous wilderness, and it seemed as if we should not have long to rejoice in our discovery of the lake'. Their guide told them it would take fifteen days to reach the northern end of the lake, which was about right, the distance being about 150 miles. But they now had food sufficient to last only eight days.

Under the circumstances they decided to turn inland in the hope of finding a group of Samburu reputedly settled on the slopes of Mount Kulal. On 9 March the party marched along the beach for another two hours before changing course for the mountain. A comparison of the Ordnance Survey map with von Hoehnel's indicates that they almost certainly walked past Loyiangalani, a Masai name meaning 'a place of trees which thrive near water'. The water is – and probably was – a spring of sweet water around which the contemporary settlement of Loyiangalani is spread. How they managed to miss it is puzzling, but extremes of heat, thirst, hunger, discomfort and exhaustion play tricks on the mind.

The detour to the mountain proved fruitless, for they found no one there. This left no alternative to a return to the lakeshore, which they followed as far as Reshiat, now known as Ileret. From Reshiat, having bought food from the local tribesmen, they headed east to discover Lake Stefanie. After returning to Lake Rudolf, Teleki decided to round its northern tip and follow the western shore southwards. But at this stage the long rains broke out, turning the Omo River into a torrent impossible to cross. Teleki would have waited, but an outbreak of smallpox among the Reshiat people sent him backtracking south, to Von Hoehnel's Bay. Then he turned north-west, crossed the Loriyu Hills to the Kerio River and headed for the Turkwel.

Jim and I decided to follow him to the Bay, but instead of going straight on to Ileret we would first head for Lodwar on the Turkwel. Because we were going to cover this leg during the rains, we hoped to find adequate water even if we got lost like Teleki. From Lodwar, Jim was to return to Nairobi, leaving me to continue south back to Baringo. I would then pick up our gear, somehow get myself back to Loyiangalani and walk to Ileret and back during the dry season. However, rain – the very factor on which we relied for the success of our plan – created circumstances which compelled us to follow Teleki to Loyiangalani after all.

At Maralal we were able to stock up with food to see us through to Lodwar, which we naïvely estimated would take twelve days. In the event, it took double that number of days just to reach Loyiangalani. God only knows what might have happened had not fate intervened between us and Lodwar.

The Maralal police assured us that there had been no incidents of violent crime for many months in any part of the area we proposed to walk through. The unlikeliness of encountering *shifta* or *ng'oroko* was reinforced by the eagerness of the men who offered to accompany us. The rolling of eyes and oft-repeated mutterings about 'enemies' were, I suspected, merely a form of salesmanship to increase the price asked for services.

The bulk of the supplies having been sent ahead by bus to await us at the Somali shop in Baragoi, we set out full of confidence with two sturdy Samburu guides to carry our gear. The week that followed was one of pure bliss, a succession of cloud-cooled days spent walking through a rolling countryside of wooded hills and rain-fattened meadows dappled with patches of gentian-blue flowers. The gentle northerly breeze fanning our faces brought with it only the lowing of contented cattle. All the rest was silence except for the trillings of birds and cicadas. The whole world seemed swathed in green, and as we passed through it I luxuriated in the unique simplicity of being a walker, a man who has disentangled himself from his spider's web of worries and obligations and stepped into a very special kind of freedom. Suddenly the past assumes a blurred irrelevancy to a future pared down to the starkness of distance and physical sensation. Sleeping close to the earth renews affinity with it and reconciles the fearful spirit to the inevitability of returning to it. Waking, still close to the earth, to the dawn chorus of the birds, the body feels charged with energy and the mind with enthusiasm. It is quite unlike waking in a bed, thrown back into consciousness by a shrilling alarm clock, made to feel listless by the prospect of another day of routine.

Samburu *manyatas* lay tucked away in every corner of the land, and our shillings brought milk flooding out of every one of them. Camel's milk, cow's milk, goat's milk, the first robustly tangy, the second blandly sweet, the third a nectar beyond description – all were there for the drinking. It was at this stage of the journey that I learned that it is possible not only to survive but to thrive on an exclusive diet of milk. A generously sized calabash of it is sufficient to fuel a ten-mile walk.

Our senior guide, Lelean, a craggy sixty-year-old veteran of Chenevix-Trench's famous horse police, knew the area well. He led us through it unerringly, finding for us every evening a dry sleeping place under a tree or in a deserted hut. We reached Baragoi without incident. All had been as peaceful as Switzerland.

The Somali shopkeeper at Baragoi told us to forget about carrying our supplies on to Tum. He would send them on his lorry to his counterparts there, Ali and Muhammad, the following day.

It was on that day that the elements brought our idyll to an abrupt end. The days that followed turned into a succession of discomforts and disasters.

We crossed the Baragoi River into a monotony of grey-green acacia scrub and headed for the ragged outline of the Kowop Hills, beyond which towered the thickly wooded slopes of Mount Ng'iro. To the north-west, white knives of lightning were slashing through an indigo curtain of cloud hanging over the Suguta valley. A young Turkana who had joined our party as a camp follower said it had not rained here for eight long years. I replied that we had brought him *baraka* (blessing); for as we were approaching his people, the rain was coming to them too. *Baraka* was all very well, but as we drew level with the hills, the wind wheeled about and hurled the storm into our faces. Almost at once the treeless plain became a delta of racing streamlets. Shivering as we squelched through ankle-deep mud, there was no way now by which we could cover the 30 miles to Tum that day.

At the base of a spur of Mount Ng'iro we stopped amid a scattering of great black boulders which looked as if they had only just rolled off the slopes above. The dreary Emurua Akirim Plateau peeled endlessly away to the west, its coppery undulations enlivened only by a pair of ostriches hastening away from the Turkana plume-hunters they had taken us for. By the time we had arranged the camp, the storm had blown itself out for the day, but the sky remained the colour of wet slate.

One feature of that day was that we had not seen a single wild mammal. A very different state of affairs reigned when Teleki and von Hoehnel arrived, for it was in this very area that they had indulged in one of their most unbridled massacres. At that time these lower slopes of Ng'iro teemed with elephants which, never having been harmed by man before, ignored his advent. The explorers, armed with massive eight-bore rifles, were able simply to walk up and execute the beasts like sitting ducks. The killings were done in the absence of every trace of remorse. In one instance, von Hoehnel describes how they watched the peaceful family life of a little herd – mothers grazing and suckling their offspring, young bulls playfully butting one another, young cows intervening when the play became too rough. But then 'the females began to move off and thus gave the signal for opening fire'.

Between them in the space of three days Teleki and von Hoehnel indiscriminately shot dead fourteen elephants. They also wounded a number of others, but did not track them down to put them out of their misery. The attitude seemed to be, what was the point of following them up, particularly when there were so many other available targets?

The explorers' motives were primarily 'sport' and amassing ivory towards recouping the costs of their expedition. A secondary motive was to provide their men with meat. But, according to von Hoehnel, only one-third of their party relished elephant meat, another third ate it with distaste, while the remaining third would not touch it at all.

The slaughter of the elephants Teleki initiated in this part of Kenya continued without respite after they left it. In 1972 I caught sight of several sizeable herds on and around Mount Ng'iro, and there were also a few on Mount Kulal. But now, ten years later, all had been wiped out. Sadly the slaughter will continue until humanity ceases to prize knick-knacks, carvings, ornaments, wind instrument mouth-pieces, piano keys, napkin rings, dagger handles, paper weights and toothpicks made of ivory.

It was a cool walk next morning under the brooding clouds to the row of tiny shops and mission school which were Tum. We found Ali and Muhammad in the courtyard of their hoteli-cum-shop. In voices as soft as their eyes they told us no vehicle had arrived or was likely to arrive for the next few days. The rain had been so heavy that the previous night the Baragoi River had swept a drunk policeman to his death. Flour and beans were available, but we had left our cooking pot in Baringo. Not a single inhabitant of Tum was willing to sell even an old tin; in such places a tin was never thrown away but was used as milking pail or cooking pot until it wore out. It was a dilemma to which there was no solution, and we could not wait because Jim had a deadline for returning.

Jim resisted my suggestion that we must change our plans. We had decided to go to Lodwar, he maintained, and to Lodwar we must go. Jim was the sort of offspring of an affluent family who had probably never known what it felt like to be hungry or thirsty. Confident in his youth and physical prowess, the prospect of the walk over the Loriyu Plateau (which Ali stated was still infested with *ng'oroko*) to cross the Kerio (which Ali said was almost certainly in spate and uncrossable) must have seemed to Jim like some kind of boy scout hike. He even went so far as to threaten to part company with me at Von Hoehnel's Bay and walk to Lodwar on his own. I tried to reason with him, but even a reminder of his impetuousness during our ill-fated attempt to climb Mount Kenya left him unmoved. A matter which did not figure in his projections was whether or not I would be able to keep up with the pace he proposed to set. About this I said nothing, preferring instead to sit back and let events decide our course of action. Which they did.

Tum was an outpost on the southern border with real *ng'oroko* country. Ali and Muhammad told us how the previous year the village had been attacked in force and in broad daylight. All the inhabitants had fled, but not before several were shot dead. The *ng'oroko* had ransacked every home. Even the police station was emptied and its communications radio destroyed. We were shown bullet holes which riddled the corrugated-iron walls of the shop's pit toilet.

Ali introduced us to John, the catechist of the Catholic mission. This spindly, twitching young man claimed to have been at the Parkati mission between Tum and the lake when that mission had been attacked by *ng'oroko* on 12 January 1981. They had swarmed down from the hills, firing their rifles to stampede five hundred children and their teachers into the wilderness. With Cornelius, the Italian priest in charge, John had fled in a Land-Rover carrying the school's funds. Halfway to Tum, where the road wound through a defile between steep wooded hills, they had driven into a storm of automatic fire. Cornelius died at the wheel. The vehicle crashed into the rocks lining the road. John escaped and hid in a thicket from which, horrified, he watched the *ng'oroko* drag Cornelius's body out and smash his head with stones. Then, after ransacking the vehicle, they set it on fire.

Inevitably, our Samburu companions were regaled with the same stories. Other Samburu in the village told them that the Turkana would deem any Samburu seen north of Tum to be a spotter for cattle rustlers and kill him without hesitation. Therefore, our guides said regretfully, they were parting company with us.

Their places were taken by two Turkana stalwarts, butchers from Baragoi. Two years before they had been living in *manyatas* in the Korante plain east of Baragoi, but after losing all their cattle in a *ng'oroko* raid they found themselves compelled to become wage earners. Of the two, one looked hungry and acquisitive, the other shy and ascetic, but both were young and strong. Hungry Moses and ascetic Sayya: unaccountably I named them 'the jokers'. The police chief said he knew them both, so we took them on.

They were not, however, willing to go to Lodwar. One reason might at a pinch have been overcome – their fear of *ng'oroko*. The other could not: they did not know the way, and no one else who did could be found in Tum. Our destination would have to be Loyiangalani. Jim was over a barrel.

Our total supplies consisted of one cooked chicken, a dozen chapatis, a packet of tea, four kilos of sugar, a little coffee, salt, cigarettes, half a kilo of Turkana tobacco and a tin of corned beef. There was no shop between Tum and Loyiangalani – a distance of roughly seventy miles. But hopefully we would be able to buy milk, fish or even a goat.

A three-hour climb brought us to the plateau's western edge, where a sudden wind swept away the clouds, revealing the broad Suguta valley with the salt lake Namakat lying like a huge lozenge-shaped diamond in its lap. It is curious that *suguta* is a Masai word meaning 'salty water', while *namak* is Persian for salt; I have found no explanation for this apparent coincidence. The rain had so enlarged the lake that it had merged with the Allalab mudflats, transforming Naperito and the Cathedral Rock into an island. North of it, the cone of Andrews' Volcano was upthrust from the valley bed, but Lake Turkana remained out of sight.

After descending into the narrow valley at the foot of Ejuk and crossing two rain-swollen rivers, we came upon Parkati, an insignificant scrabble of Turkana huts separated from the mission grounds by an ill-smelling stream called the Kitoile. Dominating the place was the deserted mission, a dozen brick buildings roofed with expensive corrugated iron imported from England, all set in a spacious compound, carefully fenced. There had been a borehole with a diesel pump to supply water to the kitchen, ablution blocks, dormitories, class-rooms, priest's house and teachers' quarters. The floor of the school store was littered with new textbooks and exercise books, lying untouched just where the *ng'oroko* had thrown them. Half a dozen Turkana men and boys were using the classrooms to sleep in, cooking on the broken kitchen range. Apart from a few heavy benches and tables, the mission had been ransacked. Windows had been shot out and roofs sprayed with bullets. A statue had been torn from its plinth in front of the chapel and broken to pieces. The diesel pump had been blown up. An atmosphere of inchoate rage still smouldered in the air. The *ng'oroko* had given expression to the feelings of the Samburu *moran* I had met in the forest near Maralal – to hell with book-learning, foreign ways and foreign gods, to hell with boys in shorts and girls in cotton dresses: let them run into the hills and learn about herding goats and weaving grass huts. With Western guns the *ng'oroko* had halted a Western intrusion.

From Parkati we headed straight up the Likaiyo Barrier, a great heap of scree and volcanic rubble between the moonscape of Ejuk to the south and the lake to the north. A series of false summits at last disgorged us into a plateau walled in by rocks the colour of burnt sienna and ringing with the harsh barks of baboons. Towards the east the ground gradually fell away to the Laisamis Valley, and there – straight ahead – was the view which brought with it a moment of triumph. It also brought back with perfect clarity that other moment when, nine months earlier, I had stood at the edge of the bay at Pangani and tried to picture Teleki first setting foot on the mainland of Africa. I felt gripped by a time paralysis, a sudden consciousness that, despite all the dramatic transformations which had convulsed the world between the moment that Teleki first caught sight of the lake and the moment in which I now hung, nothing had changed here. The milky-blue expanse of water lay placid in its volcanic bed almost as if it was conscious of its own timelessness. In the west, the Loriyu Hills filled the horizon; for me they symbolised a sculpted gesture of challenge. Marking the eastern extremity of Von Hoehnel's scimitar bay, the perfect cone of Nabuyatom sat in its watery bed like an acorn barnacle in a rock pool. From there my eye travelled north-east over the rhino back of Mount Kulal crouching between the water and the Chalbi Desert, then west along the lakeshore to the red sugar-loaf hill called Porr and the blurred protuberances of Moite and Jarigole to the north of it. What I could see from my vantage point of the lake's eastern shore was less than a quarter of the distance to its northern end. Like a long evening shadow, then, the realisation crept up on me that whatever difficulties the walk to Loyiangalani would entail were likely to be flea-bites compared with those lurking in the murky smudges of landscape beyond Jarigole.

The descent to the lake led through a vast pit into which colossal hands had flung billions of tons of debris, scoriae and house-sized boulders. It was possible to progress only by hopping precariously from one boulder to the next. I have no head for heights and found some of the chasms that had to be leaped across alarmingly deep. But there was none of the agony of thirst that had plagued Teleki on his way down, for every rock was pitted with blister holes full of fresh rain water. The stony waste ended abruptly in a glade of acacia and miswaki, beyond which, fringed by a rough beach of fragmented lava dotted by clumps of spiky grass, the olive-green water of Lokweam Inlet swam into view. It was the end of what von Hoehnel called 'a valley of death'. I walked into the water and lay down fully clothed.

Four days later Loyiangalani gradually wobbled into focus through the heat haze. Paulina's hoteli, a two-doored mud hut the size of a Scottish bothy and furnished with rough tables and benches, felt as luxurious as Claridge's.

Before you scald your tongue in it, while you are still trudging the dust up into your nostrils with the sun slapping your head, tea is a dream that steams tauntingly out of the mirages in the road. And then, at long last, it comes in a hot enamel mug and goes down, sip after greedy sip, permeating every muscle with new strength and pouring sweat into your eyes. Only then are you ready to move on to the more substantial stuff of peppery meat stew and rice at crook-eyed Chongo's Somali eating house, where Moses and Sayya wolfed their way through two plates each and never said a word for half an hour.

Around Loyiangalani's dusty main street of tin-roofed shops a hundred or so domed reed huts lay scattered among the dunes. West of them were the airstrip and the palm-cloaked transplants of tourist lodge and camping site. Well, we had got here, but before going on I had to return to Baringo to collect my equipment. The question was how to get out. Chongo said that because of the rains no lorry had arrived for weeks. There were no cigarettes, nor even newspaper for roll-ups.

A smart two-engined aircraft landed to discharge a wallow of tourists: the Italian ambassador and his guests, the Somalis at Chongo's told us, up for the weekend. Jim had a vision of a spare seat on the way back, so we walked into that other world of swimming pools and waiters in green shorts. On a veranda, one part of which was designated for 'residents only', we sank into leather armchairs by polished tables bearing heavy ashtrays. Beer, too, as we soon learned, was reserved for residents only. We sipped orange squash, watching bathing-suited heavies pouring lager into large glasses before throwing themselves back into the water of the 'residents only' pool.

Jim identified the proprietress as the quick-moving, exquisitely made-up curlyhead sitting behind us with a white-haired woman who wore a Roman nose and a *grande dame/haute couture* look. After telling me in a hoarse whisper to sit still, he interpolated himself between them and moments later had Signora Fellini smiling, twittering asides to the old girl and shooting fluent Swahili imperatives at her waiters. Jim called me over with his eyes. 'Indeed,' the signora was saying, 'after walking all that way, you certainly deserve a beer!' Were we, perhaps, through the ice all the way? 'Yes, I'm sorry about the beer,' she went on, 'but you understand the supply business is very difficult here.'

We smiled; we understood perfectly, and wondered how many crates had come up in that large aircraft. The beer tasted almost as good as Paulina's tea. Miraculously there was a spare seat on the aircraft, and the signora would take me and the jokers by road to Baragoi in a day or two. Things were really looking up.

Then the signora crossed the floor to bestow the glitter of her personality on more apposite personages, and the old lady hid herself behind the *Osservatore Romano*. Did I think we could risk ordering another beer, Jim enquired diffidently of me. My caution dulled by the first and diminished by thirst, I gave the waiter a 100 shilling note for what we had already had and requested him to ask the memsahib if we could buy another two beers. We waited a long time for the reply. It was: 'She say you have had enough.'

Next afternoon I watched Jim walking down the runway. He merged with the fatties and slid into the fuselage. A few minutes later the aircraft's roar was just an echo in the wind.

The jokers and I had been told to report at the lodge at five-thirty the following morning for our lift to Baragoi. We arrived in the dark, but found nothing astir. 'Didn't you know?' said the sleepy watchman. 'She's changed her mind. She's not going until tomorrow.'

In the afternoon, Carl, a dreamy good-natured mechanic from the East End of London, who had fled the automated world to become the manager of Loyiangalani's camping site, gave us a lift to South Horr, where we slept on the floor of a Turkana butcher's mud hut. Next day we walked to Baragoi on four calabashes of milk we were lucky enough to buy from a passing Turkana. It took me another three days to collect my gear from Baringo and to reach Nairobi.

I spent the next six weeks in my Ngong shack, feverishly making lists, assembling all the food and equipment needed for the 250-plus mile walk from Loyiangalani to Ileret and back. What I would take would be basic, but this time no essential thing must be forgotten.

To Ileret and Back

The dominant theme of Teleki's journey along the shore of Lake Rudolf was food. The same applied to mine. Teleki supplemented his rations by shooting game. All I could hope for was a few fish, since all hunting had been banned in Kenya. Teleki travelled assured of the availability of food at Reshiat. I was warned to expect nothing from the two game posts on the way, and if no lorry had managed to get through to Ileret there would be no food to buy there either.

Teleki took 24 days to reach Reshiat. The march to Stefanie and back took him another 10 days. That makes a total of 58 days for the return trip. I calculated that, unencumbered by numbers as Teleki had been, I would be able to cover the distance in half that time. As it turned out, it took 36 days, but I did not make it to Stefanie. A piece of loutishness on the part of one of my companions precluded me from obtaining the food needed for that expedition.

Probably because I have never had to go without food, the subject has always occupied only a very minor place in my mind. In this respect I resemble a dog. One meal a day adequate in quantity and content to fuel the physical and mental machinery is all that is required. Automatically applying such an attitude to the task of working out food needs for this part of the journey, I became guilty of an inexcusable lapse of imagination. Instead of investigating what would satisfy my companions, I acted on the thoughtless assumption that they would be content with whatever was made available. Thus I brushed aside such things as onions, spices, flour and cooking fat as unnecessary luxuries. Beans would be the basic staple, I decided. Protein would come out of the lake in the form of the fish – a double mistake. First, the lake was no longer snapping with tilapia as it had been a few years earlier when, using a bare hook with a white feather attached to it, an angler could feed a party of eight after half an hour's work. Second, I had forgotten the reluctance of inland Turkana to eat fish. These were mistakes for which I was soon to pay.

In the event, the food supply consisted of 30 kilos of beans, five tins each of corned beef and mackerel (for emergencies only), half a kilo of salt, a half of tea, eight of sugar, one of powdered milk, one of coffee, two of boiled sweets and a packet of powdered orange juice.

By way of equipment I brought three gunny-sack donkey packs, rope, string, plastic wrapping material, sleeping tarpaulin, cooking pot, kettle, three teaspoons, three enamel mugs, four canvas holdalls, satchel, binoculars, two petrol cigarette lighters with fuel and spare flints, magnifying glass, medical bag (quinine, aspirin, vitamin tablets, Dettol and plaster), two torches with spare batteries, radio, panga, Masai sword, flywhisk, maps, penknife, four plastic one-gallon jerry-cans, sleeping bag, hurricane lamp, fishing rod with ancillaries, cigarettes and three kilos of Turkana tobacco. A glaring shortcoming here was the omission of a tent. Setting out as I was in the middle of the dry season, I complacently assumed that it would not rain.

I drove back into Loyiangalani on 1 February 1983, accompanied by Sayya, who, true to Turkana custom, was armed with two spears. Moses was to have come too, but when I reached Baragoi he could not be found. All I needed now was to acquire three donkeys, and we could be off.

My efforts to obtain them encountered a series of curt refusals. Only one bleak, flat-faced Turkana called William (whom I was fated to get to know well) offered me one for 800 shillings, which was double what I had been led to expect. But just as dejection was beginning to set in, William brought a tiny old man, who wore a pointed red hat like one of the Seven Dwarfs. 'This,' said William, 'is Seriman from El Molo Camp. He is willing to hire you a donkey for 10 shillings a day and his brother Lepile will supply another two.'

Ever optimistic, I jumped to the conclusion that no more obstacles remained to hamper my departure. But that evening I met William again. He warned me against travelling into the land of the Shangille alone but for one Turkana companion. Towards the end of the previous year, he said, the Turkana from the other side of the lake had raided the Shangille after passing through Ethiopia. Now the Shangille were out for revenge.

William's lecture was part of the pattern of intertribal hostility which had accompanied me ever since leaving Baringo as an ever-present reminder of the need to scan the horizon, to suspect every footprint as a potential portent of violence and to lie down each night prepared to wake to the sound of gunshots. It was a pattern of suspicion, haste and fear which marred every day in the lives of every man, woman and child belonging to every community in every corner of this remote part of the world. It squatted in every empty space like a grinning hobgoblin. As an outsider, I tried to ignore it, shake it off, even belittle it. But once I had physically entered its domains, it became part of my own life too. It became the dominant theme of my journey and remained my inseparable companion all the way back to Baringo.

William suggested I recruit Laroi, a Rendile by tribe, who knew a few words of the Shangille language. Moreover, having accompanied Stephen Pern (author of *Another Land, Another Sea*, 1979) on a walk all the way round the lake, Laroi had the additional advantage of knowing the way.

In Pern's book, Laroi comes across as a trusty guide and reliable companion. Pern must have liked him very much, because the book is dedicated to Laroi. But I had met Laroi during a previous stay at Loyiangalani. He was rolling up and down the main street, shouting abuse at all and sundry, his face distorted by rage and alcohol. Alcohol brings the real man to the surface. His behaviour when drunk is a good yardstick of his potential when sober. What I had seen of Laroi was enough to dismiss him as a potential travelling companion. But Sayya, sent round the village to seek an alternative, returned to say that no one was willing to come. 'Between Loyiangalani and Ileret,' was the consensus, 'there are no people except criminals eager to kill you for your donkeys and their loads, and there are too many lions which prefer donkeys to any other food.'

Laroi came into camp sober and coherent. His face looked rounded and kindly – almost priestly. But he too was full of warnings and portents. The paraffin lamp would have to be left behind, he decreed, and fires would have to be extinguished before nightfall lest the camp be seen by bad men from afar. One man would have to spend the night on guard to raise the alarm on the approach of lions.

So Laroi it was, and thus we set out. A week later, we were back. Danger had been Laroi's sole topic of conversation, and Sayya had become increasingly reluctant with every passing day. Neither of them touched my boiled beans or the few fishes I managed to bring in. Instead, they had eaten the corned beef down to the last tin, as well as consuming the greater part of the tea, milk and sugar. On the fourth day out, Laroi dropped the jerrycan he was filling and cavorted out of the lake as fast as his legs could carry him. In doing so he wrenched his knee. While he was in the water, he said, a small crocodile had lunged at him. He had managed to evade its jaws, but his leg was so badly damaged that there could be no going on.

As soon as our feet touched Loyiangalani again, Laroi, clutching seven days' pay, sped away to the distillery with miraculous agility. While Sayya lay down under a doum palm and went to sleep, I toured

161

the shops. They were empty because the lorry had broken down on the way from Baragoi.

During my absence, however, a man arrived who was prepared to tread the perilous path northward – Naqosowe, a cadaverous, long-shanked old Turkana, narrow of nose, lip and eye. He wore the look of an alcoholic even more markedly than Laroi, and I concluded that withdrawal symptoms might attack him even sooner. To guard against this I needed a third man – and to lay Sayya's fears to rest that man would have to be a Shangille.

There was no Shangille in Loyiangalani, but Firgug the shoemaker, who plied his trade on the veranda of Chongo's Somali caff, knew one in North Horr. 'Good fellow,' Firgug assured me; 'went to school with him, so I know what he's like.'

'You'll also be able to replenish your supplies,' added Chongo helpfully. 'My sister owns a shop there and there's always plenty coming up from Marsabit.'

It was sixty miles of goat-gnawed hills and flat parched desert to the dust-swept jigsaw of hovels rattling in the wind, but at Chongo's sister's shop I was able to buy almost everything I needed. While I was eating her fiery curry, the Shangille came, lean and spivvy in a dirty tee shirt red-lettered 'FOOTBALL', sloppy old jeans, the splayed toes of his huge feet curled over the soles of rubber flipflops three sizes too small for him. He claimed to have driven his father's goats from Moite to Ileret; if that was true, he would know the way. More importantly, he was young and belonged to the right tribe. He was also the only Shangille in North Horr.

Back in Loyiangalani, Lobun, as he was named, looked through the supplies. We could not subsist simply on beans and charred fish, he said. The lorry had just arrived, so we were able to make additional purchases. Half of the beans were replaced by maize meal and wheat flour; onions, rice, cooking fat and flavouring were also obtained.

To boost our morale, Lobun energetically set about cooking us a meal. Its main component was *ugali*, the white maize porridge which is the diet of most Kenyans. Normally served up with bitter boiled kale, it looks like fairy cake and tastes like a mixture of semolina and turnip. To me it is the most insipid dish in the world, but the spicy fish curry Lobun prepared to go with it rendered it palatable for the first time.

Then, having proved his culinary skills, he assured us that we would have no trouble with the Shangille. They were, after all, his own people, and his friends would be our friends. Lions? 'Don't give them a thought. All you have to do is tie the donkeys to a tree and sleep around them in a square, so whichever way the wind blows the lions will be able to smell man.'

'Your journey will be fine now,' said William in the campsite bar, where we were celebrating with the beer I had brought from North Horr. 'You've got a Shangille, so nothing bad can happen. And if you want to cross the Loriyu Hills to Lodwar later, I'm the man for you. I'm not afraid of *ng'oroko* – they're Turkana like me, so I'll know what to say to them. It's the Shangille that frighten me.'

That evening Laroi rolled into camp, totally cured and as drunk as King Henry on his wedding night. He did not care who heard him. 'Get rid of this Shangille,' he advised me stridently. 'All Shangille are bad. You will regret it.'

His exhortation brought me to the conclusion that it had been fear that had put paid to the attempt to make the journey with Laroi – fear arising out of the fact that I had ignored a fundamental principle: take a man born in the place of your destination. Lobun was such a man. This time I would get through.

I had already named the donkeys: the mischievous Kibirenge, the ebullient and impulsive Mashurubu (who had torn himself off his nose ring when he had smelt a hyena in the Lagga Ltomia) and the gently diffident Karomaindo. Lobun and Sayya had no experience of donkeys, Naqosowe a lifetime's; but while the former immediately showed themselves deft, Naqosowe gave orders sitting in the shade. He was to prove in many things to have much experience, but little energy in applying it. He was doomed from the start and damned at the finish.

We marched through the heat of the afternoon and camped under a lone tree. I bought a bundle of thin strips of sun-dried Nile perch, each about thirty inches long, from a bent old fisherman whose companions were equally bent and old. 'El Molo,' Lobun said. 'They're all like that when they get old. That's how you can recognise them from a distance.'

My own back began hurting next day, and had I known how painful it would become I might well have turned back for the second time. We passed Ol Doinyo Nanyori El Molo – the Green Mountain of the El Molo, which was brown – and the Laba Lokwa water hole (two inches of trapped rain the same shade) to a track sloping down towards an olive-green shoreline. Although the wind had dropped, a gentle coolness was setting in. Beyond a jagged hill, we came upon the village of El Molo Camp, a score of huts shaped like upturned salad basins, reed-strutted frames covered with lake weed, animal skins and sacking. As we waited in the shade of the Catholic mission school for permission from the headmaster to sleep on the floor, the lake turned silver, and the sun sank behind the black Loriyu. A herd of donkeys, including ours, browsed on the short rough grass nearby, headropes wound round the base of their ears, making them look as if they were wearing straw hats.

With Lobun beside me on the canvas, I watched the village settle down for the night. A score of small boys had gathered in the space between the school and the huts to sing war songs and stamp in the dust. At eight, the adults, having heard enough, dispersed them. I could hear talk from every hut, with feminine laughter pealing above the low voices of the men. None of them had a lamp or radio, and every home could hear what was going on in every other. Then silence came, leaving only the honking of Egyptian geese and the metallic clacking of frogs.

The plastic civilisation was still very far away from this place. While we had been resting in the Lagga Lolporana, I listened to an interview on the BBC about a London exhibition of Italian furniture based on designs in vogue in the fifties and sixties. The designer explained that his aim in life was to make shapes to shock or amuse and thereby enrich the lives of those who used them. The people of El Molo Camp had no furniture, but clearly retained their ability to amuse themselves and enrich one another's lives. It occurred to me in this context that many of us in the West have lost this ability by having become increasingly dependent on professionals to perform the function, thus assuming a passivity of which these poor fishermen were entirely innocent.

Next day, as we pushed into a welter of rounded hills and *laggas* (water-courses), the furnace glare of the sun sent my mind into a day-dream. The honey-coloured dry grass through which we plodded in pursuit of the donkeys' bouncing haunches reminded me of the hair of the girls of the Bund Deutscher Maedel – the Nazi version of the Girl Guides. I remembered the day I had first seen them as an eight-year-old in the streets of Dresden. My father having died in Isfahan, I had been sent by my mother to stay with my grandparents, both ardent Nazis. On a ritual *Spaziergang* with them, I watched the girls walking straight-backed with their smartly uniformed Hitler Jugend counterparts. I found myself hating the neatness and conformity of those child-soldiers. 'Stay with us and we'll let you join them,' clucked my grandmother, affectionately patting my head. I said I wanted to go back to Iran and that I didn't like uniforms. I didn't like my grandparents either, and that night I cut to pieces with a pair of scissors the lace curtains in my bedroom. Next day my grandfather whipped me with a belt and sent me back to my mother. It was a small price to pay for staying out of uniform.

The ceaseless exertion required to plod in the heat and glare from one flickering mirage to the next, eyes always half-closed against the batterings of the grit-laden wind, sends the mind reeling for refuge in one day-dream after another. That morning as thus we plodded on, I relived many other episodes of my childhood which, under different circumstances, would have slumbered on, undisturbed by memory.

Naqosowe knew the way well. We did not follow *laggas*, but kept crossing ridges from one to the next. Rain must have fallen recently, for at times we waded through thick beds of flowers, largely yellow anemone-like *Pavonia zeylonica*, and the taller *Cleome allamanni* waving racemes of mauve butterfly-winged blossom. With every step we took, orange-bodied grasshoppers buzzed away on silken grey wings.

We camped in the wide bed of the Lagga Kangalimo by a knee-deep pool clean enough to wash in. Naqosowe was the last to soap himself down. 'We're not going to use that pool again,' Sayya said. 'Look, the man's got spots.'

On that day I had begun to feel the pace. After passing the last of three table mountains, I came to a standstill and rested until Lobun came back for me. From then on we should move like a convoy, at the pace of the slowest, I said; but that, like many other things, was not to be. All my companions were endowed with an ability I lacked: they could effortlessly go to sleep directly they were not doing anything else. Daily, at noon, the sun's scourge would lash us into seeking refuge in the shade of a tree, where we would stay for four hours. Preparing and eating a meal would take an hour. For the men, a three-hour siesta would then follow; for me a listless lolling as I listened to the BBC through wails of static, the leaves chittering and scraping in the wind above, the donkeys irritably stamping and tail-swishing, the lake rattling the gravel of its shores and black-shouldered kites piping soprano trills as they swooped and banked. The men could hear none of these. With their heads wrapped in *shukas* as they lay on jagged lava rock or spiky grass, they would be sleeping like angels in God's feather beds.

By seven the sun's rage would wane to a shimmer of glowing plumes waving over the broken heads of the sable hills ranked up along the lake's western shore. For another hour, then, the evening breeze would fan the day's accumulated heat from the blistered stones and boulders until the lilting Abyssinian nightjars called a respite. That was the music to relax my aching muscles and slide me from the plane of half-consciousness into the cool embrace of sleep.

Or so it would have been but for my companions, who, having had their siestas, found themselves invigorated by the absence of the sun. During the few nights I had spent with Laroi and Sayya there had also been long conversations, but for me those had been as neutral as the rumble of night traffic, because they had been in Turkana, of which I knew less than ten words. Now we had Lobun, who knew no Turkana; to include him, the talk had turned into Swahili, and I into its prisoner. That night, Sayya told how as a recruit in the administrative police he had tried to bite off his sergeant's ear for provoking him. Lobun had been caught red-handed by game scouts in Allia Bay after spearing a zebra and had spent a month in Marsabit gaol. Naqosowe had been in a fight with a gang of Gabra poachers, one of whom he had shot in the neck with a .303. The reminiscing did not cease until after two, and at four Lobun woke me to help him catch Kibirenge, who had broken loose.

The land lay always in a fever, and the stones remained warm to the touch even at midnight. Half an hour after dawn I was already sweating. By seven, the *lagga* we were walking down became a wind-swept sudatorium. Just after passing drag marks and pieces of hairy skin, where a lion or leopard had killed a baboon, Lobun shouted 'Snake!' and picked up a stone. I told him to drop it and watched the little carpet viper slither away. It was beautifully patterned with a dark chocolate zigzag on a dun background and shrank back timidly when teased with the end of my fishing rod. I took the opportunity, then, to deliver my first lecture on snakes.

The instinctive desire to kill a snake on sight has always angered me. Snakes are cryptic, retiring creatures which, with very few exceptions, only bite creatures bigger than themselves in self-defence. Manufacturing poison is a process which consumes much energy, and the snake uses the substance sparingly. Egypt is overrun with rats which destroy enormous quantities of stored grain; this is because the Egyptians have virtually exterminated their cobra population. Rats outnumber the inhabitants of Dar es Salaam by two to one due to man's habit of killing harmless, rat-eating house snakes. Perhaps the day will come when the snake's usefulness to man is recognised. Until then I shall seize every opportunity to deliver lectures on the theme.

'Lobun, the fact that you still have a stone in your hand is a sign that you are a fool,' I began.

'Why? What is wrong with trying to kill a snake? Snakes are bad and anyone who does not try to kill them is a fool,' he retorted.

'What would you do if a man tried to kill you?'

'I would try to kill him first, of course.'

'Was that snake trying to kill you?'

'No, but it might have decided to if I had not frightened it.'

'If a snake bites in self-defence, the amount of poison it administers depends on the extremity of its fear. If it thinks you are trying to kill it, it will give you the biggest dose it can. That is why most people who die of snakebite are the ones who are trying to kill a snake. And from now on, on this safari, any one of you who tries to kill a snake will lose one day's pay.'

They had listened to me, but at the end of it every face was blank. It had been, I suspected, like telling Masai that the cause of the chronic constipation from which most of them suffer is brought about by their diet of milk and blood.

After climbing out of the *lagga*, we headed north-west into a grassless plain, a patchwork of rough stony areas alternating with red and black surfaces merging into a russet brown closer to the lake. Porr and the three cathedral rocks were now little more than warts far to the south, but the dark hump of Moite grew with every mile of our approach.

Von Hoehnel does not mention Moite. He refers to the range of hills which begins with Moite in the south and ends with Jarigole in the north as 'Mount Longendoti', and *The Times Atlas* still identifies it by that name. The source of the name was Teleki's guide Lembasso. It may perhaps be derived from the Masai 'Ol-doinyo loo ndoto', meaning 'the mountain of the small rocks'. But this would be highly inappropriate, as the range is composed of huge masses of solid basalt.

On reaching the southern base of Moite, the same Lembasso advised that in order to get to Allia Bay the party would have to detour around the eastern base of Longendoti. Von Hoehnel comments that Lembasso 'apparently did not know very much about the way or the water conditions'. The little water they found during that terrible three-day march was buried under the sand in a ravine. The men were so thirsty by then that they crowded around the pit. A tumultuous riot ensued, which was only quelled 'with the help of the Somal mercilessly wielding their whips'. Distribution of the water took up a whole night.

Naqosowe wanted us to repeat the 35-mile march, but Lobun insisted there was no need. We could stick to the lakeshore, he said, so that is what we did.

Naqosowe found three mottled sandgrouse eggs in a bare nest under a thorny shrub. The one I broke was about to hatch, so I replaced the others carefully. The plain was home to thousands of these birds, great coveys of them suddenly whirring up with shrill whistles and chirps from almost beneath our feet.

During the midday stop I tried to resolve another source of irritation. The tea and sugar supply was diminishing at an alarming rate. Sayya's method of brewing up began with a large handful of tea and a mug of sugar being thrown into a pot of cold water. I laid down that instead three heaped teaspoonsfuls of tea were to be used and only after the water had come to the boil. Sugar would be individually added after the tea had been poured. No objections was raised, but trouble arose when none of the teaspoons could be found. I issued another decree that everyone must look after his own, but the result was that usually only mine could be found.

From Tinkede, the headland where we had stopped, we struck straight up the lakeshore through a mile-wide strip of rough grass between it and a range of low hills to the east until we reached the shade of a clump of doum palms near a hippo skeleton. Naqosowe and I unloaded, for Lobun and Sayya had gone off to follow the tracks of a large crocodile in the hope of finding its eggs for an epicurean supper. Naqosowe told me that a female crocodile walks several miles inland to lay her eggs in a hole she digs and covers up.

Like the snake, the crocodile is a dreaded creature, but is in fact one which itself lives in constant fear. Threats to its life are so numerous that the survivors are very lucky indeed. The female usually lays up to fifty eggs in a type of sand that hardens over them. This protects them to some extent from baboons, hyenas and men. During the three-month incubation period, the mother lurks in the vicinity to ambush such predators. When the young hatch they are too weak to burrow to the surface unaided. The mother must wait until she hears them squeaking and then she digs them out of the nest. After that begins a perilous journey as she escorts them to the lake, for there are marabou storks, fish eagles and other birds of prey circling the sky above, poised to swoop down at the slightest sign of movement. Jackals follow the little cavalcade, darting in to snatch the little delicacies. Not even if they manage to reach the water are the survivors safe, for there they have to learn to evade the scooping beaks of pelicans and the open maws of catfish and giant Nile perch. Last but not least they are even in constant danger of being snapped up by cannibals of their own kind. The chance of a baby crocodile surviving into adulthood has been estimated at one in 400. Even adults are not safe. The El Molo, Merille, Shangille and Turkana all consider their flesh to be the best of all, and spear them whenever they can. I am sure that most crocodiles, given the choice, would prefer to spend their lives in a zoo.

The clutch Sayya and Lobun were trying to find was one of the lucky ones, for they came back empty handed, having lost the trail in the undergrowth.

We woke to Naqosowe's rasping voice announcing that he was sick. Sayya unwrapped his head to say that he too was sick. The donkeys indulged in fiendish obstreperousness, sickened, perhaps, by knowing that they were to be loaded again. Mashurubu emulated my own tactic of lying down, insolently rolling on his back and kicking up his legs; Lobun and I had to twist his ears into corkscrews before he deigned to get back on his feet.

As we pressed northwards, huge flocks of red-billed Quelea birds rose before us like roaring dust devils, each flock a deep brown whirling mass casting a dark shadow in its wake. They moved, perhaps a hundred thousand in each flock, as a single body, undulating, rising, falling, then wheeling white with the reflection of their underbellies to pour like milk into the grass and disappear as if they had never existed. These tiny, weaver birds live on grass seed in the savannahs of eastern and central Africa; sometimes they migrate to farmlands, where they become crop pests as serious as locusts and are destroyed by poisons sprayed on them by aircraft.

Beyond the last headland south of Jarigole, a couple of billion tons of mansion-sized boulders had rolled off the mountain's back, forming a barrier ending in a wall which fell sheer into the lake. Naqosowe vociferously insisted that there was no way over the shoulder of the barrier, that we would have to backtrack and take the route he had originally suggested. I sent Lobun on a reconnaissance. Fifteen minutes later he was back to say he had found the path he and his father had used when they had herded goats to Ileret.

The gradient was so steep and perilous that the donkeys had to be cruelly beaten up it. Every time one of them lost his footing in the scree, my heart sank with a vision of him careening unstoppably to the top of the wall. Once Kibirenge crashed on his side, but Lobun and I got to him in time to push him back on his feet. Naqosowe expressed his resentment by washing his hands of donkey driving. He trailed behind, repeatedly declaring Lobun insane, while Sayya climbed the heights to scan the horizon. The path took us over three ridges, the last of which was bisected by a narrow gulley leading into a broad *lagga* shade-splashed by dignified old acacias. Three boats lay beached on the shore. A dozen men rested by them, one playing a lute fashioned out of a five-litre mission milk container, a piece of planking and three strings of nylon fishing line. They had piled their dried fish in a huge, five-foot-high ring like the base of a truncated brickworks chimney. Seven thousand tilapias, they said. Ebony black, nail-hard Luo, far from that other lake that was their own, they greeted us turbulently, crushing our hands with rough fingers, thumping our backs.

We would have stayed the night with them, but the suggestion was not well received. Quite suddenly they became sullen and unresponsive and started muttering to one another in their own language, casting furtive glances in our direction. I was to learn the reason for this mysterious behaviour, but not for many days. My men quickly sensed the atmosphere and drove the donkeys to the next tree-line. It had been a very hard march, and I was asleep before eight, too exhausted even to check that everything had been properly stowed.

Rain came during the night exactly at two, a massive downpour buffeted by a snarling wind. Clammy freshets soon swirled around our buttocks as we crouched under the tarpaulin amid the tumble of whatever gear we had been able to pull under it. By dawn, when we had crouched there for four hours, our teeth chattering, groaning in our cat-naps, rain was still spraying the tarpaulin from massed grey clouds, and the lake lay pockmarked like boiling porridge. First light revealed gear scattered in a chaos of mud and slush, brown rivulets winding their way round soaked donkey packs. The sight filled me with dread. If the supplies were ruined there would be no way of going on. But nothing could be done until the rain stopped.

Somehow this storm acted as a catharsis on the bickering of the past few days. All equally wet, cold, uncomfortable and depressed now, each of us could help himself only by helping the others. We got a fire going, made tea and huddled up close, steaming off first one side, then the other.

At eleven the sky suddenly cleared like a blackboard wiped with a wet cloth, and the sun dyed the lake iris blue. My careful packaging of the food in string-tied plastic had paid off, and we were loaded by mid-afternoon. After a couple of gentle headlands we reached the edge of the plain at the foot of Jarigole, already a part of the Sibilot National Park, as indicated by an iron post with a notice saying 'Turkana Camp'. My suggestion to stop there was overruled, so we continued walking until after dark. With the lights of the park headquarters dimly visible ahead, we stumbled for what seemed hours through clumps of thigh-high grass. I cursed my acquiescence to the men's unwillingness to camp earlier, for here with every step there was a very real danger of treading on a puff adder and getting a dose of poison sufficient to kill an ox. But we were lucky, for at last we stepped into a pool of light and lively talk. Game scouts and their women were sitting on stools around a fire outside one of their huts. When we made our greetings, however, they hardly bothered to look up and left us standing like a gang of tramps who had invaded a luxury hotel. There is a stage beyond the borders of exhaustion at which rage lurks close to the surface, and I had reached it. I tapped the nearest man on the shoulder. 'You,' I said, 'I said *jambo* to you. Did you hear me or not?'

'Yes, I did,' he replied, without turning his head.

'Well, then, what's the matter with you? Isn't it part of your duties to attend to visitors? I am such a one and I have a letter for your boss from Mr Leakey.'

The name worked like adrenalin. A sergeant and a corporal jumped up full of deference to conduct us to the warden's house. 'My goodness,' exclaimed the sergeant, 'you have walked all the way from Loyiangalani, aiee, aiee, aiee – *mzungu* is truly *mzungu*. What African would walk like that?'

This was something I had heard before. The first white men had come on foot, and, of those who followed, many also had this strange habit of walking, apparently aimlessly, around. Some say it is the reason why white men came to be known as *mzungu*. The Swahili root *zungu* denotes something startling, strange or clever. The verb *zunguka* means to wander about, loiter or waste time. To the sergeant I was such a one, a strange, wandering time-waster; no proper work to do, family left to their own devices, too much money and not enough sense. Writing a book? For whom? What could there be to write about in a bush full of wild animals waiting to have you for breakfast? Fool writing for fools. *Mzungu.*

'Yes, what can I do for you?' Mr Godfrey Opiata, the warden, asked me. He was lying on his bed in his bungalow, listening to Nairobi radio in the dark. His store had run out of paraffin. Dressed in white vest and shorts, he loomed through the doorway and read the letter by flashlight. Then he allocated us his kitchen veranda as bedroom and invited us to use his bathroom. There was plenty of drinking water, but would we please use it sparingly as it had to be brought in by lorry.

Opiata led me to a wicker chair. After a chairless week it was like sinking into a water bed. I was almost asleep on my feet; but as I had found with many others living in isolation, loneliness made him eager to communicate. Opiata was not one of those fat men inhabited by a thin one. An elephant can negotiate 45 degree forest trail eighteen inches wide or walk through a camp in the dead of night without touching a guyrope. Opiata was like that; he walked with consummate poise and sat with every muscle relaxed.

But he was not happy. He saw his several wives – he would not tell me how many – and fourteen children only twice a year. To do so he had to travel all the way to Lake Victoria, to one of those islands where he had his home. I pictured him sitting in the yard in front of his tin-roofed concrete bungalow, contemplating the sun as it sank into the belly of Uganda, the smell of charcoal smoke and fish stew drifting past his nostrils to an accompaniment of clanking pots, children's cries, female chatter and cajolings. Perhaps twice a year was enough, for here he could lie on his bed listening to the radio, his peace disturbed only by the swish of the surf and the grunts of hippos wallowing in their offshore gardens. A flawed paradise to be sure, but had I been made to choose between it and a bed-sit in Bayswater, I knew which way I would have gone.

There were about sixty souls living in that isolated camp. Their food came in by lorry once a month, but they were allowed to take fish from the lake. The men's job was to protect the wildlife, including the fish. 'Crocodile are the favourite food of men and lions,' said Opiata. 'The rangers ensure that only the latter are served.' The Shangille, Turkana and Luo were a menace, Opiata said. They fished in protected waters, speared hippos and invaded the park to look for crocodile eggs and turtles. The park was vast and difficult to patrol. He received fuel sufficient for only one round tour a month.

I asked him to lend me a blanket, because my sleeping bag was still soaked through. He gave me his deputy's bed and woke me in the morning with a cup of sweet maize gruel. Then he leaned over the veranda rail and hailed a man who was just landing a small boat. A 100 kilo Nile perch was brought up on a wheelbarrow, its shilling-sized eyes still glistening malachite and gold. Lobun cut off a 10 kilo steak and hung it over Kibirenge's pack.

Teleki had followed the shore of Allia Bay, but we were unable to emulate him, because the downpour had haemorrhaged the Sibilot River into a delta of a thousand swollen laggas, freshets and runnels, all bowling down to the lake. The water's edge had become an impassable morass, and further progress could only be made by turning inland.

Here again, as had been the case at Mount Ng'iro, Allia Bay teemed with game at the time of Teleki's arrival. In addition to the antelope, zebra and their predators, all of which are still relatively common today, there were large populations of rhino and elephant. One of the elephants wounded by Teleki on the shore took refuge in the lake out of effective range. Teleki resorted to naval warfare. He had his canvas boat assembled. Three men were ordered into it and told to subject the animal to a barrage at close range. Oddly the Great Exterminator himself did not participate in the manoeuvre. Von Hoehnel does not suggest a reason. Perhaps it was that the Count foresaw the consequences of the action and was reluctant to become a part of them. The elephant, having received eight bullets from a heavy rifle, 'did not budge an inch, but went on quietly rooting up seaweed with its trunk, and now and then sprinkling water over its wounds. He did not seem to notice the boat or the men in it, and was equally regardless of the bullets he received in his body.' As a remedy, the men were given a heavier rifle, and two more shots were fired. At this the elephant, very understandably one supposes, 'suddenly charged with inconceivable fury, dashing the water around into foam. In the twinkling of an eye he was upon the fragile craft, which he first shoved before him for a little distance, and then seized with his trunk. He shook it, crushed it, tossed it about, and then contemptuously flung it aside. Finally, without taking the slightest further notice of the men who were diving close to him, or of the shots which Qualla continued to fire, he marched with slow and stately steps through the water, and disappeared behind a peninsula.'

The explorers were 'very annoyed' by the loss of their boat, but made no attempt to follow the elephant, which must by then have been as thoroughly perforated with bullet wounds as Father Cornelius's Land-Rover at Parkati. The explorers found the animal's skeleton on the return march, so they did not lose the tusks, whose owner had paid the price of a lingering and excruciating death.

A curious feature noted by von Hoehnel about the Rudolf elephants was that they would wade into the water up to their bellies as a matter of course to eat the weeds growing on the bottom. The weed still exists and is the staple food of the lake's hippo. Von Hoehnel also refers to large numbers of 'big shady trees' and 'a good deal of succulent bush'. I found very little left of either. Elephant and rhino are both unknown in the area now. The reason is almost certainly man.

It was at Allia Bay, too, that the explorers and their men feasted on catfish. So did we.

Lacustrine donkeys hate opaque water. It is to them as gin is to the Muslim fundamentalist. They will approach it unresistingly, but once at its edge, they turn stubborn. It was the same each time, a turning upstream until a shallow ford could be found. If Kibirenge would cross, Karomaindo and Mashurubu would follow. If he disapproved, he would promptly lie down, only to rise again after having been convinced that no one would try to make him cross.

Walking ahead in search of such a ford, my attention was caught by a swirl and the flash of a black body. At first I thought it was a crocodile, but then there were others affording brief glimpses of fins and heads with twirling whiskers.

'Mashurubu!' a voice behind me shouts. It is Lobun's. But he is not shouting about the donkey which bears that name – the bewhiskered one – but about catfish. He has snatched one of Sayya's spears. Suddenly all three men are in the water, the donkeys forgotten, Sayya and Lobun jabbing the narrow ends of their spears into the sludge, Naqosowe laying about himself with the piece of copper piping which serves as his club. 'Over here, over there!' they shout. 'There's a whole shoal of them! Got you, bastard!'

Lobun has rammed down the spear with such force that the metal bends. Then his muscles flex as he lifts out a great wriggling catfish which is frothing with blood. He flings it over to whip-thrash on the bank. Now Naqosowe is bashing its head in, while Sayya looks on, suddenly sobered by the sight of his bent spear. But Lobun stays in the water and within moments he has impaled five more, hurling each into the grass to die while he goes after the next.

Had I not shouted for him to stop, he would have gone on killing until he was exhausted, for to him what he was doing was no longer a matter of food or a titbit. He had turned into a human cheetah, and the hunt had become a massacre before I had time to realise what was happening. Only his first victim, weighing about twelve kilos, was taken; the rest were left for the birds. What devilry is it that turns man into a killer? Does the ineluctability of his own impending death impel him to cut short other lives in acts of subconscious revenge? Whatever the reason for Lobun's bloodlust, I felt outraged and unable to excuse him.

From the delta we crossed into a treeless plain of water-flattened rusty dry grass resembling a vast wheatfield struck by a tornado. It was a lions' hunting ground, for everywhere lay the scattered remains of crocodiles – dismembered carcases, jaws dried open by the sun with every razor tooth in place, shreds of scaly skin, shrivelled intestines and claws, broken tails, whole backbones held together by desiccated sinews. It was clear that these lions feared nothing, for time and again I saw crocodile heads as long as four feet. Of the lions themselves there was no sign except the prints of their pads in the soft earth, criss-crossed by the dog-like tracks of the hyenas which had followed to take their share. Had the slaughter been the work of men, surely their feet would have left their mark also.

Under a lone, nest-laced acacia chirping and sparkling with carmine bee eaters, Lobun threw the catfish into the ashes, where it turned into a sad cadaver, the skin curling away from the flesh like a napalm victim's. The broad, flat head lay to one side, the eyes burned out of their sockets and the long prehensile whiskers charred down to knobbly stumps. Lobun cut a steak, blew the ashes off and handed it to me. The meat was firm and greasy, its taste like smoked eel. I filled myself up with the stuff; it thickened the blood and recharged the muscles.

It was hot. Very hot. It felt like being in a bath in need of a dash of cold water to render it tolerable. The blisters on my legs had burned dry, leaving the skin looking as if I had recently recovered from chicken pox. But the heat did not matter. It was there all the time and inescapable to the extent that even immersion in the lake conceded only a very transient solace. What mattered was the exhaustion it induced, a lassitude so heavy that even my desire to smoke was often curbed by reluctance to expend the degree of energy necessary to grope for the lighter.

Afternoon brought us into a land of undulating dunes and scraggy bushes. When the sun was nearly down, we halted by a wind-stunted tree. We spread the canvas on a flat patch of sand free of shrubs and snake tracks. We had done about eleven gruelling miles that day, but there had been the mercy of rain-water pools everywhere. It is no good looking at such water; all of it is the colour of beige emulsion paint. Take a mouthful; if it tastes sweet, it is fit to drink. Tea made with it looks milky before it has had a drop. But tea made with lake water is yellow, brown, green and even blue, depending on the concentration and type of salts it contains, which seem to vary markedly.

Morning found me feeling morose and resentful. Until after midnight I had been kept awake by loud talk and rumbustious laughter. I had kept feeling the urge to call for silence, but refrained, knowing only too well that the tension which would ensue from expressing my rage would keep me awake even longer than if I exercised patience and waited for the men to stop.

Lobun handed me a mug of tea. It was as bitter-sweet as saccharine and treacle-heavy with milk. Again my rules for brewing it had been ignored. Now there was something else to be angry about. I wanted to lecture, harangue and threaten, but then I heard a familiar whooping in the distance. At seven in the morning, hyenas? They were there all right, two of them, no need for binoculars. Only a hundred yards off, yowling and looping straight for us. I looked at Lobun. We laughed. Bloody stupid beasts. In a minute they would see us, and the terror of it would send them scuttling off like rats. Not so. They kept coming, coming, big now, black, spotty and heavy. Sayya handed Lobun a spear; the men rose and stiffened and suddenly they were off like sprinters, spears held high at the ready. Still the hyenas came on like a pair of hungry wolves. Then they halted. The men were still running, only yards between them now. The men stop too; their spear blades flash. The scene freezes to a still, then breaks again with the hyenas turning in noiseless flight, stunted backsides bouncing to keep up with the thrust of their powerful forelegs. They recede and diminish, juddering black smudges now, dissolving in the mirage.

Lobun and Sayya strode slowly back to camp, smiling and elated, sweat trickling down their thighs and flat stomachs. From the drudgery of camp chores and donkey driving, they had risen like phoenixes briefly to become the warriors of their dreams. They had routed the enemy and safeguarded their companions, happy that fate had given them the chance to prove their loyalty. And they knew that on that day at least, my gratitude would dissipate my anger.

Hyenas are not cowardly. A pack of them will drive a lioness off her kill. I had heard of them attacking women and children in the dark, but a frontal attack on four men in broad daylight was to all of us unprecedentedly bizarre. The incident left me feeling afraid of hyenas for the first time.

Koobi Fora is a base camp for scientists searching for human fossil bones under the auspices of the Nairobi museum directed by Richard Leakey, whose work in this field is now world famous. Built in the early seventies, it is situated near the water at the end of a low headland and comprises staff quarters and kitchen, an office with a radio mast, workshops, several bungalows with spacious verandas and an airstrip. Had we arrived there in a Land-Rover laden with sugar and oranges, I suspect our welcome might have been warmer; but as impecunious-looking donkey drovers, we were probably suspected of being short of supplies and likely to become a nuisance. Asked for permission to use one of the verandas, Francis, the grumpy man in charge, said we were welcome, provided we paid him 800 shillings. My assertion that I was known to Mr Leakey was curtly dismissed; had I been telling the truth, I would have brought a letter. Mr Opiata had retained my letter, I said. Another lie, I was told. Childishly piqued by his attitude, I turned on my heels and marched the party inland as far as a rocky hollow beyond the tree-line, but no sooner had we unloaded and the donkeys were rolling on their sweaty backs than a messenger arrived to say we could use the staff-quarters veranda and kitchen. Lightning was already flashing to the north, so I ordered the beasts to be reloaded. Sayya was furious. Inspired by his defeat of the hyenas, he had become, for the first time, unreservedly content to camp in the open. 'Why do you let those dogs mess you about like this?' he chided. 'When they say go, you go, and now when they say come, you come.' I pointed wordlessly to the rainclouds looming in the north, and he said no more.

Lobun cooked beans, which we ate with the remains of the catfish. Thunder growled, and lightning lit up the darkness, but it did not rain. There was nothing to be bought or traded, but Lobun found a friend who lent him a good pair of jeans and a teeshirt for his homecoming to Ileret. Three years earlier Lobun had eloped from there to North Horr with a girl engaged to be married to another man. It had been love, Lobun told me. The aim of the borrowed clothes was to pose spurious prosperity in mitigation of a soiled reputation.

In the morning we walked north-east through a grassy plain wrinkled by wet *laggas*. The first herd of oryx we had seen on the march observed our approach before cantering off inland, their leader playing rearguard. Beyond them we reached a stony brown headland overgrown with stunted trees. At the top of it we found the Kokoi game post, a huddle of half-derelict huts with an aerial connected to a broken radio. A friendly sergeant with a handlebar moustache showed us to a campsite into which a herd of fat goats was being driven by women dressed Boran style – tight-bodiced long dresses and black headscarves. There was not enough milk for us to buy, but the sergeant brought us each a plate of rice with meat so delicately juicy and tender that it was certainly neither goat nor mutton. He said the hyenas had probably attacked us because they were rabid. He and his colleagues had found the carcases of several which had died without apparent cause. More recently, a pack of them had invaded the camp and attacked the dogs. One or two of the dogs had subsequently turned rabid, so the rangers had shot every one. They were worried now, because they had none left to warn them of poachers creeping in to steal the goats.

Finding to my dismay that we were into our last packet of tea, I ruled that from then on only I would make tea and no one else. I was to be informed when the water came to the boil and would then measure out the precious leaves. On that, the first occasion I applied the rule, my fingers slipped, and half the water in the pot spilled over my bare foot. The men laughed when I had to change from boots to plimsolls. 'The price for making silly rules,' Sayya commented. I put on woollen socks and forgot about the foot, excited by the knowledge that Ileret was only a day's march off now. We kept to the volcanic ridge starting in Kokoi for about three miles before descending to the lake again. From there on it was one of the most beautiful walks of the whole journey. The water lapping the black rocks lining the shore was glass clear. I was intrigued by a black strip twenty yards across, starting only a foot or two from the edge. Moving and undulating unceasingly, it extended all the way to Ileret and beyond. Like an enormous python, it coiled away as we approached and closed in again after we had passed: it was a solid shoal of catfish. Crocodiles in large numbers, some as long as fifteen feet, lay sunning themselves in crowds like bathers on the beach at Cannes. I counted thirty-eight plunging into the water from one small headland as we drew near. Their panic ceased about a hundred yards out, where they stopped and floated on the surface to observe our passage.

Only once did I get a close look at one and that was after cresting a piece of dead ground. The crocodile slid into the water without delay, but then, apparently having decided I was too near for safety, suddenly put on a burst of speed with enormously powerful lateral movements of the tail, leaving a wake like a power boat's. His behaviour and that of the others made the stories I had heard of crocodiles attacking people on dry land hard to believe. The ones I saw moved stiffly and clumsily on the shore, but once in the water they were as agile as sharks.

We followed the beach to a point where it turned sharply towards the west, from which we made for the Lagga Ilkemere and lay cool in the shade of its old acacias. In the afternoon we traversed a grass-and-bush-clothed alluvial plain spreading westwards from the base of a range of bastion-shaped hills on which topi and Grant's gazelle roamed in herds of forty and fifty. Then to the shore again, where, a mile on, we came upon three boats, a parked lorry and a crowd of people. We were on the last lap to Ileret and could already see the mission house on the skyline with the police lines and huts farther down the ridge.

Lobun, smart now in his borrowed clothes, was greeted like a sailor returning to a familiar port. The lorry belonged to the police, who had come to buy fish, but now it refused to start. The people milling around it to push were fishermen, both Turkana and Shangille. A policeman told me that rivalry between the two had not yet penetrated the sphere of fishing, but for cattle they would kill one another. Lobun led up a tall, pretty young woman dressed in a blouse and *kitenge*, whom he introduced as Fatumah Solomon, the wife of his friend at Koobi Fora; it would be by her house that we would be camping.

Ileret was a three-tier village. At the top of the ridge were the police lines, dispensary and mission house. Halfway down were the square, tidily thatched mud houses of the middle class – those of the dispenser, the distiller, the teacher and the police canteen manager. Below these sprawled a mass of beehive huts built of wood, skins, sacking, shreds of plastic sheeting and flattened tins, the entrance of each about two feet high with a leather flap serving as door – the homes of the Shangille and a few immigrant Samburu and El Molo.

A crowd of all ages watched us unpack; they were curious, but exceptionally polite. The women wore nothing to cover the upper part of their bodies, and almost all of them were very small and thin with tiny breasts. Those over thirty were as flat-chested as boys, their shoulders the narrowest I had ever seen. Their skirts were of leather, a long one down to their ankles at the back and a short one hanging down to crotch level in front. Much less heavily decorated than their Turkana counterparts, most of them wore only two or three bead necklaces and a bracelet or two above the elbow; a few also wore plain brass anklets. One little girl's anklets had little 'singing bells' attached; her mother explained that she was naughty, always running off at night. The women's hairstyle was very similar to that favoured in Eritrea – braids clinging to the scalp from the forehead with ends brushed free at the back. Girl children were dressed like their mothers, but all the boys were stark naked.

The men were as thin as the women. Most had their hair shaved round the head down from a point about an inch above the pinna of the ear, leaving what remained standing free or plaited into two pigtails. About one in three had plastered their heads with mud painted green or red and decorated with ostrich plumes. One had covered his mud cap with two curved ridges of ostrich down like a double-plumed Roman centurion's helmet.

Fatumah's house was one of the middle-class group, about twelve feet square with a full-length entrance and divided into two by a partition parallel with the door. To the left of the entrance, three cushioned stools made a tiny sitting room; when you sat on one and someone else entered you had to draw back your legs before he could pass. The first space to the right was the kitchen, a three-stone hearth, utensils hanging on the wall and stacked on the floor; but Fatumah was comparatively well off, for she had a teapot, thermos flask, plates, cups, glasses and a hurricane lamp. To the left, past the partition entrance, stood a large bed, with spare clothes hanging from a nail above it. To the right, most of the space was taken up by a wooden chest of drawers draped with an embroidered cloth. Between them hung a large picture of the Pope and family photographs, including one of Lobun.

Sayya said he had been defecating blood. His forehead felt very hot. We took him to the dispensary, where we found the health assistant sitting outside in the cool evening breeze. The casualty book, being a leftover from colonial days, required Sayya to state his tribe. Samburu, he said, later confiding that he had been afraid of telling the truth in case he was given poison; what he got was quinine and piriton. On return to the house, he promptly ensconced himself in Fatumah's bed, from which we had great difficulty extricating him. She lent him one of her blankets, and we all went to sleep on the canvas spread outside her front door. There were no mosquitoes, but the sand beneath teemed with small beetles which scratched interminably as they built themselves new homes.

Naqosowe was displeased by the arrangements. 'Why do we have to stay with these *washenzi*,' he whined, 'when we could have camped in the police lines with civilised people?'

Sayya was too sick to lend him support, but on the following day he, too, made his point: 'What primitives these women are! They wear nothing under their skirts, and when they walk you can see everything.'

After so many mornings chorused in by wild birds, the Ileret dawn was strange with crowings and bleatings. A grey light hung over the lumpy little dwellings below as women and girls began to slip out of their flap doors like silk moths from cocoons. As they reached each corral, the massed pleadings of the sheep and goats subsided like classroom chatter with the teacher's entry. Soon only the swoosh of milk squirting into scores of tins could be heard and then more voices stirring out of sleep as the village twitched back to consciousness. Figures began to hurry from hut to hut with breakfast milk and embers for cold hearths. Mothers emerged and sat on skins as they breastfed babies. No quarrelling here, no shouting or tearful cries: a dignified order seemed to hold the denizens of that jumble of ragged shacks together.

The Shangille (or Reshiat, as von Hoehnel called them) were no longer the food-rich tribe they had been in Teleki's day. Now they grew a little millet, grazed their livestock on the grassy plain between Ileret and Banya and took their toll of the lake's catfish. Those who lived on the Ethiopian side of the border around the Omo River delta, being able to irrigate their crops more easily, were better off. 'The Shangille have been given a bad time by everyone,' Njoroge, the police chief, told me, 'the governments and, worst of all, the Turkana. They used to have their settlements farther north, around Banya, but in 1956 the government moved most of them down here to give them better protection. Now it's more difficult for the Turkana to attack from the south, but there's still hardly anything to stop them from crossing into Ethiopia from Namuruputh and coming at the Shangille from the north.'

A wild-eyed woman as thin as a wire doll passed by where we were sitting in the police compound, her walk fast and jerky. 'That's what she does all day,' Njoroge said. 'She doesn't know where she's going, but she goes all the same – the only mad woman in Ileret. The boy who brought our tea is her son, her only son. Eight years ago she and her family lived between here and Banya. They had a good herd of cattle and were never short of milk. One afternoon she went into the bush to search for a lost goat. When she got back, she found all her cattle gone, her home in ashes and the bodies of her husband and nine of her children strewn around the compound. Only the tenth, that boy, then a baby, who had been speared in the shoulder and left to bleed to death, survived. But her sanity didn't. He was about eleven when I found him here. I tried to help the woman by sending the boy to the mission school in North Horr, but the priest gave up after he failed standard four three years running. The only way I could go on helping them was to employ him as my servant. So, my friend, you can see why the Shangille hate the Turkana.'

Two years later, to the day, the Nairobi *Daily Nation* reported the following: 'Cattle rustlers killed 40 people in a *manyata* in the Ileret area of Marsabit District and stole 6,000 cattle and goats and 2,000 camels. Reports reaching Nairobi from Marsabit yesterday said that police have recovered 3,800 cattle, camels and goats stolen in the raid on Monday last week. Police reports added that nine people wounded during the attack were recovering at Marsabit Hospital.

'Immediately after reports reached the police, they deployed light aircraft and the rustlers were spotted at Darade water well. Reinforcements of regular and administration police from Marsabit were rushed to the area and intercepted the marauders between the Sabarei and Buluk Administration Police posts. Ileret is on the north-eastern side of Lake Turkana and, according to police, the raiders were intercepted at Sabarei, about 100 miles from Ileret and a few miles from the Ethiopian border on the eastern side of Lake Turkana.

'Police said all the animals except those which may have died during the gun battle between the security forces and the raiders had been recovered.

'Earlier reports reaching the *Nation* from Marsabit said several of the cattle rustlers were killed in the encounter with the security forces. The rustlers are believed to be Hamar Kuke tribesmen from a *manyata* at Nyamber water well in North Horr Division of Marsabit District.

'Those killed during the night raid included men, women and children. The marauders took the villagers by surprise as they slept.'

Njoroge's police lines were dilapidated. A predecessor had built a concrete swimming pool and planted trees around it, which were the only aspect that had improved with age, and I was happy to be able to sit in their shade. The pool was empty now. Men had painted their names on its walls in the hope of being remembered, curiously certain, I thought, that it would never be filled again.

Most of the windows of the building were broken. 'My station is falling to pieces,' Njoroge explained, 'and nothing is being done for its upkeep. When furniture wears out, it is not replaced. I asked for a carpenter, but none was sent. The men have nothing but their truckle beds now. The roofs of the quarters used to have a double layer of corrugated iron, but during the tour of duty of one of my predecessors,' he said, carefully shifting his muscular frame in the chair and the mood of his account into the passive, '. . . one complete layer was removed from every building and somehow sent away. The post's refrigerator was also relocated at the same time.'

Next day I went into Njoroge's house to use his bathroom. The bedroom in the pleasantly spacious bungalow contained one truckle bed, a wardrobe, a hardbacked chair and a table on which six empty beer bottles stood in a row. The rest of the house was as empty as the bottles. The shower did not work, but there was a tap in the wall and a stool to sit on while soaping oneself. No toilet except a hole in the centre of a sacking-palisaded whitewashed platform in the garden.

Like Opiata, Njoroge was far from his home on the misty slopes of Mount Kenya and his family of six – another administrative exile, just like his predecessors of the colonial era. Perhaps Ileret was some kind of punishment station, for his communications radio had broken down, and no one had been sent to repair it. His Land-Rover had been taken away at the orders of his headquarters. Before being posted here four years earlier, he told me, he had been in charge of the police at Isiolo, where he had fallen foul of the local military commander. He hinted that that individual had been behind his transfer, adding with evident satisfaction that the man was now in prison for his role in the August 1982 coup attempt. 'I was here on that terrible day,' Njoroge said. 'I had no means of communicating with my headquarters, so all I could do was put my men on standby and pray. I was expecting something to come over the border from Ethiopia at any moment, but thank God things took the course they did. If those fools had succeeded, Kenya would have turned into another Uganda.'

Njoroge introduced me to the manager of the police canteen, Ngolo, who sold me sugar, tea, maize meal, sweets, ginger and a two-kilo tin of Italian powdered milk on the understanding that I would give him half a kilo of tobacco for the privilege he was according me. On returning to Fatumah's to stow these treasures, Lobun introduced me to his parents, the one a pathetic, reeling old man, the other like a wizened ten-year-old girl. At Lobun's request, I gave them twenty shillings and half a kilo of tobacco.

Njoroge, splendidly turned out in uniform and carrying a Greener riot gun, took me in his Mercedes lorry for a tour of the border. 'We go up about once a fortnight,' he explained, 'and quite often we cross to see our Ethiopian colleagues. As police, we can understand one another, for we have the same interests. We catch criminals who cross the border and hand them back on a mutual basis. The only difficulty is communication; the Ethiopians do not know Swahili, so we can only talk in broken English.'

'What about the Shangille? What do they think about the border?'

'Shangille? All they know is that there is a row of markers. The politicians and surveyors did not consider them when they drew lines on their maps. The Shangille are united by blood on both sides and still have no understanding of being the citizens of any country. Neither we nor the Ethiopians interfere with their cross-border wanderings unless some crime has been committed. The only difference between the Shangille living in Ethiopia and those on our side is that the Ethiopian lot are still armed, because the government is too weak to protect them against the Turkana. Ours were told to bring in their weapons for registration and repairs. We locked all the rifles in the armoury and simply told their owners they couldn't have them back.'

After crossing the yellow sand of the Lagga Ileret, we drove into what seemed like a solid wall of wait-a-bit thorn along a track so rarely used that the branches of the trees on either side formed an unbroken low ceiling. As we bulldozed through, thousands of carmine bee eaters flashed away in every direction as if we had been ploughing through a field of carnations. Quite abruptly the trees ended, and the lorry sped us into a flat, grassy alluvial strip about two miles across between the forest and the lakeshore. This, the Sapari Plain, was dotted with livestock and *manyatas* all the way to the border and beyond. Each homestead consisted of a cluster of delicately woven reed-and-grass beehive houses with tiny straw-framed entrances. Miniature replicas of the residential huts perched on long stilts to serve as stores and hen houses. 'We keep the stilts polished,' an El Molo/Shangille half-caste told me by his lakeside home, 'to keep the mongooses off the poultry and the rats away from the grain. That way the mongooses stay hungry enough to hunt the rats and snakes and so long as they can't get at the chickens they don't bother us.'

On the way back from the border (which was marked by white pyramid-shaped concrete blocks at intervals of a kilometre, each numbered, with 'Kenya' in Roman script on one side and 'Ethiopia' in Amharic on the other), we passed a small tin-roofed building standing empty and forlorn in the wilderness. 'In the days of Emperor Haile Selassie,' Njoroge said, 'a missionary named Swart lived and worked among the Shangille on the Ethiopian side. They liked him because he spoke their language and provided the only available medical treatment. He was left alone until Mengistu took over. But Mengistu, being an atheist Marxist, liked neither Christians nor missionaries, so he gave Swart his marching orders. In 1980 Swart moved to Ileret, hoping to help his old friends from this side. He built a bungalow for himself and a store for the Ileret fishermen. He set up a workshop to maintain his transport and the fish store refrigeration. And then he built as a clinic that little place we just passed. Every two or three days, he would drive there to treat the Shangille of Ethiopia, who came to him because their liberators had done no more for them than the ousted monarchists. But the sight of their liberated populace crossing the border in search of what the progressive rulers did not provide proved too embarrassing. Swart received a message from Ethiopia, informally verbal, but to the point: you have a week to get out before we kill you. Swart went, leaving a workshop full of tools no one knows how to use, a new pick-up no one knows how to drive, a fully equipped fish store no one can operate and a beautiful residence no one is allowed to live in. So, thanks to Mengistu, the Shangille of Kenya can no longer store their fish and their relatives over the border have had to revert to traditional medicines.'

The juxtaposition of thus depriving the Shangille of medical facilities on the one hand and allowing them to retain their arms on the other epitomised for me the basic nature of Mengistu's regime. It had been from the outset and nakedly remained the rule of the gun, regardless of the political fancy dress he had continued trying to disguise it in. Mengistu's era is bound to go on record as a tapestry of death, terror and deprivation of liberty unprecedented in the history of Ethiopia.

The most sought-after commodity in this part of the world is, after food, tobacco. What is desired is the roughly cured leaf, which the Turkana, Shangille and El Molo like to chew, while the Masai, Pokot and Samburu grind it into snuff. It is always in short supply and therefore received with disproportionate enthusiasm and gratitude. However, failure on the part of the traveller to carry a good supply is universally regarded as the height of niggardliness.

We had arrived in Ileret with three kilos, of which I had given half a kilo to Lobun's parents and some to Naqosowe along the way. Sayya and Lobun both smoked cigarettes and therefore had no need of it. I owed Ngolo half a kilo, and the rest would be kept in reserve for the march to Lake Stefanie (which I had yet to discuss with Njoroge) and the return to Loyiangalani. The supplies I had been able to buy from Ngolo were barely sufficient for the Stefanie leg. No one in Ileret was willing to sell food for cash alone, but cash supplemented by tobacco was another matter altogether.

What happened next was almost unbelievable.

When we got back from our drive with Njoroge, we found Naqosowe asleep on the tarpaulin, dead drunk. The brown paper bag which had contained the rest of the tobacco lay beside him, and it was empty. Two bottles next to it were empty too. There could be no march to Stefanie, and the supplies I had been able to buy from Ngolo were barely sufficient to last as far as Allia Bay. At that moment I would have enjoyed feeding Naqosowe to the crocodiles. It was an irreparable disaster.

Njoroge wanted to lock him up, but I needed Naqosowe for the return march, and that earned him a reprieve. As we made our farewells, old men approached me with upturned palms into which I would have liked to put pinches of tobacco. Instead, I pointed dumbly at Naqosowe; they understood instantly, but with sad faces. Then, after promising to write to Njoroge and to meet him in the big bad town if he succeeded in getting a transfer, I turned south for the first time since leaving Pangani.

The two Turkana forged ahead with the donkeys and the comradeship of their shared language. Lobun and I lagged behind in a newly discovered togetherness of shared disappointment, for he had been as keen as I had to go on to Stefanie. He was also as angry as I not only because Naqosowe had frustrated our plan to do so but that his action had also served to cut short our stay at Ileret.

Once we stepped across Ileret's southern pale and out of earshot of its last cock crow we returned once again to our own isolation in a land where men are but hasty transients. But backtracking soon proved to be every bit as inspiring as the outward journey, for every feature and vista, now seen in reverse, was entirely new. It was a bonus as delightful as accidentally discovering a fine landscape whose existence had never been suspected painted on the back of a familiar canvas. I felt more confident too, for nothing untoward had happened on the way up to engender disquiet during the return, and my skin was proof now against the brandings of the sun. The only doubt nagging me on that day was whether we would be able to replenish our food supplies at Allia. But the shadow lifted when I remembered the great stack of dried fish we had seen on the way up. Even if nothing else could be found, a few of those would see us through. Provided they were still there, of course.

The rapidly climbing orb of the sun had already sucked up the sparse drops of dew spilled on the scorched grass by the dawn. The shore of fragmented fossils of pachyderms, pterodactyl, fishes and men embalmed in lava by the past stretched timelessly into the future, its very desolation a refuge from the present. Not even the slightest ripple creased the lake's primordial waters lying undisturbed in their dark-edged basin of yellow hills. But then the wind stirred a little in its sleep. It would soon shake itself awake and resume its impetuous daytime buffetings.

As we ambled on, I felt myself drifting gradually into a dream-like mood. It was as if I was straying into a landscape where nothing moved, nothing sounded and nothing signified but the realisation that destiny and despair are synonymous. And yet there remained the perplexing paradox of freedom of choice with every step taken – the choice, for example, of deciding to sit down and transcending into a state of Sufic unity with I knew not what, or simply lying down to die. But even that would not have mattered, for a man's death in a place such as this would have been as insignificant as the death of a baby crocodile.

Or so I thought until the piercing cry of a fish eagle and a hand grasping my elbow with sudden urgency jolted me out of my reverie. Half a mile inland to the left of our vanguard, two black spots hovered in the mirages splashing the dun-coloured slope. 'Shangille,' said Lobun, 'with rifles.' We studied them through the binoculars: great busbies of hair standing straight up from their heads, *shukas* worn to crotch level – Shangille fashion. One had a .303, the other an Italian rifle with long barrel and ramrod. Now they had stopped too, looking first in our direction, then towards Naqosowe and Sayya, who had stepped up their pace. Lobun handed back the binoculars. We did not speak, for each knew the other's thoughts. *Those men ought not to be here. They are dismayed that we have seen them.*

For three years, during the emergency in Aden, I had worked and slept with a Stirling submachine-gun never out of reach. Never once did I have occasion to fire it in anger, but the weight of its curved magazine and the roughness of its perforated barrel housing never failed to transmit a sense of security. Now I could feel it again and had to look down to disabuse myself of the illusion. I felt totally vulnerable.

The Shangille started walking diagonally towards the shore. I estimated they would pass us at a hundred yards – too far for explanations, too near for comfort. Lobun gripped my arm again. 'Look,' he said, 'they are my own tribe. I'll go and talk to them. When I raise my hand, come over too so that they can see you're a European.'

Through the binoculars I watched him approach the pair. Their bodies were well fleshed, their skins shiny with grease. Their rifles were slung over their shoulders, muzzles up. Each carried about a hundred rounds in leather bandoliers. 'About as *shenzi* as they come,' my diary says. Lobun shook hands with them, and seconds later his arm went up. They stood still as I approached with outstretched hand and took it in turn without opening their mouths.

It was indeed a tense moment. The elder of the pair held my eyes in his for what seemed a very lengthy moment, knowing, as I did, that his weapon was as illegal as his errand and that I was witness to both. We also knew that he could make certain in only one way that my share of this knowledge was not passed on. Lobun was a fellow-tribesman, but his status as such was diminished by what he too now knew and by the company he kept. Our meeting place was a hyena paradise, and the favourite food of hyenas is bones. By morning ours could be just a few dusty splinters – and the riflemen could be in Ethiopia.

'*Habari?*' I said with artless inspiration. 'You must be Home Guards.'*

They glanced at each other, the younger one looking puzzled. The other turned back to me. 'Yes, that's what we are,' he affirmed in Swahili. His reply was a reprieve, for if I was stupid enough to believe him, then I might also forget his face. Lobun said a few words to them in Shangille and then we parted. 'Go with God,' I called after them, hoping they were not in the process of changing their minds. But they did not take their rifles off their shoulders and before long they had faded once again to just a couple of black spots in the distance.

'They've been in the park after zebra,' said Lobun. 'The Shangille believe zebra meat makes a man very strong and its fat can cure

---

* In Kenya's outlying regions certain trusted locals are armed by the government to protect their districts against raiders and intruders. Known as the Home Guards, the force was originally established by the British during the days of Mau Mau to protect villagers.

gonorrhoea. But we were lucky. If we'd had any cattle with us . . . weee – that would have been something else!'

It took us an hour to catch up with the Turkana. Together then we entered a piece of open ground patched with clumps of waist-high grass and thickets. 'That looks like a perfect house for a lion,' I remarked to Sayya as we passed a particularly luxuriant and shady miswaki. At that moment a lioness leaped out of it. Sayya, spear up and bounding in great strides, was instantly in pursuit, but she vanished in the grass as effectively as a crocodile in the depths of the lake. However, a search of her tracks revealed that before we flushed her she had changed beds several times, each within striking distance of where the donkeys had been browsing not long before.

That evening, at the Kokoi game post, the sergeant told us that he too had met up with poachers. 'It was yesterday afternoon, six of us on a routine patrol. We stopped in a *lagga* about twenty miles east of here. Suddenly eight Shangille opened up on us with four rifles from under a tree where they'd been sleeping.'

I realised then that we had been even luckier than we thought, for the two we had encountered had almost certainly belonged to that gang.

'We fired back and they ran away,' the sergeant went on. 'But now we're afraid they are preparing to raid our goats, so I want you to tell Opiata. Our radio is still out and we don't have enough petrol to drive to Ileret.'

It was a six-hour walk, but my suggestion to emulate us evoked derision. Government officers travelled by Land-Rover, he informed me; when there was no Land-Rover, the journey was cancelled.

A one-time governor of Kenya, Sir Richard Turnbull, whom I had got to know in his capacity of Aden's penultimate High Commissioner, once paid a visit to a newly appointed district officer in North Horr. They went on a Land-Rover tour of the district. After twenty miles or so, Turnbull ordered the driver to stop by a Sudan gum arabic tree. 'What's the name of that tree?' Turnbull asked the district officer. He did not know. A few miles on, a man flagged down the vehicle for a drink of water. 'What tribe is that man?' Turnbull asked. Again the district officer did not know. When they had gone fifty miles, they stopped under a tree, in the shade of which a group of Boran were bargaining over a camel. Turnbull wanted to know what language they were speaking. 'I don't know, sir.'

'Then get out of the Land-Rover.'

'What is it you want me to do, sir?' asked the now distraught young official.

'You're going to walk back, and by the time you get to North Horr you'll know the answers to my questions and a few more besides.' With that, Turnbull drove off in a cloud of dust.

I told the story to the sergeant, stressing that in those days government officers were expected to walk. 'Very strange man that Turnbull must have been,' was his comment. 'Why should a district officer be expected to know the name of a tree?'

Halfway between Koobi Fora and Sibilot the donkeys suddenly became frisky. Far from having to be beaten to maintain our walking pace, they now had to be restrained from exceeding it. 'They know they're on their way home,' Sayya said, 'where all they'll have to do is roll in the grass and fuck their mothers and sisters.'

The donkeys were soon to demonstrate that they were less logical than Sayya supposed. At midday we stopped by an isolated acacia near a water hole a mile inland. To the east, the ground rose to debouch into a ten-mile-wide plain extending as far as the bases of three large hills – Nderet, Sililorenya and Alya, the last like a giant round table tipped to one side where one of its legs had broken. The donkeys were grazing in an alluvial plain about 150 yards to the south of us. To one side of them, close to the lake, were several topi, and between them and the donkeys stood half a dozen zebra. To the other side of the donkeys, nearer to the tree-line, was a small herd of Grant's gazelle. In the middle of the afternoon the sun relented, and we decided to move. Lobun set off to drive the donkeys back for loading. I was watching the wild animals through the binoculars. So were the donkeys, backsides facing me, ears alertly erect. The topi began walking inland. When they levelled with the zebra, the latter followed suit, but at a trot. Suddenly the Grant's gazelle pranced off in alarm, triggering the zebra and the topi into a panicky gallop. That set off the donkeys, which started chasing their wild cousins with all their might. Within a minute the whole lot were through the tree-line and over the top of the slope.

Lobun ran back to camp. He and Sayya snatched up their spears and dashed off in pursuit. I tried to follow, but could not keep up due to my scalded foot. From the top of the slope I was able to see a wooded plateau descending to a bare plain, but a thorough search with the binoculars revealed not a single movement. To go on, I risked getting lost myself, so I returned to camp, where I found Naqosowe on his back amid an unsorted jumble of supplies and equipment.

Night fell like a theatre curtain. The easterly wind, which had been battering us all day, died with a sigh, leaving a stillness broken only by the crackling of the fire. At eight the moon rose, hooded by hazy cloud at first, then gradually brightening. Naqosowe picked a smouldering branch out of the fire and, facing inland, waved it from side to side to the accompaniment of an incantation. I felt a surge of guilty affection as I watched him; there was nothing he could do in our predicament, but at least he had thought of trying to conciliate his God, poor man, and had done so in the knowledge that to him it would make little difference whether I lost the donkeys or not. Either way, it would take just as long to return to Loyiangalani, and so his pay would be the same. But what was happening over there beyond the slope in the moonlight? Had the men lost the tracks, or were they waiting for dawn? Had they come up against lions? Perhaps the donkeys had been killed and the men had gone to Sibilot for help. And I remembered that they had run off without water bottle, torch or cigarettes.

Recalling Sayya's assertion that donkeys could run just as fast as zebra, but were less alert to the danger of lions, I asked Naqosowe if donkeys could see in the dark. He said they could not. So, I reasoned miserably, the lions stood an even better chance.

The camp was not far from where the hyenas had attacked us, but that night our only weapon was the Masai sword. We piled large stones between us on the canvas as potential artillery. For once the night was quiet, but I could not sleep. It was past midnight when I dozed off, only to be startled back to consciousness by the growls of a lion. I reached for a stone, and Naqosowe woke too. Silence again. The growls had been Naqosowe's snores.

In the morning I found myself alone. The acacia's foliage was very sparse. Making shade would have to be the next thing; it would soon get devilish hot. A family of ravens were sitting on the topmost branch, the parents alternately caressing each other and nudging their two fledglings into daring a take-off. The hen flew off and returned with titbits, which her children gobbled down with hoarse cries of gratitude. Then a black-shouldered kite swooped out of the sky and sent them all flapping off. The first to return was the cock, who settled on the firewood and studied me with beady eyes as if he was sizing me up as a potential meal. Joined by his family, he turned his attention to the pot of beans, trying to get the lid off; a stop-gap substitute for me, I supposed.

I threw two donkey packs over the lower branches, but hardly had I settled in their shade with my travelling mentor, Thomas Hardy, before the wind snatched them away. The same wind brought the sound of voices. I began to climb the slope, sick with apprehension. If I was not to see donkeys, I would see disaster.

Yet again I was lucky, for at the top I met them all. 'They ran into the thick bush with the zebra,' Lobun told me after gulping down several pints of water. 'We followed until it became too dark to see the tracks. We stayed put and did not go to look for water for fear of losing our way back to them. Then, when the moon rose, we went on for another two hours until, again, it became too dark. We slept by the tracks. At dawn we started again and followed the tracks until we found the donkeys. They were standing all together under a tree at the very base of Nderet.'

Had the hyena incident remained the sole example of the men's loyalty, I might have concluded that they had acted out of a sense of self-preservation. But this time they could easily have given up the search and been none the worse off. By persevering and succeeding, they had merely assured themselves of another week of hard work, which failure could have rendered much less irksome.

At Allia Bay, we found Opiata, as before, lying on his bed. His response to my message from Kokoi was a shrug. 'All they're worried about is their bloody goats,' he said. 'If there were six of them, and only four of the Shangille had rifles, why didn't they just finish them off?'

He was in a sardonic mood. The radio had just quoted an official as promising that five hundred elephants which had been making a nuisance of themselves in the Laikipia agricultural area would be 'transferred' to a game park. 'They can transfer me,' Opiata commented, 'but how do you transfer elephants?'

He was short of water, so we washed in the lake, but his store was overflowing with food. I bought enough to ensure that we could afford to dawdle all the rest of the way back.

When we halted again where two-headed Jarigole leans his buttresses into the wind-ribbed lake, Lobun said he had heard it whispered at Sibilot that the game scouts had attacked the fishermen's camp we had passed on the way up. My impression of the benign Opiata militated against belief, but as we approached the site Sayya picked up a freshly fired .303 cartridge case. A few hundred yards on, we reached the narrow strip of shingle where we had met the fishermen resting. All that was left of their catch was a yawning black greasy patch with a few half-burned tilapia curled up by its edges. A single rubber sandal, almost new, lying abandoned at the water's edge, told of a terrified rush to the boats. Lobun nudged the sandal with his foot. 'Tsk, tsk, tsk,' he muttered with shaking head. 'By God, if ever I get any money together, I'll collect a gang of my friends and we'll kill every animal in this park. What kind of a system is it that sends men to burn people's property?'

I empathised with his rage. He could grasp only the concept of his friends' wasted sweat – the 7,000 fishes worth nearly 10,000 shillings which had been piled up there on the beach, food for the hungry, new shirts for the fishermen and *kitenges* for their wives – all wantonly destroyed. It was pointless trying to explain that the lake was well on the way towards being fished out due to greed, hunger and absence of management: Luo using small-mesh nets, Turkana famine-stricken, no patrol boats.

A few miles on, a dozen Turkana over from Kalokol on the other side of the lake beached their two sailboats to greet us. They told Sayya and Naqosowe they were on their way to fish the forbidden park waters that night. They were aware of the fate of their Luo friends, who had shied away from letting us witness a night-time poaching cruise. 'We know all about them,' the Turkana said, 'but what can we do? There aren't any fish anywhere else.'

They were right. And if Opiata gave up trying to stop them, the day would inexorably dawn when there would be no fish left at all. Anywhere.

Halfway through the precarious climb to circumvent Jarigole's lakeside precipice, I forgot all about the fish. Ever since passing Porr, three days after leaving Loyiangalani, I had been intermittently troubled by stabbing pains in the back – something I attributed to the cracking pace of my companions, men inured to walking in deep sand and clambering over jagged volcanic rock. So far it had been no more than a nagging discomfort, but floundering up that scree-strewn slope now, I suddenly felt as if I had been skewered by a witch-finder. I staggered through the next few days in a sort of trance, noticing nothing, remembering nothing. Each evening found me so debilitated that I was quite unable to write my diary. Sleep became almost impossible. Even Naqosowe took pity and kneaded me with gnarled hands. I was touched by his ministrations, but they did not bring relief. By the time we reached Moite, I began to doubt that I would be able to go on.

On the way, Lobun had picked a sprig of slender cactus bearing yellow flowers edged with red, called in his language *gorkuled*. That evening he boiled it up with the leaves of a tree called *alang'* in Shangille and *epuu* in Turkana. 'That,' said he, pointing at a mugful of fluid blacker than Turkish coffee, 'is the bitterest and most powerful medicine in the world and it will even cure gonorrhoea. If you can drink it all, I promise that you will get no more backache, starting tomorrow.'

It tasted like a distillation of scorpion's gall, but I wanted to believe that it would work and managed to get it down without vomiting.

Next morning I got painlessly to my feet. Was it the result of faith-healing?

Alang'lepuu, I found out later, is *Cadaba rotundifolia*, one of the *Capparidaceae*, a family of herbs and shrubby trees common in the sandy soils of Turkana land. *Gorkuled* was identified for me as a recently discovered new species, *Euphorbia tescorum*, by Dr T. Reynolds, who is researching exotic herbal remedies at the Jodrell laboratory in Kew Gardens. According to Dr Reynolds, there is growing interest in the potential medicinal value of various types of euphorbia and aloe. It is perhaps worth recording in this respect that I have not suffered from severe back pains since the day I took Lobun's medicine.

Three days later we left Porr glowing like a heap of charcoal embers in the setting sun. The nearer we got to Loyiangalani, the more obsessed Sayya and Lobun became with the subject of sex. Sayya told of his success with a Maralal policeman's wife; he had paid for it by spending two nights in the cells. Lobun in the bush with a thirteen-year-old shepherdess: failing to penetrate her, he had used his index finger, upon which she had run home bleeding, and his father had been obliged to pay hers two goats. Naqosowe lamented the demise of the old tribal disciplines; these days, the women had got out of hand and would double-cross their husbands for the meanest of trinkets. Having proudly given accounts of their own aberrant exploits, Lobun and Sayya heartily agreed. It was up to men to guard their women, they said, or reconcile themselves to feeding bastards.

We made our last camp by a hollow knee-deep in water as sweet as any we had had during the whole of the journey. In the morning we were told of Europeans camping at Losichoi. They were three middle-aged West Germans and their wives, who gave us white bread and bierwurst. Herr Breit stood up, saying they needed to stock up with water. 'I'll try the springs first and if it's no good there, I'll go on to Loyiangalani.'

I told him the Losichoi water was not much better than the lake's. 'But you've got good water right here on your doorstep,' I added, pointing towards the rain pond beside them.

He looked surprised. 'No, we can't drink muddy water, so we'll go to Loyiangalani.'

I overcame the temptation to remind him that back in Stuttgart he would be content again to drink filtered sewage, while here he was turning up his nose at water which had fallen straight from heaven into a hollow of cauterised sand.

In 2,000 miles of Tanzania and Kenya I had never seen human

excrement near water. Zigua, Chagga, Masai, Kikuyu, Samburu, Pokot, Turkana, Rendile, Shangille – all would assault anyone defecating near water, but in Iran you cannot approach a river without first walking into swarms of bluebottles and then putting your foot in a turd. Muslims have to wash their hands and anuses immediately after relieving themselves. Consequently, Egyptians defecate into their canals, Kashmiris into mountain streams – and then use the same water for making sherbet. Pigs eat shit, and dogs like rolling in it. The Prophet Muhammad noticed and condemned them as unclean animals to be neither eaten nor touched. But unaware of the danger of drinking contaminated water, he did not warn his followers against doing so. Today, they all continue to observe his strictures on cleanliness, but too many of them remain as ignorant as he was of the dangers of fouling their water.

I put the gear into the back of the lorry and sent off the men to walk the donkeys to Lepile at El Molo Camp. Herr Breit drove me to Loyiangalani. The journey was like a jet flight as the familiar landscape was ripped past my eyes like a cinema film gone out of control. Suddenly I was in Chongo's caff with the gear all over the floor. I could hardly see and felt slightly mad. Chongo and all the other Somalis came to shake my hand. 'How was the Shangille?' Firgug wanted to know.

'First class. Didn't put a foot wrong.'

'And Naqosowe?'

'Well, you know what he's like.' I told him about the tobacco. It was vindictive, perhaps, but had we been unlucky enough to have found Opiata's store empty, we might have had to give up and scrounge a lift back. To each of Lobun and Sayya I gave a zipper bag and half the remaining food and cigarettes as a bonus. Naqosowe got nothing, but I did not carry out my threat to fine him. 'What about me?' he asked crossly.

'You had your bonus in Ileret,' I replied, handing what was left of a tin of 500 aspirins, 'but you can have this. If you wake up with a hangover tomorrow, eat them all.' We shook hands before parting all the same.

No Time to Stop and Stare

The finest house outside Loyiangalani's tourist and mission enclaves was built of smooth grey stone. It had a proper wooden door and glazed windows. Inside it was a sofa, armchairs and every other sort of furnishing. When I was invited in, tea was served in white china cups. None of the hoi-polloi enamel mugs here. The mistress of the house was Mama Shanga – Mrs Bead – the most dignified, well-oiled and meticulously ornamented Samburu matron one could ever hope to meet. 'All this,' she told me with an expansive sweeping gesture of her generously braceleted arm, 'I bought with the profits of my trade in beads. I am Loyiangalani's number-one bead seller.'

Love of beads is, like love of livestock, shared by all the tribes of the Northern Frontier District – men, women and children alike. The beads come in various colours and sizes. They are worn either as necklaces strung on wire, or sewn in patterns on cloth and leather as ear rings, head decorations, bracelets, belts and anklets. Every kind has its own significance. A man, for example, wears a special type of dark blue bead to show that his children have been initiated. Their beads, in turn, tell the same story. An unmarried girl wears beads defining her status, and they are different from those worn by a married woman. The quantity of beads a wife wears reflects how much her husband loves her. In the remoter parts of Turkanaland, few men bother with clothes, but I rarely saw one without a string of beads round his wrist, neck or waist. Beads are a universal requirement. They were in Teleki's day, too, and if he had had the right sort in Reshiat he would have been able to buy the cattle he needed for the return march. He did not, so he went without.

Agostinho was a twelve-year-old Turkana schoolboy, who made a bit of pocket money showing tourists the sights of Loyiangalani and serving tea at Chongo's caff. He became my friend and was happy to run errands for me. His home was one of the many grass beehive huts, where he lived with his mother, Eng'omo. Like most Turkana, she was named after a tree. John Hillaby (*Journey to the Jade Sea*, 1972) had a different name for her. He called her the Lolita of Loyiangalani. He greatly admired her as a dancer and tells how, after she had outdone

195

every man in prowess and endurance, she 'strode from the dance floor like a queen'.

Hillaby's book includes a full-length photograph of her. She stands propping herself with her left arm against the trunk of a doum palm. A string of beads, each end attached to an ear, passes under the nether lip of her gently smiling mouth. Barefooted and wearing nothing but an ostrich-shell bead-fringed triangular leather miniskirt at the front and a robe falling down to her ankles at the back, her figure is a perfection of symmetry. Now, eleven years later, she had become Loyiangalani's number-two bead seller.

When, on 6 June 1983, I brought for her at Agostinho's request half a kilo each of red and blue beads, I saw her for the first time. She stepped out of the door wearing the same style of leather skirt as she had worn for Hillaby's picture and she was still stunningly beautiful. Head held high and back as straight as a guardsman's, her eyes were fearless and direct. She took my hand. The beads I had brought, she told me through Agostinho, would be put aside to make necklaces for his sister.

But that had not been the idea. It had been for her to sell the beads, undercutting Mama Shanga's prices. Then I would send more from Nairobi. That was what Agostinho and I had planned. Her trade would become brisk, and that would help towards her son's school fees. Eng'omo smiled broadly and nodded her head in vigorous agreement. 'She says yes,' Agostinho translated, 'but next time you should send her white beads as well.'

It was not until the following afternoon that I came to understand the terms under which her request had been made. A Swahili-speaking woman approached me in Chongo's caff to say that Eng'omo wanted a word with me. I was led to a tree under which Eng'omo was squatting behind a cowhide spread with her wares, including, I was relieved to note, the beads I had brought. She addressed a few words to the woman, who turned to me. 'Eng'omo says she wants you to give her some money to buy wire for stringing the beads.'

Until that moment of truth I had only thought of Eng'omo as an exceptionally beautiful and graceful woman. I had forgotten that she was also a Turkana and that in Turkanaland the 'give that ye may be given' words of the Sermon of the Mount read 'give that ye may be asked for more'.

'Tell her to buy the wire out of the proceeds of the beads,' I said.

Eng'omo's face creased with displeasure, transforming her beauty into the ugliness of a child thwarted. She was outraged. 'You were rich enough to buy the beads,' she informed me with irrefutable Turkana logic. 'Are you not still rich enough also to buy the wire that goes with them?'

On the way back to camp with Sayya, I met Lepile of El Molo Camp, to whom I owed some money outstanding from a donkey deal. He stood in our path, stately in his indigo toga, staff in hand, bald head reflecting the sun. 'You are setting off on another long and dangerous journey,' he pronounced, 'but you have already proved yourself. A good traveller has nothing to fear.' He spat into the palm of his hand, then raised it like a Roman emperor signalling the start of a gladiatorial contest. 'I call on God to protect you throughout. Go with God's blessing,' he added.

I thanked him and placed my debt into his wetted hand. As I turned to go, I felt a tap on my shoulder. It was Sayya. 'Lepile says he wants another five shillings for his saliva.'

Nothing is free in Turkanaland. Rapacity is the common denominator controlling every thought and movement. Generosity is a virtue, but it is the product of surplus, or at least of sufficiency. Those who were generous to me in Tanzania were, compared to the Turkana, possessed of at least such a sufficiency. The Turkana has nothing to spare. Most of the time he gets less than he needs. He lives in a land so hard that to survive in it he must be even harder. He must search for every crumb, remain ever strong enough to snatch it up and defend himself from other would-be takers.

In my experience, Turkanaland represents the most clear-cut example in human terms of Darwin's 'survival of the fittest' theory. During the rainy seasons, which are often unreliable, the Turkana lives mainly on milk and blood. During the dry season, which is most of the time, grass becomes scarce and udders shrink. If he has been able to grow a little millet, he is lucky. If not, he must rely on the fruit of the doum palm, which has to be pounded to make it soft enough to chew, and those of *ebei* (*Balanites pedicullaris*), *erdung* (*Boscia coriacea*) and *eng'omo* (*Grewia tenax*). I have tasted all of these. They are as hard, bitter and astringent as the Turkana character. No one who has had the ill fortune to have to subsist on them can be blamed for yielding to rapacity.

From Loyiangalani, Teleki's route now pointed south to Lokweam at the southern extremity of the lake, then north-west over the mysterious Loriyu Hills to the Kerio River and finally to Lodwar, all of it through the Turkana heartland. The walk was to be, as I had feared from the start, not only a back-breaking physical struggle but an unremitting guerrilla war on minds narrowed by climate and environment both equally harsh.

Apart from the stretch to Lokweam, I knew nothing of the way except the red line on von Hoehnel's map. To be sure, I was better equipped with maps than he had been, but there was no way of telling if the water holes they showed still existed or that they could be found. For that I should have to rely on William, the Turkana who had refused to accompany me to Ileret but was now to be my guide.

I was now more experienced than on the day I had set out for Ileret. I had learned that donkeys are rough and that travelling with them is dusty, that the nature and quantities of supplies must be rationalised to the demands of the consumers and reconciled to what the donkeys can carry. Dried food is more weight-effective than tins. The best staples are maize and wheat flour and beans. I had also brought adequate supplies of tea, sugar, coffee, dried milk, dried Nile perch, corned beef, cooking fat, salt, onions and flavouring, plus tobacco for barter and ingratiation. To be dust-proof, rain-proof and donkey-proof, every fragile packet of staples was carefully wrapped in plastic and tied with string.

I sent William off to buy donkeys. There was no question of hiring this time; the ultimate destination was Baringo, from which they could not be returned to their owners. By lunchtime the day after my arrival he had bought two and by the afternoon of the next he had secured a third, who turned out to be none other than Mashurubu.

Trouble started that very day. My supplies had been calculated for a party of five, consisting of Lobun, Sayya, Moses, William and myself. Now William declared his intention of taking his young assistant, a cheeky, bow-legged adolescent. 'If you don't take him,' William said, 'I'm not coming either.'

That piece of blackmail was the first blow in a battle of wills fated to be fought all the way to Lodwar.

'What's his name?' I asked.

'We call him Arroghoy Muzhi – the one who hasn't eaten yet.'

I never found out his real name. He was to be given food and a token sum of money on arrival in Lodwar.

The donkeys were soon loaded, about thirty kilos apiece. William worked deftly, but I did not like the way he tightened the crupper ropes. 'It's better than damaging their thighs,' he said. 'It's the thighs that keep them going. That bit under the tail doesn't matter.'

He had spent the whole of his boyhood dealing with his widowed nomadic mother's donkeys. Next to his experience, my journey to Ileret counted for nothing, and his mouth's loudness told me that he had already been at the hair of the dog. He roped the donkeys together for the walk through the village, Mashurubu in the lead.

A dreary three-day tramp took us first along the road by the lakeshore between stony desert hills and a wind-scarred beach until it turned east to disappear in the red Longipi Hills. Then we headed inland through a range of naked ochre-and-yellow hills to a plateau sloping gently down towards a beach pitted with the five-toed stompings of hippo. Finally, having climbed through a hellish jumble of boulders, we reached a grove of miswaki and acacia in whose inviting shade whined millions of gnats and mosquitoes. Beyond it, edged by a rough lava beach clustered with spiky grass, lay the cloudy green water of Lokweam Inlet. Here I declared a two-day halt.

Two Turkana men, naked but for a single string of white beads round the waist, were just finishing their meal of roast Nile perch. Neither was circumcised. Moses said very few Turkana practised circumcision, although he himself had had the operation performed on him by an 'American' at Maralal known as *Bwana Juu* ('the tall gentleman'). I had already heard of this famous surgeon, but it was not until much later that I learned he was none other than Wilfred Thesiger.

Each of the Turkana men was equipped with a long-barbed wooden-hafted spear and a coil of rope. They described how they harpooned the big perch which strayed into the shallow inlet. What about crocodiles? 'Well, yes, they're there all right and if they get a chance they will pull in a goat, a donkey or a cow – even you if you're not careful. So you've got to watch out all the time.'

Three leather-clad girls lifted and put to one side several flat stones. Grinning conspiratorially, they uncovered the biggest perch I had ever seen. To show me how it had met its end, the eldest inserted her forefinger into a spear gash in its side. Using a leaf-shaped knife, she slit along the fish's lateral line and cut me a three-kilo steak, then put the ten-shilling note I gave her into a leather purse suspended between her plump naked breasts.

The first people Teleki met on the lakeshore expressed amazement at what to them was a fact – that all the members of his party were women, because all of them were wearing clothes. Sitting now with the naked men, observing the girls severing the fish's head by smashing through its two-inch-thick vertebral column with a stone, made me realise how little had changed here since Teleki's day. The remoteness of the spot and the apparent absence of anything in it that an outsider might wish to possess would hopefully ensure its preservation for at least another century.

My own efforts to catch fish were nothing less than a fiasco. Arroghoy Muzhi and I tried the channel with handlines. We started by using grasshoppers to catch tiger fish – striped pike-like predators much sought after by sportsmen for their fighting qualities. Tiger-fish flesh served as bait for small tilapia. These we flung far out into the deeps, where they were instantly taken by Nile perch. But the surge of excitement stirred by every heavy pull was almost as instantly followed by empty disappointment as time after time the fish sliced through the nylon traces. We returned to camp empty handed with eight hooks lost.

In the cool of the morning of the next day, I set off with Arroghoy Muzhi to explore the surrealist volcanic scenery. No one else wanted to come, for they preferred to spend the sizzling day to come sitting in the shade. We took a path over the rocky wall on the far side of Lokweam Inlet to a sand flat bounded by a fifteen-foot wall of gunmetal-black lava, gnarled, whorled and twisted, convoluted and intertwined as if the guts of a stupendous tyrannosaurus had spilled out here and fossilised. After passing a blue pond which heaved and guggled with pelicans and cormorants, we walked between the sheer slope of Nabuyatom's ash cone and another wall of lava to Von Hoehnel's Bay and a gravelly beach sloping down to glass-clear water. Gentle breakers swished us as we splashed and rolled in the shallows, lazily watched by a ten-foot crocodile cruising on the surface of the deeps. However, the cooling effects of the swim hardly survived the moment of re-emergence into the parching wind. The whole of the bay, which curved towards the south, west and north from where we stood, was bounded by a huge lava field gaping satanically in an eternal rigor mortis under the blazing sun. 'If there really is a hell in the hereafter, I imagine it probably looks like that,' I said.

'Funny you should say that,' Arroghoy Muzhi remarked, 'because we Turkana call this place Lokweam, which means home of the devils.'

Teleki's Volcano no longer existed, the Nairobi experts had told me; it had been flattened by erosion, they said, but the black bulge on the horizon to the south was clearly a volcano, and the map confirmed it as being Teleki's. From my vantage point now, I could see that Teleki's Volcano had been the source of all the lava which had flowed to form the triangular field descending into the lake over a three-mile hypotenuse between Nabuyatom and Abili Agituk. Just north of the volcano's asphalt slopes, we crossed the lava field at its apex. The very edge of it looked daunting enough, five feet high and like an overspill of clotted pitch. Fractures and fissures criss-crossed the whole of the field's surface. Many were as much as ten feet across and breathtakingly deep; a donkey falling into one of these would die.

It was a magnetic corner of the world, this. Here, instead of pointing north, the needle of the compass did a confused little dance. But to me the spot was magnetic in another way. Rather than seeming in any way devilish, the sparkling blue bay and the dragon-black lava field fused together in everlasting wedlock assumed the status of a very special place. It looked still magically near in time to the day when, millions of years ago, the earth had split open here and let the waters in. I could think of no other place in the whole world I could revisit, changed by age myself, and be certain of finding it unchanged both atmospherically and physically. Its timelessness has haunted me ever since, and its vistas are so imprinted on my mind that simply by closing my eyes I can perceive them just as they lay before me then in all their stark and terrible beauty.

That was a blissfully dream-like day, one of the best of the whole journey. Refreshed and exhilarated by a cool breeze which unexpectedly sprang up in the evening, I began for the first time to feel more sanguine about the walk to Lodwar. But this feeling was brutally short-lived. Three old men with grizzled hair and smooth skins came to sit by our fire, their spear shafts mellow with handling. They told us how the *ng'oroko* had marched into this very spot in 1978, driving its inhabitants into the hills between the Serima Valley and South Horr to languish there for four fishless hungry years. Not until the previous September had the refugees returned to their old haunts, relieved to find that the *ng'oroko* had moved elsewhere. The *ng'oroko* had cleared out of the Loriyu too, the old men said. But now there were gangs of *shifta* in the Nachurogwai desert between the lower Kerio and the lakeshore.

From the moment those words were said, fear became the leader of our caravan.

The next day dawned with a clear sky which filled with apprehension as we picked our way among the boulders and clumps of thebaica palms at the bottom of the Lokweam gorge. After crossing the lava field without incident, we skirted Van Hoehnel's Bay. Then the Loriyu Hills faced us like a wall rising straight out of the lake. We turned west and up. Two of the donkeys had bleeding cruppers when we started, but William was shaking with tension, deaf to the world.

The going was rocky and steep. Over and over again a donkey would slip and fall on its side. Loads kept sliding, and Sayya quarrelled with Lobun over the right way of adjusting them, each telling the other he knew nothing about donkeys. Lobun gave up and started lagging behind with me, while Sayya kept pace with William. We made it to the top in exactly the three hours it had taken Teleki, but when we got there William and the others were nowhere to be seen. Lobun, who had tracked the runaway donkeys in Allia Bay, now did so again.

William was waiting at Nardid, a meadow between two hillocks. He was annoyed. We had delayed him. Him? Yes, I thought, I shall find a way of curbing this man's haste. And his generous disposition of my supplies; four visitors were supping our tea.

On the way to Nardid, a sick woman had approached me from a *manyata* and asked me to give her medicine for malaria. She sent her brother with me to collect it. Now that I was able to extract it from one of the loads, I handed him a packet of quinine. He took it from my hand, wordless and unsmiling, turned on his heels and went. He left me feeling that if he had found me dying of thirst, he would have waited until I expired, then stripped me. Every day, meanwhile, a little more of the Turkana message: give and keep going.

As we made to move off, a man came up carrying a ram. It had broken its leg in a scramble to get to water. We bought it for a song, but it had to be carried for another mile. William did not take part. It was done by Sayya with a sense of imposition, Moses with resentment, Lobun as a member of an inferior tribe and Arroghoy Muzhi out of fear that were he to refuse he would get none of its meat.

The ram died like a Muslim fundamentalist, in silence. Soon the air reeked of blood and wet dung. The cliffs enclosing us amplified the liquid sounds of avid hacking and chopping. The soup I was handed in a mug lay under an inch of molten, yellow fat, the first scalding mouthful of which brought me to vomit point. Putting the mug aside, I supped on a single dry chapati, while the others gobbled up chunks of meat, laughing as the grease ran down their chins. That night they wolfed down the ram to the last shred of marrow, squatting bloated round the fire amid a debris of bone splinters. God willing, I thought, morning will find them prostrated by colic.

William had chosen as camping site an execrable heap of broken rocks by a hole full of water so foul that even the donkeys balked at drinking it. They had not had a drink since leaving the lakeshore, and their haunches were streaked with blood. That day they had been given barely an hour to graze, and here in the ravaged lap of the Mugurr gorge there was no blade of grass.

William had also decreed that on the next day we would reach the Kerio in a single march. That was seventeen miles as the crow flies. Wending one's way through such a maze of bristling hills could easily double the distance. Near the western edge of the Loriyu Plateau were the Gautoro water holes, but a northerly detour would have to be made to reach them. We would make that detour, I resolved as I sank into a small grave of flat sand amid the sharp stones. If there was to be a single march to the Kerio, William would do it alone with his water bottle.

The longer I lay there, the more bitter I began to feel. Having crossed the lava, we had spent the previous night at Nangholi Bay in a comfortable campsite of doum palms. Arroghoy Muzhi had proved his worth by spearing us a fine meal of fish. There had been milk aplenty and fodder for the donkeys. The shore was dotted with shallow holes full of good drinking water. Yard-high foam-capped breakers crashed up against the pale beige sand.

The bay was one of the most spectacular I had ever seen. Just to be able to be there was worth the sum total of all the sweat and effort since setting out from sleepy Pangani. Here, so very far from that beguiling place, the lake held me with one arm and showed me its vastness with the other. The lion-gold slopes of the extinct Abili Agituk volcano turned the colour of flowering heather as they caught the rays of the declining sun. Behind me in the huge sweep of the *lagga*, the dark doums and acacias fell into sharp relief against the haze of the green-and-dun foothills of Kalolenyang. I found myself mumbling gratitude to whatever it was that had brought me so far.

When I told William that I wanted to stay another night, he threatened to return to Loyiangalani. I would have parted with him with relief even then, and would have done had not Sayya taken me aside and confessed that without William he would be too afraid to go on. I was over a barrel, just as Jim had been at Parkati. Now, as I lay feeling claustrophobic, walled in by the gorge's dark bastions, I was overcome by a mixture of rage and helplessness. For God's sake, I said to myself, what is the use of this march if there is to be no time to stop and stare? Again I swore to curb William's panic-stricken haste.

But in the morning, William surprised me by agreeing that we should camp by the Gautoro water holes, which, according to the map, were seven miles from Mugurr. The way to Gautoro? Somewhere to the west. No one was sure. We were in a piece of moonscape as desiccated as a ship's biscuit under a sky just as hard. All five jerrycans clonked hollow against the donkeys' backs. No birds flitted among the crumpled shrubs. No life here, just five unattended camels, which scowled down at us with the contempt we deserved. We had hardly started marching when Arroghoy Muzhi stopped to consult with William in an exchange of long faces and clipped words. Then we turned back and began heading south-west, our throats dry as the sand crunching beneath our feet, until we reached a *manyata* in a grove of acacias. The sight of coveys of buffalo weavers and namaqua doves honed my thirst, for these birds are never seen far from water. After a brief talk with a group of men, both William and Arroghoy Muzhi seemed nervous and in a hurry to get away. 'The water is *karibu* now,' said William, 'so let's get moving.'

Karibu is Swahili for 'near', but the word can mean anything up to six miles.

The *lagga* would turn into a torrent when it rained. Now it was a dreary furrow, seemingly leading nowhere, but gradually broadening as we went along. At dusk a sharp bend led us into a deep gloomy gorge. Three surly women drove a flock of goats past us; there were no greetings, but I was relieved to see that the calabashes they were carrying were heavy. Then, just beyond them, at the base of a sheer hundred-feet-high basalt cliff with a doum palm poking out of a crack in the middle of it, I caught sight of the donkeys, heads down and noses buried in the gravel. We had reached Gautoro.

I threw myself flat and drank in deep gulps until breath failed me.

There were about ten holes in all, some containing clear, others cloudy water. The rules were strict. There were holes for humans, holes for animals and holes for washing. A man who failed to observe the categories laid himself open to assault, for in all of that parched land there was nothing so precious as water.

Opposite the cliff was a platform shaded by ancient umbrella acacias, an ideal camping spot, but William rejected it. 'What you must understand, Tom, is that this is the only water for miles around. Everyone and everything has to come to Gautoro – animals both wild and tame, good people and bad. It's a place to keep away from.'

Blinded to logic by fear, he led us fifty yards up a crooked flinty gulley to halt at a spot from which our fire would be in full view of anyone visiting the water holes. Had it been William alone who was thus obsessed, I would have rounded on him, but the others were equally affected, all poisoned and all looking to William as their natural leader. Were I now to quarrel with him, I risked bringing about the defection of all. There remained no alternative to the biting of lips.

In contrast to the lakeshore, here on the Loriyu there was no breath of air. It was almost as if the sun rammed its rays into the ground, which in turn exhaled invisible fire. The heat was so intense that it rendered muscles flaccid and goaded the emotions. But William forced us through it like a barefooted fakir walking over burning coals, conscious of no one in the world but himself, desiring nothing other than getting this walk over and done with and the devil take the hindmost. I was beginning to learn what it felt like to be a Turkana.

During the last lap to the Kerio at a time when I was reeling with heat exhaustion, I stopped William from leading a detour to a *manyata* where he wanted to buy milk. My action was taken as high-handedness, and a shouting match ensued. It was a stupid episode, detonated by the sun. I had thoughtlessly attributed to William the power of exercising empathy. But empathy is not a quality one is born with; it has to be learned, and there had been no one to teach William. Life had taught him only one way, which was his way.

'William,' I said to him later in an attempt at reconciliation, 'you are very strong.' The statement was to have been the prelude to an explanation of heat exhaustion and age differences, but he would not let me go on.

'Oh yes,' he countered, 'I am very strong. I can walk forty miles in a day under the hot sun and will not even feel tired at the end of it.' His impenetrable self-enshrinement vanquished me again.

Our resting place hummed with a rising buzz of voices as each fallen log became a bench for curious men and women, each bush a conspiracy of whispering children. There was no road to that place. Whites did not come to it because it offered nothing to attract them – no inspiring vistas or elephants or lions, only dusty people, goats and cattle and the acrid smell of dry dung, all trapped for centuries under the doum palms in an unchanging routine interrupted only occasionally by birth, dance, violence and death. We had evoked curiosity only because the equipment we carried suggested that something might be gleaned from us.

A wizened, stooping woman, a centenarian perhaps, stopped on her way to fetch water to inspect me intently at close quarters. Had there been a far-off day when she had watched von Hoehnel bargaining for sorghum with her parents? But her tired eyes showed only an ephemeral interest before she shuffled away, knowing that we would be gone before she returned from the river.

The features of the people varied enormously. There was nothing which could be described as typically Turkana, except that most of them were lighter-skinned than their fellow-tribesmen of the lake and the Loriyu. Some may even have been non-Turkana; one, who wore no ornaments, looked like a Kikuyu from Nyeri – straight-nosed, thin-lipped and eyes set wide apart. Another, short and middle-aged, his hair clipped to a stubble, wore shirt and shorts. His bearing was unmistakably military, and he spoke basic Swahili, imbuing me with the suspicion that some of our visitors were deserters or *ng'oroko* whose rifles were hidden in the bushes.

The men's ornaments ranged from nothing to the full regalia of painted mud caps, ear rings, necklaces and bracelets – some of brass or aluminium, but most of plastic. The oldest, being also the richest, were the most heavily decorated. Nearly all wore wrist knives and brass rings on each finger and thumb. Their footwear was buffalo-rawhide sandals with wedge-shaped soles protruding several inches beyond the tips of their toes and tied to their feet with thongs.

The women and girls were more stereotyped, every one loaded with bead and ostrich-eggshell necklaces from jaw to shoulder. Their colourfully bead-patterned leather dresses swept the ground and crackled with every movement.

All that remained of the river here was a series of pools near the edge of its bank. The washing pool was full of what looked like dishwater. It reeked of rotten perfume reminiscent of a dirty shower room. Soap had reached the Turkana, even here. I noticed that a group of girls filling their calabashes from the drinking-water pool were free of ochre, their limbs ungreased. Remembering Mrs Loteka of Tangulbaye, I felt sure that the change introduced by the use of soap would be followed by cotton dresses directly there was enough money to buy them. When a couple of boys approached me asking if I had any clothes for sale, I felt even more certain.

We camped that night in a sandy place below a *manyata* set on a high ridge a mile from the river. It was too dangerous to camp near water, William had insisted, and by this time I was too cowed by exhaustion to argue with him. In contrast with the river bank, there was no grass here. It angered me to see the donkeys despondently nibbling miswaki leaves, which would give them diarrhoea instead of nutrition. But I knew that William did not care, provided they did not collapse before getting him to Lodwar.

'The town is near now,' he proclaimed triumphantly next morning, wantonly thrashing the already trotting donkeys, which were all bleeding now from deep crupper abrasions. There was a streak of vicious cruelty in William, but I had become too apathetic to try to prevent him from indulging it. I had somehow lost my place and felt as if I was just being carried along like a tourist in a minibus; sheer tiredness and depression had burned up my morale. The journey, so unique in potential and time-consuming in preparation, had become a dull slog. I could have fought off William's determination, but his fear was too strong for me. Now he was already sniffing the aroma of refuse heaps. 'Today we shall camp in town,' he chanted, 'and we shall have *chang'aa* (Nubian gin) and *miguu* (legs)!'

'*Miguu*' was our stock joke. It had originated during the afternoon of 30 November the previous year when we reached Lokweam for the first time. Sayya had cut his foot and asked me to treat it. '*Lete mguu*,' I told him in Swahili; 'shove your leg over.' He laughed. I did not ask why, but during the days that followed he and Moses laughed every time I changed the plaster. Later, in Loyiangalani, Sayya explained. 'When you're in bed with a woman, you tell her: *wacha mchezo, lete mguu.*' Which means: stop fooling around, let's have your leg.

Approaching the lake, but still out of sight of it, we came upon a sprinkling of miserable villages, fishtraps perched on every roof. Flocks of sheep and goats stood motionless in the glare. In one house, an emaciated mother and two children were pounding the roots of a tree for porridge. Outside another, a woman frantically chased her children beyond the peril of photography.

A couple of miles on we reached the lakeshore. Cattle were grazing, guarded by boys lolling in the grass, and there were dwellings scattered among the meadows. At least five hundred yards of mud flats intervened between the limit of the grass and the edge of the shallow water. The donkeys foundered and turned back, but we walked ankle deep in mud until we reached it. The lake lay hazy, the dead calm of its surface interrupted only by the blurred outline of a fishing boat shimmering in the rays of the receding sun and the figure of a small boy, who waded knee-deep towards us, carrying a fish.

Nayapunetebu was a village about the same size as Loyiangalani, but distinguished from it by the presence of many domed huts woven from palm fronds. The largest of them turned out to be a beer hall, its braided windowless walls standing ten feet tall and the apex of its mosque-like roof a good twenty feet above the floor. Fat, sweating women poured sorghum beer into Kimbo tins for men who sat on planks balanced on stones. (Kimbo is a brand of vegetable oil, and the empty tins commonly serve as drinking vessels.)

A big, tin-roofed building was the fish store, guarded by a red-capped watchman, who showed us several stacks of sun-dried tilapia putrid enough to discourage a more detailed inspection of the interior. A line of shops, all but three and including 'Elizabeth Chepchirchir's Lodgings', locked: no one knew where she had gone or if she would ever come back. In the shade of her wall half a dozen women in greasy leather were selling calabashes of curdled milk. Babies slept on mats as slim, affectionate dogs played around them in the dust. The 'Kerio Valley General Store' looked deceptively superior. Inside it, a be-frocked Turkana girl, her hair tightly braided Mombasa style, told us she had no sugar, no tea, no flour and no maize meal. I could not understand why the next two shops, being totally empty, were open.

'Is this Tanzania?' I jibed at one of the shopkeepers.

'No,' he replied unsmilingly, 'you are in Kenya.'

An acacia scratch on my leg had ulcerated, so our next destination was the dispensary, a clean, two-roomed building with steel-framed windows and a floor of concrete. Striding purposefully between a row of patients sitting on wooden benches and an aluminium trolley was the health assistant. A baby belonging to a worried young couple wailed in helpless outrage on being injected. An elderly pair were given tablets in little twists of paper; the man's necklace was a fan-belt and the woman's bracelets jubilee clips. A downcast young man, who had left his spear outside, got an injection in the next room. The dispenser's case book disclosed that his name was Edome and his complaint gonorrhoea. My ulcer was cleaned with acriflavine, anointed and bandaged.

Surprised to find Sayya and William in the queue behind me, I asked what was wrong with them. 'Nothing at all,' said William, 'but the medicine is free, so why not have it?'

They were both given tablets, all of which, days later, I found loose in the bottom of my satchel. They had spent an hour acquiring them, the triumph of acquisition being sufficient compensation for the uselessness of the loot.

Outside another beer hall, an official-looking man wearing a navy blue beret was waving a polished swagger stick over the heads of a listless group of men and women. He was haranguing them with the fierce energy of a Hyde Park agitator, emphasising points with both hands. When I asked William what he was saying, the answer was, 'Oh, nothing.' William replied so not because of a disinclination to tell me but because he genuinely did not know. He had been too busy concentrating on what he himself was going to say next to take in the man's words. It happened all the time, and not only in the case of William. There would be a conversation full of laughter, dismay, derision, shock, surprise, astonishment, but when I would ask what it had been about, no one would be able to tell me. William communicated with me constantly, but on topics demanding decision, action, advice or argument. In those other conversations, which concerned emotions, the reaction of each speaker obliterated the memory of the words evoking his response, because by then the speaker deemed only his own words to be of relevance and worthy of attention.

William directed us to a clump of doums near the ruins of several abandoned huts. The ground beneath the fronds was strewn with bones, rags, broken glass, turds, dung and vulture droppings. It was here that we were to camp. Being so close to beer halls and *miguu*, William was delighted with the site. Grass being something he was not interested in eating himself, he did not remark upon its total absence.

208

Within minutes a score of men and boys arrived and placed under close surveillance every muscle we moved and every eye we flickered. One of the men was a fully accoutred Turkana warrior, whose equipment consisted of one *shuka* (clothing and bedding), one wooden headrest (pillow and chair), two spears (security), one sword (butchery, manicure and surgery), one leather purse (overnight case), one wooden comb stuck in the hair (cosmetic) and one ball of tobacco lodged between eartip and skull (recreational stimulant). William called him over and declared that he would be our new guide to lead us to Lodwar and that his pay would be 10 shillings a day. Too tired to argue, I made his recruitment conditional on his leading the donkeys to the lakeshore to graze as his first task.

When the first jerrycan of sorghum beer lay empty and the talk inclined towards *miguu*, I disclosed what I had seen in the dispenser's case book. If William was unlucky, he would get home just in time to infect his wife. Undeterred, he and Sayya went off to hunt among the hurricane-lamp-lit shanties, but returned accompanied only by bottles of *chang'aa*. 'Better to knock ourselves down with this,' William said, 'than to collect a disease.'

The last lap to Lodwar was a mosaic of frustration, exhaustion, discomfort and rage. We set off without brewing up. Tea later, said William. Our supernumerary 'guide' marched us straight down the main road. By noon I had reached my physical limit. But how to curb the demonic hysteria driving my companions into such a rush to eat the forty burning miles separating us from our destination? I found myself unable to think of any course but to declare war on every Turkana in my company and on William in particular. Weaponless, I seized inspiration from Gandhi and lay down on my back. Lobun returned to look for me. I would not take another step, I said, without tea. William's gift of time to brew it was as grudgingly given as had been my surrender to his authority. That night, in our waterless camp, Lobun said he would not cook, but his own hunger and the realisation that none of the Turkana intended lifting a finger persuaded him to change his mind.

Next day I was cheered by the knowledge that before the end of it we would reach Lodwar and a parting of the ways with William. I feigned indifference to the insane donkey beating. The fragrance of meat stew, beer and Bint El Sudan perfume had already filled every Turkana nostril, and nothing I did or said could now change anything. After marching thus for five hours, our guide turned us towards the tree-line, which could only mean that we must now be very near to the sanctuary of 'town'. As we left the road, I stumbled upon a child's skeleton lying bleached and forgotten in the sand, its bones scattered like a goat's. The sight blended well with the landscape and my own mood. And yet, however harsh the sight seemed to me, it was fully consistent with the harshness of everything else in Turkanaland. The Turkana – unless converted to Christianity – always abandon the dead of their kind. The custom reflects the irrefutable logic of the Turkana. This dictates that a living person is always useful in some way, but of what use is an inedible carcase? What, moreover, is the use of wasting precious energy digging a hole for it in the iron-hard ground when the land teems with vultures and kites, hyenas and jackals (and, one is tempted to suspect, even Turkana dogs) to dispose of the corpse efficiently and hygienically? The Turkana see death as a piece of bad luck. The homestead where it occurs is an unlucky place. The body of the departed one is left in his grass hut, and his relatives move to build a new homestead in a hopefully more fortunate place elsewhere.

A mile or so of glaring pebble plain ended abruptly where the doum palm forest began. As its sombre shade cooled us, the men's voices dwindled away into the breeze as each of them cocooned himself in a lonely trance to contemplate the imminence of his journey's end. The Turkwel River was soon reached. Swollen by scarcely imaginable rains somewhere upstream, its honey-coloured waters surged past in frenzied haste. Briefly we followed the bank until a well-trodden path appeared out of nowhere. It led us into a savannah sprinkled with beehive huts woven from the branches of the round-leafed *epuu* and the spiny acacia trees among which the dwellings nestled. To the Turkana every tree is a tree of life in the absolute sense of the term. To build his home he must have trees. To survive the hardship of drought, he must eat their fruit and feed their leaves to his animals. His father named him after a tree, he himself gives his children the names of trees and, concomitantly, he knows the name of every tree in his land.

Suddenly the path spilled us into a spacious clearing stripped of all vegetation but littered with the harbingers of urban affluence: discarded cigarette packets, plastic wrappers and broken glass. Before us stood a row of four half-completed identical staff houses of steel, concrete and tile. Beside them a brand new cement mixer lay motionless like a sleeping watchdog. The site was deserted; it must have been a Sunday. But at the edge of it I spotted a hut which so blended with the surrounding foliage as to be almost invisible. From its dingy doorway emerged a young Turkana woman, barefooted, beaded and dressed in scuffed goat leather. She watched us with uncurious eyes as we passed her by. But moving thus through her field of vision seemed like crossing an unmarked frontier between her Iron Age world and the world of the microchip which was mine, and the moment of doing so encapsulated the enormity of the contrast between the two.

As we approached the last of the houses, I conjured up for it a metamorphosis of completion, as in one of those trick films which reduce to a matter of moments the process of a bud opening and becoming a mature flower. I pictured the house curtained and inhabited. Visible through the plate-glass window of the kitchen is a young housewife. Her hair is beautifully combed, and she wears a cool summer dress. A blood-red coral necklace accentuates the velvet texture of her coffee-coloured skin. With manicured fingers she carefully adjusts the gauge of her eye-level grill, then turns to the window. Her gaze travels towards her Turkana counterpart, whose hut is now situated just beyond the fence of an incipient garden. The Turkana is stirring sorghum porridge in a convex-bottomed earthenware pot balanced on a hearth of three stones enclosing a fire. She looks up, and through the smoke there is a meeting of eyes. I glance from one face to the other. That of the woman in the house betrays neither pity nor contempt, the Turkana's neither envy nor resentment. Each is so remote from the other in psychology, condition and place that none but a feeling of static neutrality can be shared. The two are physical contemporaries and fellow-citizens, but the gulf of alienation separating them is wider now than that which lay between the nineteenth-century colonialist and the first indigenous individual he met.

The tableau faded into the heat haze as we passed on to cross a girdered bridge, at the far end of which we found a building advertising itself as the 'Lodwar Staff Canteen'. Ice-cold beer was quickly served by a smiling girl. Then a white-shirted young man sitting opposite asked me where I had come from and why. On being told, he drew back as if to distance himself from me. 'You Europeans can afford to use your time like that,' he sneered with heavy sarcasm. 'Your pockets are always full of money and that is why you have never felt hunger, thirst or any other hardship.'

I remembered that John Hillaby had evoked the same sort of reaction during his walk through Britain (*Journey through Britain*, 1968). Having walked all the way from Cornwall to the Welsh border, Hillaby met an old man whom he told about his exploit. The man was not impressed. 'Shaking his head sadly, he said: "Then all I can say is it's a pity you couldn't be doing something useful."'

I left smugly, intending to sleep for three full days. But at the Mombasa Hotel in Lodwar next day, well before dawn, I was kicked into consciousness by a Koran recital. The hotel's tape recorder had been tuned to maximum volume, its speaker seemingly hung on the wall of the adjoining room. What was this onslaught when the sun's first ray had yet to climb over the courtyard wall? I had forgotten; it was the fasting month of Ramadan, so there would be no respite for the rest of the day. A Koran recital is not a constant sound of the kind the captive listener can channel away from his consciousness. On the contrary, each passage is separated from the next by silences of varying duration, some so prolonged that he is tempted into sighing with relief. But then the sonorous voice inundates him again, reminding him that the intention of the words is not to soothe or entertain, but to set upon the mind of the fasting believer the seal of God's severity.

There was no more sleep. Instead I walked to the hospital to visit Doctor Clement English, who for the past decade had been studying hydatid disease: tiny worms entering the human body through contact with the faeces of dogs to form gross cysts, treatable only by surgery. The biggest he had ever excised weighed 27 kilos; he was looking for a less drastic cure.

The Turkana, Clement said, have an intimate relationship with their dogs. He believed that the nature of it was influenced to a great extent by the chronic shortage of water suffered by those living out of reach of the lake. The symbiosis begins immediately after birth, when the dogs eat the human afterbirth products. Babies are placed in the care of dogs immediately after entering the world, for protection and also to be licked clean after defecating or vomiting. Dogs lick the pots and dishes clean after the family has eaten and help to look for stray animals. They are also deemed to possess curative properties; their faeces are used as an ingredient of herbal medicine, which is sometimes smeared on women's necklaces. Such customs only education can change, but it is a slow process, and schooling is not much sought after by the Turkana. Meanwhile, Clement had decided to poison all the dogs in Lodwar.

My men were on a binge. William, having run short of money, had resorted to *chang'aa*, a bottle of which cost no more than beer. He sneaked up, Arroghoy Muzhi like a drugged puppy by his side, to whisper that he had been thrown out of the lodging. I replied that it was none of my business, but we would talk next day when he was sober. William was, of course, perfectly sober right then. That might be so, but he would get no more money from me.

Having watched him, Clement remarked that *chang'aa* contained amphetamine, which made it a double-action drink. The alcohol content reduced responsibility, while the amphetamine stirred up aggressiveness, thus tending to turn the drinker into a violent maniac. William, who was not far from becoming one, walked away.

He left next day with Arroghoy Muzhi to return to Loyiangalani by boat. Moses, too, dropped out. 'People here have told me that not far south of here there is a place called Arami, where there are Turkana who will kill anyone – even fellow-tribesmen if they are not of their clan,' he explained.

Had I been able to foresee what was to happen to the rest of us within the next week, I too might have decided to take the boat to Loyiangalani.

The departure of Moses was of little significance. Lobun and Sayya sufficed to handle the donkeys, but to cross Turkanaland we needed a man with local experience. Such men were by no means uncommon, but my offer of thirty shillings a day plus food and cigarettes was repeatedly met by shaking heads and clicking tongues. Arami was the word, and no one would go south along the Turkwel.

After three days of my fruitlessly combing the town, a man came to the hotel and offered his services. He could do with the money, he said. Sam Chopiri was lean, almost to the point of emaciation, but his eyes smiled forth with rare warmth from beneath a thatch of grizzled hair, and his hand's firmness transmitted a message of dependability. 'We might meet *ng'oroko*,' he said calmly, 'but on the other hand, we might not.'

We did.

Ng'oroko

As we walked south through receding signs of habitation, the Murua
Ngisigerr Mountains to the west and the Kafigithigirir Hills to the east
clasped us ever closer in their embrace. Two men and a woman were
driving a half-grown donkey towards us. The animal was frightened,
its nostrils bleeding. Sam explained that its nose ring had only just been
put in so that it could be controlled during slaughter. To the Turkana,
donkey flesh is just as acceptable as goat meat, beef or mutton.
Suddenly the donkey broke free and galloped towards us, then quietly
took its place behind Mashurubu as if it believed we were on the way
home. One of the men ran up and seized it with a savage swoop. Sam
exchanged a few words with him as he held on to the trembling beast.
'You can have it for a hundred shillings,' Sam said. I was tempted, but
being short of cash, and the donkey untrained to carry loads, I let them
drive it to its death.

The incident brought to mind how Teleki travelling in this region
had bought as many donkeys as he could, having learned from the
Turkana that donkey flesh is perfectly palatable. When the foreman of
his caravan protested that none of the men would eat donkey meat,
von Hoehnel snidely retorted, 'Never mind, when there is nothing left,
Count Teleki and I at least will eat it; the rest of you can satisfy
your hunger with beads, wire and merikani.' Von Hoehnel goes
on to remark in his description of the Turkana that they 'are by no
means dainty about diet; they eat everything, even their dogs'. I
asked a good many Turkana if this was true, but all vehemently
denied it. And I never saw a Turkana treat a dog with anything but
affection.

A buxom girl sold us a calabash of camel's milk, which we drained
on the spot, except for Lobun who was afraid of catching hydatid
disease. Then, as we briefly rested, a couple driving an unloaded
donkey stopped to ask our destination. 'To Juluk,' Sam replied.

'Fine, we are going the same way, so we can go together,' said the
man, whose name was Lopeyo. He was about forty and over six feet in
height. A little red-and-khaki porkpie hat somehow made him look
even taller, while his prominent Roman nose and hooded eyes lent him

the expression of a bird of prey. There was much sharpness in those eyes, but little feeling.

Lopeyo's young companion was a flawless Turkana beauty, with skin as smooth as polished soapstone. Her almond eyes were of a perfection that Persian poets have described. Like a trained model, she walked as smoothly as milk poured from a calabash. She smiled often, an uncommon habit in this region where few had much to make them happy – and it was then that the whiteness of her teeth lit up the symmetry of her rounded features. Her name was Akiru, the daughter of a famous rainmaker, Sam said, which was easy to believe. Had a Sasanian king campaigning with his army chanced upon her guarding her flocks in the desert he would have given her a horse and celebrated his victory by making her his queen. As for me, I instantly became her captive.

I asked Lopeyo to tell me about his life, and particularly about dogs, which I had promised Clement to enquire about. 'Just now our *manyata* is near Qotaru beyond the Kateruk River,' he said. 'There's still some grass left, but we'll have to move if it doesn't rain properly soon. Dogs? We just keep one to warn us against animals.'

'What else troubles you?'

'Pokot. They come here from the hills – all those over there.' He pointed to the Murua Ngisigerr Mountains and south to the Karasuk Hills. 'No one can go up there and come back alive, even you. Look, you can see the smoke from their fires, they are so near. It was just recently – at the beginning of May – that they raided us. They took cattle and killed four women, one of them Akiru's sister. They speared her through the lungs; when we found her she was still alive, but by the time we had carried her home she was finished. The Pokot always kill, because they want us to be afraid, to run away and leave everything. Pokot are bad people. They have no mercy.'

'But don't you Turkana raid the Pokot too?'

'No, we are a peaceful people, and even if we wanted to, we have no rifles.'

We made camp in a deserted *manyata* west of the river at a place called Qaqurodeh. One of the huts was almost intact. We spread the tarpaulin over it. Our march had been disrupted by a sharp thunderstorm, which had left us shivering and every lagga racing to the Turkwel. Now the sky was still frowning.

Sayya and Lobun took me aside. 'Akiru asked me,' Sayya said, 'why are you taking the old man down this path? Don't you realise that if you go much farther you will all be killed? She has lived here all her life and knows the people. It is a *tanganyika*. They will kill you for what is on the donkeys and in your pockets; that is what she said. And she said we must get away from this place.'

Lobun stepped in. 'Tom, you know I don't easily believe what people say, but this time it's different.'

'But you heard all this from Akiru. If it's true, why hasn't Lopeyo said anything?'

'That's the whole point,' Sayya insisted. 'What you've just asked shows that you understand nothing. Only women tell the truth. That's the way it is with us Turkana. After Akiru heard Lopeyo telling you about the Pokot, she told me not to believe him. Even Lopeyo has a rifle and so do most of the other men at Qotaru. They kill the Pokot and take their cattle whenever they can. Tell your old man not to go to Juluk, she said, but say nothing to Lopeyo.'

An uneasy silence befell us. Unequivocal acceptance of the warning was written on the men's faces. I recalled a similar look on Sayya's after listening to Laroi's fantasies about lions on the way to Porr. Sayya had believed him just as he later believed Lobun, who had told him the opposite. The Njamus had warned me against the Pokot, the Pokot against the Turkana, the Turkana against the Shangille – and yet I had walked through all their lands unscathed. But now there was a difference. All the previous warnings had come from men of one tribe against those of another. Today a woman was alerting me against the men of her own clan, perhaps even against Lopeyo himself.

I told Lobun and Sayya they were right. We would change course and head for Katillo. But Katillo was on the other side of the river.

Sam was relieved. Akiru smiled. Lopeyo stretched himself and said, 'Tomorrow morning Akiru and I will cross the Kateruk with you. Then we will show you a path to the *manyatas* of peaceful people, who are cultivating near the river. You stay by them until the water subsides and they will help you cross.' He paused to give me a steady look, then added, 'I should like you to give me a bit more tobacco.'

I went to sleep in the open, but it soon rained, and I crept into the hut with the rest. We slept like six rats in a nest, sprawled amid the gear.

At dawn, some women brought us a calabash and a half of camel's milk. The full one was sour, but Sam and Sayya drank it with relish. There were three mugfuls of the fresh, and I had it all.

Then we headed south again, mostly over wet ground through thickening bush fluttering with birds. I saw an Abyssinian scimitarbill and a blackbilled wood dove, but there were others I was unable to identify. A fox flashed across the path, and Lopeyo showed me the tracks of hyena and warthog. After squelching through two rain-swollen laggas, we reached the Kateruk, which swirled menacingly, but proved to be only a foot deep. The donkeys had to be beaten to persuade them to cross, but we did not have to unload. An hour later we stopped by a patch of dried-up grass for the sake of the donkeys. Sayya, Sam and Lobun were abnormally unresponsive. I said the sort of things that usually made them laugh, but all I got was blank looks.

By mid-afternoon the Karasuk Hills stood before us like a russet wall of China some thirty miles to the south. The wind lurched from north to west and threw several showers at us. As we walked, Lopeyo stopped to talk with a man. Akiru began speaking excitedly to Sayya, who turned to me. 'Did you notice the strip of goatskin tied to that man's arm?' I looked back and caught sight of a sliver of white. 'Akiru says that's a *ngawamaye*. It shows that he has killed a man.' Further explanations followed. A similar strip tied to the left elbow denoted the killing of a woman, and others worn like wristbands indicated children. Sayya had never heard of the custom. It was foreign to the Turkana of Baragoi, he said.

Two men walked across our path, neither glancing in our direction. One, wearing a hat like Lopeyo's, had a *ngawamaye* on his right arm. The other had his hair plaited crosswise like an urban woman's and carried a short forked stick. Akiru looked strained. She said the stick was a rifle rest. Lobun had also noticed it. 'She's right,' he said. 'I've seen sticks like that around Ileret. The poachers use them to improve their aim, which is important if you're short of ammunition. Tom, we must get over that river today.'

I was nervous myself now. We had crossed the border of warnings into a land of tokens.

Whatever doubts I had left were dispelled by a group of men sitting under a tree, talking loudly. As we drew level with them, every head turned towards us, and every tongue fell silent. Almost everywhere I had walked in Turkanaland, hands had been extended in greeting or supplication, but here was an indifference tinged with a hostility which made me feel like an intruder in forbidden territory. Even the landscape had become menacing. I caught myself scanning the bush, not for birds or animals now, but for men. Our party was as vulnerable as a scarab rolling its ball of dung across a main road.

Lopeyo and Akiru stopped. Lopeyo pointed south-east. 'See that path? Just follow it and you will reach the people we know.'

Ever since I had decided to change course, Lopeyo had repeatedly commended those people, but Akiru had not mentioned them once. Could there be something wrong with them? I jumped to the insane conclusion that if only Akiru could stay with us we would be safe. I turned to Sayya. 'Tell her I want her to walk with us as far as Katillo.' It was a joke born of hysteria but, like all jokes, half serious.

Akiru turned on her beautiful smile. 'She says,' Sayya translated, 'that she would if she could, but who will look after her children and sick husband?'

With that she flicked her donkey's rump with her little stick and strode purposefully away, her long leather cloak, so redolent of musk and curdled milk, slapping her legs. The tall figure of Lopeyo loped off behind her. When I heard his word of encouragement to the donkey, I knew we had already been forgotten.

We had just pushed into a tangled jungle of doum palms whose fronds dimmed the light of the late-afternoon sky, when we came upon the head of a freshly decapitated buffalo. Its glazed eyes gazed up from the base of a palm. Wordlessly we stared at the head and at one another, for this dismal relic was confirmation of every word we had heard from Akiru. First the *ngawamayes*, then the rifle rest and now this third token of menace. There is no animal more skilled in killing men than the buffalo; no man will try to kill one with spear or bow if he has access to a rifle. Given the choice at that moment between meeting a buffalo and meeting its hunter, all of us would have opted for the buffalo.

In a flooded clearing where ragged palm stumps and clumps of grass stuck through the surface of the water stood three small thatched shelters from which children had scared birds off last season's harvest. Now the shelters were empty and falling to pieces. Beyond them the milky-brown Turkwel roared frothing to the north, full five hundred yards across. The nameless donkey bent his head to the water, nostrils twitching like a tea-taster's. Mkulakamba and Mashurubu drew up on either side to emulate him, but not one of the three ventured to take a drink. Eyes wide with dismay, the men gazed across the torrent towards the frog-green reeds and grass which waved wistfully from the far bank. 'What shall we do now, do you think?' Sam said, with one of his wry smiles.

I began taking off my shoes and socks. Lobun too began to strip. Of the three of them, only he could swim. 'You two stay here,' I said as though I had a perfect plan. 'One of you guard the donkeys – you, Sayya. Sam, take a walk and look for a place to camp in case we have to stay this side. Lobun and I are going to try the river.'

Naked we slithered down the steep bank into the current, gasping at the sheer power of it. Keeping close together, we let ourselves be swept towards shallower water. Then, with the river hissing past our thighs, we struggled towards a low reed-shrouded islet in midstream. As we thrust ahead, the current snatched past us every kind of flotsam – sticks, branches, even a dead hare. The sandy bottom undulated, varying in depth from shin to chest level. Past the islet another deep patch, then shallow again, then deep and out and over the bank into the coarse wet grass. It had taken us just ten minutes, but we both knew it was too deep for the donkeys. We moved back even more swiftly.

Sam and Sayya were standing with a tall grey-haired man, watched from a few yards' range by two unusually plump girls. The stranger's face was bony with high cheek bones, a deep line cleaving the inner edge of each cheek from nostril to the corner of a downturned mouth. His eyes were hard and cheerless, their dourness underscored by a white metal lip plug. 'This is Etirai,' said Sam. 'He says his *manyata* is nearby and we can camp by it. Then, in the morning, if the river has receded, he and his sons will help us cross.'

I shook his hand twice with the conventional gripping of thumbs and expressed gratitude, which he acknowledged unsmilingly. There was an oddly caustic look about him.

With Etirai leading and Sam and Lobun driving the donkeys, we retraced our steps. The forest closed in about us so tightly that the animals had to thrust and scrape their loads past the low-hanging fronds. Just as we entered a little glade, a young man stepped into our path. Slung over his shoulder was a G-3 rifle.

The advance party had already vanished. Sayya's face was like cardboard. My mind stampeded. I offered my hand. '*Ejoqaa?*' I enquired. 'Is it well?'

'*Ejoq,*' the man replied, grasping it. 'It is well.' He accepted a cigarette, and we all lit up. He was wearing a green shirt with military pockets, a checked *shuka* tied at the waist, Somali style, a good pair of suede boots and a sky-blue denim hat; no ornaments except a necklace of orange beads and, on his right arm, above the elbow, a *ngawamaye*. Drawing on his cigarette, he looked at me hard. 'Where are you going?' he asked in Swahili.

'To Etirai's *manyata*.'

'Good,' he responded. Then he stepped back into the trees and was gone.

Sayya and I hastily caught up with the rest. I shook Sam by the shoulder and told him what we had just seen. 'Ask Etirai who he is,' I said.

'He says he has no idea.'

The reply stunned me. How could he fail to know? The answer came like a clap of thunder; he did not know which of the men carrying rifles we had seen.

The forest ended in a sandy area of low bushes and medium-sized acacia. 'Etirai says we can camp here,' Sam informed me. 'He'll have the donkeys taken to the *boma* and kept there for the night. Tomorrow his women will take them to grass till we need them.'

The loads were hardly off before men, women and children began flocking in. Soon there were at least a hundred. Women brought water, but there was no chance to make tea. We were walled in by faces and assailed by a hubbub of voices. Wherever I looked, bunched fingers were digging into cheeks. There was no doubt then that we would pay heavily for Etirai's hospitality. We had two and a half kilos of tobacco in three packages. Sam and I began putting pinches of it into outstretched hands, even those of five-year-old boys.

This was no agricultural *manyata*. The man with the blue hat was there together with a braided fellow, both with G-3s. An oafish-looking teenager walked in with a Kalashnikov, followed by another with a Second World War Italian rifle. The first wore a *ngawamaye* on his left arm, the other one on his right wrist. None of these men requested; they just beckoned and helped themselves. Bluehat even took the package out of my hand, and there were nasty looks when all that remained was the brown paper bag.

The expansiveness which normally followed a tobacco hand-out did not ensue. Only the women were smiling. 'Bring more,' Etirai snapped when he had pointedly shaken the empty wrapper. Sam opened the second package. Bluehat and his companions made themselves comfortable on our tarpaulin. They unclipped their magazines and emptied the contents into their laps. Sam tore them each a piece of foam rubber from a cushion with which they cleaned every round before recharging the magazines.

Sayya told me next day that, while this had been going on, one of the spearmen had called out to the oafish one, 'Why don't we kill this lot tonight?' The oaf had smiled and caressed the stock of his Kalashnikov, but an older man had shouted angrily, 'How can you think of killing our guests, particularly when two of them are of our own blood!'

But I knew nothing of this at the time. I studied the people around me, noticing others with rifles at the fringes of the crowd. At least a dozen, armed and unarmed, were wearing *ngawamayes*. From the moment the tobacco was finished we were ignored.

When Sam and Etirai led me up to a gangling, emaciated octogenarian, I hoped perhaps to hear a few words of wisdom, or at least to see a smile, but all I got was a red-rimmed stare. A two-inch silver plug, curved like the sheath of a Yemeni dagger, protruded from beneath his

221

nether lip. We shook hands, and he croaked a few phrases, which Sam translated: 'He is the old man of the *manyata* and he wants to be given some tobacco.'

Luckily, in addition to the kilo I had managed to hide, I still had in my satchel a small emergency package, which I now handed over. After raising it to his nose, the old man waved a dismissal and tottered into the murk, leaving me with a feeling akin to despair. I could detect no characteristic among that group – young and old – other than aggressive acquisitiveness. Was it this that had drawn the philanthropists of the West to the outposts of Turkanaland? Was importunacy a balm for conscience? Was forcefully expressed need a Turkana secret weapon? Everything in me rebelled against replying to these questions in the affirmative. I had come here, I told myself, to see how people fully pitted against their environment lived and thought. But did not such a life dictate exclusive concentration on what could be wrested from that environment? How then could I, an intruder of no apparent relevance, expect to be treated as anything but a windfall?

My thoughts were interrupted by Sam. 'Etirai needs you. He says there is a baby which needs medicine for its eyes.'

Clement had told me that conjunctivitis was rife, but could easily be cured by washing the eyes in clean water. This was not a course I could recommend, for Etirai would assume that I was withholding something I could afford to give. The same would apply if I told him the truth – that I had no eye medicine. What I did have was an empty bottle, which I gave him with ten chlorine tablets: half a tablet to the bottle of water, eyes to be cleaned with a rag three times a day. This satisfied, yet I felt guilty lest he decided on a double dose just to be on the safe side.

There were no stones for a hearth, so Lobun dug a hole and put on the tea water. Bluehat and several of his friends were observing our every move. Sam tried talking to them, but they were not interested. 'Make tea for us. We thirst for tea,' Bluehat commanded.

It was after nine before we had the camp to ourselves. Lobun hastily cooked *ugali* and watery corned beef. We could not find the salt, so we did without.

Sayya could not eat. He wrapped himself in his blanket, complaining of headache and cold. I knew his symptoms well by now, but gave him four quinine tablets all the same. I too was very much afraid. 'What if the elders fail to control the young men? Do you think they could attack us during the night?' I asked Sam, who was sitting by the fire peering into the embers.

He thought for a long time. It was his way to be cautious over giving an opinion, and I respected him for it. 'I don't know,' he said at length, 'but probably not. Now that we're by their *manyata*, we're their guests. They would be breaking tradition if they killed us here. But if we had met them on the road, I don't believe they would have hesitated.'

We were a mere ten yards from the *manyata*, but no sound emanated from it. Only the steady throb of the river adulterated the night. For the first time since leaving Lodwar I felt a twinge of nostalgia for its Koran recital.

I woke to the voices of women. We had slept peacefully, and their presence suggested that the morning too would be peaceful. '*Ejoqaa?*' the eldest called to me before addressing herself to Sam. 'She says,' he interpreted, 'that you have made them very happy. You are a good man because you gave them tobacco yesterday.'

They nodded vigorously in response to my smile. 'They have brought you fresh cow's milk,' he added. We bought it for twenty shillings, an unimaginable luxury, for we had not even set eyes on a cow for a week, let alone milk. The women's visit sweetened my mood.

But not for long. Bluehat and his gunmen stormed into camp. The women picked up their babies and hastened away.

'We have come for tea and we are hungry too. Give us tea, make *ugali*,' Bluehat orders. They settle down to unclipping magazines, polishing rounds and rattling bolts. I give up my habit of listening to the news, for the radio could prove too tempting a prize if seen. Instead I pretend to doze; I am still in my sleeping bag.

Lobun nudges my shoulder. 'Tea,' he says. The first sip of the day is an untarnishable delight, and with it goes the day's first cigarette. As I raise my head to light it I find myself looking into the muzzle of Bluehat's rifle. The magazine is in place; the threat looks real enough.

Somewhere I have read that it is harder to kill a man if he is looking at you, so that is what I do. Nothing stirs. I am surprised to find my emotions seized by a sense of terminality rather than fear. But I am still spliced to life, organs working, blood coursing – all waiting on what lurks behind those neutral eyes. I sip tea. Bluehat looks away and lays down the rifle. He flips a word to his friends, who burst into laughter. I put the mug down and inhale deeply. Sam is sitting on the far side of the tarpaulin. Like Bluehat's, his expression is neutral. Sayya is stirring *ugali*, Lobun squatting beside him.

A movement from Bluehat draws back my eyes. Again they meet the muzzle of the G-3. It moves a little, first pointing over my shoulder, then edging back to my head.

Dying in the course of living out my dream of many years has always been a possibility, but the thought that a bullet from this blockhead's rifle can stop me from completing that dream sends my pulse racing. I light another cigarette, and the rifle goes down again.

More laughter. Bluehat has made another quip. Our eyes meet again. Without diverting his gaze, he picks up the rifle and, very deliberately, aims it at my head. Click! He grins; he has pulled the trigger on an empty chamber.

Simultaneously, Sayya looms into my field of vision, carrying the breadboard with a steaming lump of *ugali* on it. He puts it down for the gunmen. 'Tea!' one of them shouts. 'Bring tea quickly.'

Their appetites satisfied, they get up and walk away with neither a word nor a look.

Directly they were out of sight, my fury boiled over in curses. Sayya and Lobun were standing, arms adangle. Sam, still lying down, shook his head in a gesture of deprecation. It was now, I decided, that there was going to be a response. The incident could not be allowed to pass. I turned to Sam. 'Go right now to Etirai and tell him what that dog did. And tell him this: I am here because he invited me, so he is responsible for the way I am treated. Say that if any of his young men bring their weapons into my camp again, I shall strip and put my clothes at his feet. I shall hand over to him my donkeys and their loads and then I shall walk to Katillo naked to demonstrate the quality of his hospitality.'

Stripping is the last-resort protest of Kikuyu women – the infliction of shame on the strong by the weak. I thought perhaps Turkana women might do the same *in extremis*. My position among Etirai's people equated to that of a woman, for I had no means of defending myself. If threatened again, I would feign madness, for I knew that many tribal societies deem it unlucky to harm the insane.

Sam returned. 'Etirai says we are his guests and, as such, have nothing to fear here. He also says the river has risen again, so we should wait before trying to cross. These people are going to move from this *manyata* tomorrow because the grass is finished, but Etirai says they will help us cross before they go.'

It made no sense to me. 'If we're guests, what the hell does he mean by letting his men intimidate us?' I said.

'I don't think he realised what was going on.'

A shot interrupted our conversation – from close by, near the river. A ricochet wailed into the distance, but no one remarked upon it.

'Sayya, what shall we do?'

'I don't know,' he said in a numbed voice. 'I'm afraid of this place.'

'He's right,' Lobun cut in vehemently. 'I say this place is bad, these

-people are bad. Even that old man, Etirai, is bad. He must have known what was happening. Maybe he even told them to do it. He's a liar. Now he's telling us to stay and at the same time he says they're moving tomorrow. That means whatever they've decided to do, they won't be staying around for any explaining. I tell you we've got to get out and do it quick. Look, if the river's too high, why don't you and I go to Katillo and leave Sam and Sayya here? We could tell the police and bring back help.'

'No,' said Sayya, suddenly alert. 'Don't do that. We've come this far by sticking together and that's what we've got to do now.'

'OK, OK,' Lobun conciliated. 'Let's do what he says. But we don't even know that it's true about the water level. Let's go and look for ourselves.'

He was right. If the worst were to befall us, Sam and Sayya, as fellow-tribesmen, were the most likely to be let off. Lobun and I had the most to fear, and without them we had even more. 'I agree with both of you,' I said, 'but those thugs are somewhere near the river. We need Etirai.'

Sam brought him. On the way down, Etirai said he needed a rag for washing the baby's eyes. Remarkable. Here was a man who possessed every kind of livestock and had relatives with rifles worth at least five cows apiece – but he had no rag. I had none either, until I remembered my khaki shirt. I tore off the tail of it, and Etirai stowed it in his rawhide purse. Had I offered him the shirt itself, he would have accepted it, but would then have pointed out that I had forgotten to give him the rag.

On the previous afternoon I had poked a little stick to mark the water's edge, which was a foot down from it now. 'You'll never get those donkeys over,' Etirai said grimly. 'Their hoofs will stick in the mud and the current will sweep them away.'

Lobun and I waded beyond the middle. Not only was it shallow enough, but we were sure we would be able to get the animals across without help. The only remaining problem was our hosts. 'Why do you think Etirai lied to us about the water level?' I asked Lobun.

'Because he has a plan and all of them are in it. The idea is Bluehat's: that's what his behaviour has shown me. I think he's persuaded Etirai to break tradition. They want us to stay another night and attack us in the dark. They fired the shot to keep us away from the river. Etirai came with us hoping we would not notice that the level had subsided.'

'What will they do when they realise we're set on leaving?'

'They'll probably let us go. Too many witnesses about during the day. But what I know for certain is that we've got to get out right now.'

Etirai led us to a group of men. Only one, a braided fellow wearing a *ngawamaye* on his left arm, had a rifle. Another held a bow and arrows, the rest spears. Eighteen of them there were, including Etirai. A harsh-featured man, who might well have been a younger brother of Etirai's, stood addressing them as he fashioned a pot from a rough piece of wood with the blade of his spear.

Another man walked up. In spite of my earlier misgivings, I was overjoyed to recognise Lopeyo. He had shared my camp and food for two days, so it must surely now be he who would solve our immediate problem. But Lopeyo said he had urgent business and could not stay. He left with long and rapid strides.

'These are the men,' said Etirai to Sam, 'who will help you cross. For this you will pay them twenty shillings each.' Which was outrageous. Sam bargained him down to five.

The donkeys were messily loaded, and we trooped platoon-like to the river. Then, off again with the loads, 'helpers' standing inertly aside.

By some coincidence, two girls were pulling a female donkey and a foal into the water. Sayya and Lobun tried to persuade our nameless donkey to follow, but his obstinacy defeated them. I moved up Mashurubu, a more compliant soul, talking to him and pulling his ears. The mare and the foal were already ten yards out when he finally relented. The nameless one and Mkulakamba followed with Sayya and Lobun, Sam being left to guard the loads.

Ten minutes later the donkeys were over, and we returned. The gear was still littered in the mud. We picked up what we could and staggered back into the river. Looking back, I made out Sam and about five others following. Another ten minutes and everything lay on the far bank.

Sam identified the men who had helped, but our money was refused; they had decided on ten shillings each. Not only that, I was told, but nineteen others who had done nothing must be paid.

A stranger, who had been lying in the grass watching, addressed Etirai. He spoke in Turkana, so I was unable to understand either what he said or the ensuing exchange, which is based on Sam's subsequent account. 'Look,' the stranger said, 'you men agreed to take five shillings each from this European, so why don't you stick to your deal?'

'You keep out of this, it's got nothing to do with you,' Etirai snarled back. 'Shut up or we'll throw you into the river!'

'Why don't we ask for fifty shillings each,' a young man suggested, 'and if he refuses we can go back for our rifles.'

'Don't be stupid,' Etirai retorted. 'Can't you see we've got a witness?'

They stood, tense-muscled, in a long crooked line with Etirai squatting at one end. I felt like a motorist halted by drunken soldiers on a lonely road. 'Pay them ten each,' I said, 'and let's get the hell out of here.'

Most of the money was in twenty-shilling notes. They did not trust one another, wanted to be paid in tens. Their voices rose in anger, Sayya shakily explaining that we had no change. Etirai got to his feet. 'Let's go,' he shouted. 'We're wasting our time.'

They raised their voices in unison, turned and plunged into the river to plough through the current like a shoal of porpoises. The sight of their receding bodies drew the tension out of me.

Kaikir, for this was our new friend's name, grabbed the frantically grazing Mashurubu by the ear. 'Come on,' he urged, 'get these donkeys loaded fast. I know those fellows. They might try anything, even now.'

'But they've taken their money and gone. What more can they do?' I protested.

'Don't be a fool,' Sam snapped. 'One of them has already suggested fetching their rifles. Kaikir is right and but for him we would have lost everything.'

Soon we were storming through the doum forest bordering the river. The two girls and their beasts, who had attached themselves to us, were in lively conversation now with Sam and Sayya. All through the altercation on the river bank they had stood demurely by; they had not counted as individuals qualified to make decisions, but only as pliant executrices of male will. During a conversation on differing customs during our march over the Loriyu, William had put the attitude of Turkana men in a nutshell. 'Would you throw away your Land-Rover?' he asked me. I replied with a laugh. 'Of course not,' William said patronizingly, 'and neither would I throw away my wife. She is my Land-Rover.'

I grieved for the donkeys, which had been thrashed away from the juicy grass. By now we had left the doum to march through scraggy acacia and miswaki bush. The ground underfoot was as hard and dry as last week's bread. It was late afternoon when we made camp near the *manyatas* of Agitankori. The donkeys sniffed the miswaki leaves and hung their heads. They were as scrawny as stray dogs.

My anger had yet to subside. When three men visited the camp, I itched to lose my temper if they so much as dared to beg as little as a pinch of tobacco. Being asked for a cigarette was enough. 'Why don't you ask me if there's anything I want instead of asking for what you want?' I said rudely. 'None of you people can set eyes on a stranger without turning into beggars.'

Sam reproved me. 'This man didn't come here to beg for anything,' he said. 'I've told him what happened and he says we're lucky to have got past Etirai. Anyway, he says he'll try to bring us some milk, but there won't be much because there's no grass left here either.'

That shamed me. I would have been far too cowardly to be so aggressive had I caught sight of just a single round of ammunition. I offered my cigarettes round and, when the men came back with two tins of goat's milk, I added three large handfuls of tobacco.

We marched at full tilt across the four dry *laggas* called Aqaropus, Qaraqereteh, Loqopil and Qaqeteh, which Etirai had said were all in spate. By mid-morning, the landscape had changed completely. Trees were taller and more varied. Grass waved in the breeze, butterflies sucked at flowers and birds twittered everywhere. We passed over-grown acacia branch corrals enclosing abandoned homesteads. The sight of them, combined with the presence of long grass and the absence of cattle, frightened Sayya. In a land where grass was a scarce and much sought-after commodity, such a combination invariably denoted insecurity.

Sam and Kaikir forged ahead with the nameless donkey. Sayya, desperate to force Mashurubu and Mkulakamba to hurry, beat them hysterically every time they dared to snatch a mouthful. He walked swinging his heavy stick, his face tight with apprehension. Mkulakamba halted. Sayya attacked him so furiously that the stick broke, but the donkey refused to move. He must have felt like a Gulag prisoner running a gauntlet of tables set with plates of steam-ing steak-and-kidney pudding. I told Sayya to leave the donkeys alone; my feet were painful, and I needed a fifteen-minute break. Luckily for me and the donkeys, a group of men and girls caught up with us and started talking. There being safety in numbers, my quarter of an hour turned into half.

We arrived in Katillo at noon. It was like reaching the end of a severe bout of malaria. We unloaded under a thick-trunked fig tree fifty yards from the river, with the Karasuk Hills rising dark purple a few miles beyond its thicketed banks. Between us and the water's edge stretched a meadow steaming with moisture. Now at last the donkeys could graze to their hearts' content. I would not move again until they were fully back in condition. They would need their strength, for little did I know that even harsher ordeals of endurance lurked ahead.

The Gauntlet of Teleki's Ghost

Katillo lies on the right bank of the Turkwel some fifteen miles south of the Kateruk's mouth. It is one of quite a few new settlements in the area. The 1973 survey map does not show it. But in 1983 Katillo was already a district headquarters complete with hospital, government quarters and a United Nations Food and Agriculture Organisation agricultural scheme. New buildings were going up everywhere. There were two rows of shops, nearly all owned by members of the Meru tribe from the eastern slopes of Mount Kenya. One shopkeeper said he had first arrived twelve years before when Katillo was still in its infancy. Now he could speak the Turkana language well, and his trade was brisk; he was a typical example of the inter-tribal penetration process taking place all over the country. He did not believe that Etirai's men would have killed us. 'They would have been content with taking your possessions and scaring you off with their guns,' he said. 'But Pokot always kill first and then rob.'

Maina, the district officer, was unassuming and helpful. 'That is a well-known gang,' he said after hearing about our experience. 'They are also very angry. In May they went as far as Nginyang in the Pokot country and stole a few hundred cattle. The stock-theft people traced them back to the Kateruk. There was a fierce gun battle; several rustlers were killed and all the cattle recovered. If they sold you cow's milk, then they must have had another crack at the Pokot. This sort of thing happens all the time and one lot's as bad as the other. On 21 June the Pokot came here and raided right into Katillo town.'

One of the district clerks told another tale. Earlier that year the district officer was ordered to commandeer all unlicensed weapons in his parish. The Turkana brought their rifles and machine-guns. 'Now before we hand these in to you,' said their leader, 'we want you to tell us who is going to protect us from the Pokot and the Karamojong, who are better armed than we are.' In reply the official pointed to the small group of policemen standing behind him with semi-automatic rifles. The Turkana spokesman looked them up and down. 'If that's all you can offer,' he said, 'then you've no right to disarm us, but if you want to use force, you're welcome to try.'

'Look,' said the clerk as he came to the end of his story, 'there are some of them over there across the river.'

My eyes focused on half a dozen men leaning their rifles against a tree before stripping for a bathe while their cattle drank. But for some intervening trees they would have been in full view of the government offices.

For four days and five nights the donkeys munched their way through the meadow while we lolled on the river bank. I went to sleep and woke up to the sound of their unceasing mastication. On arrival they had been as emaciated as Napoleon's horses during the retreat from Moscow; but donkeys have amazing powers of recuperation, and by the time we left, ours were plump and fighting fit again. It was as well that they were so, for the forty miles of bush between Katillo and Loyapat, the southernmost outpost of Turkanaland, were a vacuum containing nothing but fear. We were to move through it at the pace of fugitives.

At the halfway mark lay Kaputir, a fragile doum-frond refuge at the edge of superlative pasture lands vacated by Turkana fleeing from Pokot and inhabited now only by antelope, buffalo and elephant. Cowering in their beehive huts on a bleak hillock, the Turkana refugees gazed longingly over the valley which had once been theirs. The smoke from Pokot fires curling up with lazy insolence from the slopes and thickets of the brooding Karasuk Hills was a daily reminder that there could be neither a return nor a release from apprehension, that the night could suddenly be split by the whip-cracks of rifle fire, the drumming of feet and the wails of victims.

Sam left us there. He was too old to stay the pace. I was sorry to lose him, for his calmness and sense of humour had steadied the impulsive Lobun and the nervous Sayya. As replacement I took on Orogai, a short vigorous man of about sixty, whose forthright manner emanated an aura of confidence. 'I will take you to Kainuk,' he declared, 'but remember we are in a *tanganyika* and there will be no halting until we reach Loyapat.'

If I did not take at face value Orogai's diktat of no halting, I was soon to learn that he meant what he said. Waist-high grass arched over the seldom-trodden path through abandoned pasture invaded now by a burgeoning tangle of acacia. Orogai's hairless pate reflected the sun like an aubergine as it bobbed incessantly up and down ahead of the donkeys. He was a man of iron, with the gait of a runaway convict, whom we were forced to follow like a posse.

After four hours the path dipped for the first time to the river bank. There the Turkwel had carved a broad bend through a tunnel of old fig trees. Orogai grabbed my shoulder and pointed to a path leading to the water's edge on the far bank. 'That's where the Pokot cross when they come to raid Kaputir,' he whispered as if we were in earshot of the enemy.

My feet were throbbing as if they had been bastinadoed. Words had failed to stop Orogai even for a moment, so I impulsively stripped and threw myself into an eddied pool. Lobun, supportive as ever, followed suit. Orogai and Sayya stood by, their eyes full of consternation. 'This is no time for bathing,' Sayya said grimly.

No sooner had he spoken than he raised his stick high and slashed the unsuspecting Mashurubu's flank. The donkey sprang away in terror, and then in a trice the beasts, Sayya and Orogai were gone, leaving Lobun and me in the water. It took us half an hour of trotting like bushmen to catch them up again.

And so it went on for another four hours with the hound of fear snapping at our heels every inch of the way. Not until we came upon a beehive log in a tree – the first sign of a human presence since Kaputir – did the tension ease. From a nearby cluster of deserted huts a track bearing fresh tyre marks led to a mission school, where a young and well-washed teacher lamented that only the previous week a gang of Pokot had burst in during the night and seized everything they could carry. Loyapat was only a mile on, he said. Coming as it did from a teacher, the information proved to be correct.

From Loyapat it was a mere five miles to Kainuk, a substantial market village straddling the Lodwar-to-Kitale road, and the border between the Turkana and the Pokot. Orogai, true to his word, had brought us there safely, but I was relieved to see the back of him. My feet were soggy with blisters which the night-stop in Loyapat had been too brief to relieve.

There was no grazing at Kainuk. The police advised us to walk another five miles to Amolem, where there was plenty. Amolem was, at first sight, a little paradise of spreading trees and dewy grass reclining on the right bank of the Wei Wei River in the shade of Nasolot Peak, which crowns the eastern wall of the Turkwel gorge. 'Welcome!' Chief Jacob Kamkele, a slight Pokot in his twenties, announced expansively. 'Here we have everything and you have no worries. Just unload and let the donkeys graze. They can wander anywhere and no one will take them – unless, of course, the Turkana come while you are here.'

It did not take long to find out that their visits were frequent and unwelcome. The latest had taken place on 19 June, just two days before the Pokot raided Katillo. I was told about the incident as I was lunching with my host, a Masai policeman named Richard, at a doll's house-sized restaurant. Maryam, the ancient Somali lady who owned it, mourned that business was poor. 'No one has any money because everyone keeps losing cattle and everything else the *ng'oroko* can lay their hands on. That last time they emptied the shop at the end of the street completely. Now the people are so terrified that they leave their homes at dusk and hide in the bush to sleep.'

'All we policemen could do was jump into our foxholes and start shooting back,' said Richard. 'It was too dark to go out looking for them – we'd have ended up shooting at one another. This is a small place with big problems we are ill equipped to deal with. There are only fifteen of us, so there's not much we can do, particularly if a really big gang comes. The *ng'oroko*'s weapons are as good as ours, some even better, so it's become a matter of self-defence more than anything else.'

We had made camp on the earth floor of Richard's rondavel. A sheet of plastic had been tied to the rafters to reinforce the leaky thatch overhead. Opposite the doorway stood a truckle bed half hidden by a cotton curtain suspended by a wire. By it were his rifle and a pair of black boots. A table next to an upright chair was stacked with a few items of crockery and an enamel teapot. A broom, hurricane lamp and radio completed his household equipment.

'I've been here four years now,' Richard told us, 'and I'm seriously thinking of resigning. Life is crushingly dull. Apart from raids, the radio is my only entertainment. I can't save even though I neither smoke nor drink. The pay just about covers food and general living, but buying something like a shirt nearly cleans me out. It is all getting too frustrating and I feel sick in my heart that in spite of our presence the people we are supposed to protect can't even sleep safely in their houses.'

It was market day when we set off again. Hundreds of Pokot women streamed past us as we went. In dress and ornament they favoured styles as varied as London's punks. Most striking were the multi-stringed necklaces. These were similar to those of the Turkana, but instead of reaching the lobes of the ears they fell away from below the chin to drape over the shoulders like capes. To set off the colours of the beads – blue interlaced with red, orange with black, or green with yellow – a brilliantly white shell was worn as a centrepiece. Rings of aluminium, brass or copper, some as much as four inches in diameter, so stretched the ear lobes that part of the weight had to be carried by beaded leather bands fastened to the hair on the crown of the head. Some women left their hair free; others had it braided into rats-tails,

Turkana style, while a few wore heavy pigtails hanging down all round their heads. Most were dressed in brown goat leather fastened above the breasts, but quite a few made do with skirts, leaving the breasts bare. Some wore plain cotton dresses and no ornaments at all. But every one carried produce in rucksacks made of leather or paraffin tins.

The few men with them tended to be more uniform in their turn-out: black *shukas*, a few strings of beads round the neck, wrists and arms adorned by metal bracelets. The younger ones wore a bead-studded strip of leather encircling the head with a flap hanging down over the nose. The chignon – a hairstyle first noted by von Hoehnel – was still favoured. The wearer plaits the hair of his ancestors into his own and compacts it with mud, cow dung and animal fat. Some of these chignons hung well down the back like a spine pad.

An ornament common to nearly all – men, women and children – was a single black cock's tail feather worn on the crown of the head like a symbol of defiance. And defiance there certainly was. On approaching us, all their chatter ceased, and all turned their widely spaced glittering eyes on us. High-bridged noses rose in disdain. No one smiled. It was as if the sight of us brought to the surface a silent rage that they wanted us to feel. As we trudged past these shoals of grim faces, so unlike any I had seen throughout the whole of the journey, I found myself gravitating towards the conclusion that there was real hatred here – hatred for Sayya, who was pretending to be a Samburu (but was almost undoubtedly recognisable as the Turkana he was), and hatred for me as a white man.

In Turkanaland, Sayya had been a Turkana like all the rest and, as such, part of the landscape. I was just a poor white, who was frequently asked what goods I was carrying for sale. Here in the land of the Pokot, however, we were both traditional enemies. Experience was to prove that we were walking on very thin ice indeed.

Hostility towards Turkana was axiomatic, but how did I fit into the picture? The reason is to be found in the behaviour of Teleki, the first white man the Pokot ever set eyes on. It was among the Pokot that Teleki spent the second half of July 1888. The party had run out of food a month earlier, and the Pokot's crops had not yet matured. There was nothing to eat but berries, weeds, half-ripe figs, acacia resin, birds' nests, fledglings, mushrooms and the odd zebra or two Teleki managed to shoot. As time passed, things became desperate. Men were dying. Von Hoehnel was completely prostrated by fever and had to be carried in a hammock. The Pokot in the Kolowa area had cattle, but refused to exchange them for the trade goods offered. What they wanted was tobacco, which Teleki had not included in his inventory of supplies. That was the last straw. Teleki reacted by sending a party of armed men to take by force what was needed. It was a raid the Pokot have never forgotten. Oral tradition preserves an exaggerated account of it, and the Pokot continue to associate aggression and injustice with the white man.

Another incident in the same area half a century later hardened that attitude. In the late thirties Elijah Masinde, a member of the Luhya tribe living on the southern slopes of Mount Elgon, founded a new religion, which he named Dini ya Msambwa – 'the religion of the departed spirits'. Its theme was a return to the ways of the ancestors in the belief that the spirits survive to influence the living. Imported religions like Christianity and Islam were anathematised.

In common with most other tribes in Kenya, the Luhya had suffered the depredations of Arab traders and subsequently the punitive expeditions of the British colonial government. Thus, when in the early forties Masinde called for the ejection of the British, promising his followers possession of everything left behind, he received an enthusiastic response in the form of acts of arson and civil disobedience.

Lukas Pkiech, a Pokot convert to the Dini, spread it among his tribesmen inhabiting the area east of Lake Baringo. He persuaded several hundred of them to march to Mount Elgon, where they would find heaven. They would receive gifts of livestock; the barren would conceive; the blind would see again, and the sick would be healed.

The British, already worried by the growing popularity of Dini ya Msambwa, were alarmed. They decided to halt the migrants at Kolowa, disperse them and arrest Pkiech. The plan misfired. On 24 April 1949 a mêlée took place. The British-officered force opened fire, killing – according to official reports – Pkiech and twenty-eight of his followers and wounding another fifty.

Two alleged survivors gave identical accounts of the incident. When they reached Kolowa, they were singing hymns of joy. They refused to obey the district officer's order to turn back. Who was he to tell them to go back to hell? When he threatened them they did not flee, for they believed their faith had made them bullet-proof. With their bare hands they attacked the cordon blocking their passage. It was then that the policemen opened fire.

One of the survivors claimed that the government later sent in reinforcements who killed 50,000 Pokot, releasing a spate of blood that dyed the Kerio red. Then all Pokot men with cicatrices (etched into the skin to record a killing) were arrested and taken to Kabarnet and Naivasha to be executed. The British exhibited their heads at

Kolowa to cow the remaining Pokot into handing over a fine of 500,000 head of cattle. That was why, the survivor said, the Pokot held the whites responsible for impoverishing and reducing their numbers, thus rendering them more vulnerable to other tribes. Now the Pokot rejected all forms of religion, despised official chiefs and deemed all non-Pokot suspect.

A chance encounter about a week after leaving Amolem dispelled any remaining doubts I may have had over Pokot chauvinism as a fact of life. We were on our way from Maron to Nginyang, a village south-east of the Chepanda Hills. Sore feet had brought me to a halt under a tree. My companions, now including Kasyaluk, a Pokot boy I had hired as interpreter and guide at Amolem, had stopped about fifty yards ahead. An old Pokot accompanied by a woman silently passed them by. Drawing close to me, the pair hesitated. The man said something to the woman, then came to squat by me on his portable stool. For what seemed like a full minute he studied me gravely. No greetings. 'Where have you come from?' he asked at last.

'Lodwar,' I replied innocently.

'Hm.' Another silence. 'In that case you must be either a *ng'oroko* or a thief.'

I burst into incredulous laughter. 'How can you believe that?'

With great deliberation, enunciating each word carefully in his bush-Swahili, he repeated the accusation.

'But why? Has anyone told you that I'm up to no good?'

'No one has told me anything. I have met no one who has seen you. But you have walked from the land of the Turkana with donkeys. That is the land of the enemy. The enemy did not kill you. You left his land alive and therefore you are an enemy of the Pokot.'

It was fantastic. 'But I'm a European!' I protested.

My words immediately made me think of Teleki's raid. The man's thin careworn face suggested he was about seventy – old enough for his father to have been one of Teleki's victims. And what European had travelled with donkeys along the banks of the Turkwel and the Wei Wei into the land of the Pokot since Teleki, the white *ng'oroko*?

I glanced at the woman. No smile on her face. Nor on mine now. I turned back to the man. 'Look, if I'm a *ng'oroko*, where are my rifles? I've got nothing but the bow and arrows that boy is carrying and, what's more, he's a Pokot like you.'

The man got to his feet and picked up his stool. 'It makes no difference,' he said, glaring down at me with eyes full of the hatred I had seen in the expressions of so many others by now. 'I don't care what his tribe is – or the other two. What counts is that they are your men and therefore the same as you. And there is no need for you to be armed. Tomorrow you will go to Marigat in the land of the Tugen. From there you will drive your car to Lodwar and tell your Turkana brothers where you have seen the best Pokot cattle. You are a *ng'oroko* and a dog.'

The encounter shocked me deeply. If he believed what he said – and he had given me no hint for supposing that he might not – and if he was not mad, which he did not seem to be, then I could well meet others who shared his views. If my role was to be interpreted as one of cattle-spotting, then there could be real trouble. A shiver down the spine dispelled all sense of outrage. I put my shoes and socks on. Suddenly I felt just as keen to reach Nginyang as the men did.

An even more explicit expression of Pokot feelings lay in wait just round the corner. The track led into the village of Chemolingot, which I mistook for Nginyang. Through the heat haze a building with a flagpole swam into view. It looked like a police station. Kasyaluk was nowhere to be seen, but that didn't matter any more; law and order were once again in reach.

A gangling youth in trousers and a red shirt stepped out of a building site, carrying a workmanlike panga. Such a relief, I thought, to see a chap in trousers with a panga instead of a fellow in a *shuka* carrying a bow and arrows. I greeted him and passed on. Suddenly he leaped into my path, his arms stretched wide, staring with bloodshot eyes – a youth turned in a flash into a raging man. His mouth opened wide to emit a screaming voice: 'You, *mzungu*, stop! Who are you?'

I reeled back, astonished. Kasyaluk was still nowhere to be seen. Lobun and Sayya were a few yards ahead with the donkeys. I made to move, but a palm pushed against my chest. I staggered and nearly fell. I could smell the reek of *chang'aa*.

'You, *mzungu*, who do you think you are, bringing Turkana here? Don't you know that no Turkana can come here?' A trail of saliva trickled from loose lips down his chin. 'All Turkana who come here will be killed and those who bring Turkana will be killed. I will kill them myself!'

Spectators gathered. He brandished the panga. I knew no one would intervene even if he used it. I was the odd man out, like the pickpocket tripped up on a Nairobi pavement. I had seen a stone dropped on the head of such a one.

'Who are you?' I asked. 'Who are you to stop me?'

'I will show you,' he shouted. As he fumbled through his pockets, I noticed Lobun beckoning from a shop. I stepped into it. Lobun whispered that we had lost our sword. 'We don't need swords,' I whispered back. 'What we need is a policeman.'

'Turkana!' the man roared. 'I will kill Turkana!'

Lobun leaped past me and confronted him. 'Who the hell do you think you're talking to? OK then, I'm a Turkana. What are you going to do about it?'

I pulled Lobun back towards Sayya. 'Look, you two,' I said in a low voice, 'you just stay here and let me try to sort this out. He can't say I'm a Turkana, can he?'

Lobun's outburst seemed to have produced the calming effect that a vigorous response often exerts on aggression. The man's arm curled itself fraternally around my shoulders, his face drawing close to mine. His voice became patronising. '*Mzungu*, you don't know Turkana,' he was saying in a schoolmasterly tone. 'They are very bad people. Therefore, if we see them here, we kill them, do you hear?'

Behind us now, Sayya and Lobun were driving the donkeys slowly towards the police post. Good; the sooner we got there the better. But the hand on my shoulder moved to grasp my shirt. I was being shaken. The man's face was a rictus, the panga blade an inch from my nose, his voice a siren. 'Anyone who brings Turkana is worse than a Turkana even if he's a *mzungu*. If you have brought Turkana, I will kill you right now!'

'Police!' I shouted at the top of my voice.

A man ran up. 'I'm a policeman,' he said.

I was shaking in a combination of rage and relief.

He addressed my assailant in Pokot. Both were using the word 'Turkana'. Tribal identity was clearly an issue here, even if the police were involved. We were joined by a middle-aged man dressed in a safari suit – the uniform of civil authority. It was then that I learned we were in Chemolingot and that he was the chief of it. He inspected my papers in a manner neither friendly nor reassuring. Then, with a bluntness which implied that there had been some justification for the assault, he asked me what tribes my men belonged to. Sayya's Maralal-issued identity card was turned this way and that. Lobun had lost his, and the chief had never heard of the Shangille. The drunk burst in again, and again I heard the word 'Turkana'. The chief mildly rebuked him, and the policeman led him away.

That incident at Chemolingot epitomised for me what life was all about in the cattle-raiding lands of north-western Kenya, where blood had flowed for centuries before Teleki and now continued to flow a century later. The guns that followed Teleki's guns in ever increasing numbers and with ever increasing killing power unleashed a permanent state of terror from which there was no escape. And because there was no escape every mind was permanently full of suspicion, fear and hatred.

Only one philosophy could be relevant to such circumstances. It was: weaken your enemy. Kill as many of his kind as you can and seize their wealth. Do not spare the little boy, because he will grow up to become a warrior. Do not spare the little girl, because she will grow up to become the mother of a warrior. Be merciless, because compassion is a betrayal of your own tribe.

Such a philosophy generates rock-hard materialism. The Turkana or Pokot man must move with the grass and the water. In order to survive, he must participate in a series of logically orchestrated communal acts. To these his woman must contribute the last drop of her sweat. She lives exclusively to work and bear children. She is bought by her husband and is expected to spend the rest of her life labouring to replace what she cost and to generate a surplus.

The Turkana apply a kind of hire-purchase system to marriage. Sam described how it worked in Katillo: 'If you fancy a girl enough to want to marry her, once her father has accepted a deposit of cattle, you can take her away immediately. But you are expected to hand over the outstanding balance within about three years. If you default, the father starts looking around for another suitor. If the father succeeds, he is entitled to send his sons to collect the woman, who is then handed over to the new husband together with all her children. Once the second man has paid the full price, you get back whatever animals you have already given, but you will have lost your wife for ever. The children are returned to you once they come of age.'

At Maron in the Pokot country, I repeated Sam's account to Njaramba, the headmaster of the school where I had camped. 'That's really quite advanced compared with what the Pokot do,' was his comment. 'First of all, the bride price must be paid in full before the girl is handed over. It is a kind of auction which the richest man always wins. Once the father has accepted the bride price, the girl has no say in the matter whatsoever and she must marry even if she hates the groom. She never knows what is going on until one morning her brothers and their friends drag her out of class, strip off her uniform there and then and dress her in the leather frock she's to be married in. I can remember only one who tried to resist, but after a few slaps and kicks she went quietly enough. One of our best pupils. We were sad to see her go, but if we'd tried to interfere they'd have beaten us too.

'A by-product of such a custom is of course that it provides an additional motive for cattle raiding. Turkana husbands who have failed to pay up, or Pokot suitors afraid of being outbid, face the choice between celibacy and theft if their fathers cannot or will not pay the bill.'

In this context I told Njaramba about a letter I had received from Stephen Pern (author of *Another Land, Another Sea*), saying: 'If you could get some good stuff about Turkana life, especially if you could go on a cattle raid, I reckon you'd have a winner. I am toying with this idea myself, so hurry up!' I had replied that he would get no competition from me; instead I would try to publicise the bloodier aspects of the bride-price system in the hope of encouraging the government to legislate against it.

Njaramba was amused. 'That's a noble thought,' he said, 'but even if you could persuade the government to do so, such a law could hardly be enforced. First of all, the government would face the enormous task of disarming the tribes. Don't forget the tribes have to be able to defend themselves against raiders from over the border. And arms are coming in from Uganda, Sudan and Ethiopia. Disarming the people here could only succeed if those countries co-operated, which none of them are in a state to do even if they wanted to.'

Njaramba believed that education, particularly that of girls, was the best weapon against the scourge of cattle raiding. 'But it's an uphill task,' he said. 'Just yesterday, for example, we ran out of food, which the government provides, and by this morning nearly all the children had gone. This school has been here for years, but the Pokot are still wary of education. They send their children to eat, not to learn. Most of the boys are taken home directly they are big enough to be useful, while the only girls that stay on are the ones no one wants to marry. A boy usually leaves school after five or six years. He is then encouraged to become a warrior and marry as many wives as he can afford. For him there's glory, but for a girl the future holds out little more than drudgery. It is only school that makes her aware of other possibilities, which she might pass on to her son. But even then, it will still take a long time for such a son to gain any influence over his peers or elders. Today, the handful of men who have been to secondary school are barely accepted. You know nothing, the illiterates tell them (that is to say, nothing of what is important to the tribe); what you know is useful only to foreigners (meaning members of other tribes) so go and serve them. By the time we get any change in a place like this, I will be an old man and you will be dead!'

I thought Njaramba was right in believing that educating women was the key to future change, but also that he probably underestimated their impatience to bring it about. A few days earlier, at Chesegon, another teacher had convinced me that, far from accepting their traditional status of subjection, the women were itching to throw off its shackles at the first opportunity.

Joseph Masai was not a Masai in spite of his name, but a Kony from the southern slopes of Mount Elgon. It was very difficult, he told me, for teachers like him to live far from home in remote places like Chesegon. How was that? I asked. 'It's the girls,' he replied flatly.

Why should they be a problem? 'Sex,' he replied cryptically.

The darkness and the inability of my companions to understand English encapsulated Masai and me in the kind of privacy available in the otherwise empty compartment of a train in which two strangers sometimes exchange intimate confessions, never to meet again.

'If it's sex,' I said, 'then all you need is a wife.'

'I've already got one, but she's at home where we've got a farm and the children go to school, so I stay here alone. In this place all the women are married and if you got mixed up with one of them you could be beaten to death. But then there's the girls – the ones at school. They all know they're going to be married off and then it'll be up before dawn, work all day, fetch water, cook, always the last to bed and pregnant most of the time. But at school they don't only have their lessons. They also get to see how the teacher lives. His house has a metal roof; he has a proper bed, kettle, charcoal brazier, paraffin lamp, utensils, cups and plates, plastic basin, towels and soap – each item something the girls do without at home. In their eyes the teacher lives in luxury and possesses things they desperately want themselves. They see him being paid just for talking and writing on the blackboard: that's not work, they think. You know, some of these girls are big, they are in standard four, but they are thirteen, fourteen and some are very beautiful. They start dreaming about becoming the wives of teachers. How? Simple. All they have to do is to get pregnant by one and tell their parents.

'One will come to you after school and say: Mr Masai, I'm having trouble with long division, so would you mind if I come to your house and you help me a little? She is attractive; you would like to sit near her and help her, so that is what you do. Then, one day she says: Mr Masai, you are being very kind to me, you have helped me a lot. I have noticed that your house needs sweeping and your pots are dirty. You feel tired, so let me do it. One evening it all takes a long time. It gets dark and you haven't even noticed. She says: Mr Masai, there was a lot of work today and I've only just noticed how late it's got. I'm worried, because if I go home now, my father will beat me. That doesn't matter, I often get beaten, but if I say I've been with you he might make trouble for you. So, Mr Masai, you just let me stay here and very early in the morning I'll go to school and pretend I'm the first to arrive. Then, when my parents ask me where I've been, I'll say I went picking berries with my girlfriend and stayed with her because it got late.

'So, Masai agrees. He's only got one bed and they both get into it. He hasn't had a woman for three months. The girl does not resist – quite the opposite – and two months later she tells Masai she's missed her period. When he hears that, Masai knows he's ruined.'

'How so?'

'Don't you know the ministry's rule? Any teacher who impregnates a schoolgirl is sacked. It's all right for an unmarried teacher; he can keep the whole thing quiet by marrying the girl, provided he can pay the bride price. In my case I could only do that by selling a piece of land, but for that I would have to face the land board. My wife would object and I would be refused permission. And in any case my pay's not enough for keeping two women. So, Mr Tom, what's the answer?'

The only thing I could think of was vasectomy. I told him about Mrs Gandhi and men being given radio sets.

'No, that's no good at all. If I told my wife I'd had an operation like that, she'd leave me.'

'And if you didn't tell her?'

'Then either she'd start asking me why she wasn't getting pregnant any more or one day she'd get pregnant – and then what would I do?'

Accept it, I supposed, but that was inconceivable to him. He pointed out that a valid role remained for prostitutes to help men in his position.

There were such women, but they existed by default rather than by choice.

On the evening of our arrival at Katillo, Lobun and I went to the shops to buy meat. We also found a bar and tasted beer for the first time since leaving Lodwar. After disappearing for a while, Lobun turned up with a soft-featured girl. Her name was Margaret Emoria, and he had invited her to our camp. It was dark by then, and as we wandered back another girl stepped out of the bushes and grasped my elbow: Margaret's friend, who also wanted to visit the camp. I could not see her, but her voice sounded husky, and her arm felt very thin. It soon slid round my waist, which denoted either that she had become my property or I hers. I did not protest; it was better than having a rifle pointed at one's head.

She said her name was Josephine, but soon confessed that she used that name only when visiting the Catholic mission for hand-outs. Her real name was Khadijah, which her mother had given her in honour of a kind Somali neighbour.

Next morning I found Khadijah by the river, washing my clothes. The scene was confirmation of the rapidity with which a chance encounter with the opposite sex tends to assume domestic proportions.

Khadijah was no beauty. She was emaciated, and her hair was done up in a host of little spaghetti plaits hanging like a fistful of bootlaces over her forehead and the nape of her neck. A broken jaw had left her face crooked. Her right arm had been broken at the elbow and set askew. Her left leg had been fractured at the hip; it too had knitted slightly out of true, leaving her with a limp.

'It all happened three years ago,' she told me. 'I was travelling from Lodwar to Kitale in the back of a lorry which collided head-on with another. A sack of sugar fell on my chest. The next thing I knew I was in a sort of box flying through the air and there were tubes stuck up my nose and into my arm. I was in an aircraft, but I didn't understand that then. I spent the next six months in hospital in Nairobi. My father sold eight cows to pay the bill. When I got back I was told my mother was dead. She was a Turkana and my father is a Karamojong. He works in Molo looking after a European's cattle. I was sent to my aunt in Katillo. The doctor had told me I'd never be able to work properly again, but I'm lucky because my aunt is kind and understanding.'

Sam and Sayya made no secret of their contempt for Khadijah. 'What do you want with a smashed-up old crone of thirty?' Sam snorted. 'I don't want to see her face. That woman was thrown out of Lodwar for fighting. That's how she got her injuries. She was taken to court and told never to show her face in Lodwar again. That's why she's here. Have you checked your pockets? She'll steal anything, that bitch. Why don't you let us chase her away and we'll find you a nice young one like Lobun's. At least we can look at that one without feeling sick.'

Khadijah was down and should therefore be out. She was nothing better than a *malaya* – a social reject fit only to be picked up and thrown away after use.

Their open derision hurt Khadijah. She wept that life was so cruel and that she often wished herself dead. Her training had been for the part of a married woman within the tribe. But the tribe had no place for a crippled woman who could not work. She had become an outcast, and it broke her mind. Now she revved up with *miraa* and blocked off with *chang'aa*. She could see the day when she lay dying in the road, watched from a shop veranda by men drinking Coca Cola.

Khadijah's tears and the men's callousness were integral to the generalised misery which continued to come out of the barrel of the gun. It was that same misery which had so appalled the Westerners who floated into the area on the tide of the British colonial presence that they soon set about trying to put matters right by giving assistance. As early as the nineteen-twenties, philanthropists began writing cheques. Missionaries and experts arrived to feed the hungry, dig wells for the thirsty, build for the homeless, cure the sick and teach the children better ways for the future.

Much effort was and continued to be put into alleviating that misery, but throughout the years less than satisfactory progress was made. One obstacle encountered was apathy on the part of the inhabitants. What, to them, could be the point of building anything for a future which could be shattered by a hail of bullets at any moment? It seemed more profitable and logical to go out and round up a few of your enemy's cattle. That way you at least had something tangible in your hand; and if in the process you were able to do away with a few of the enemy as well, so much the better for the future. Thus apathy continued to exist side by side with insecurity, and neither the British colonial government nor its independent successor had succeeded in resolving the conundrum.

By the time I arrived on the scene, the successors of those do-gooders were still there, beavering away at the same tasks. In Lodwar they were as thick on the ground as crocodiles in Allia Bay. I noticed they had three characteristics in common: they were all white, they were all rich and they were all cruising around in shiny four-wheel-drive vehicles.

Turkanaland, Clement told me, was a favourite target for what he called 'the aid industry'. Some of its activities were even counter-productive. In 1973, for example, a British organisation had sent a team to study the lake's fish resources. Its report had not yet been published, but was about to be. In the meantime, a Norwegian team had built a plant at Ferguson's Gulf capable of freezing 30 tons of fish a day. The Turkana were sold nylon nets at cost price and promised that all the fish they brought in would be bought. The catches proved inadequate, and the plant ran at a loss. When the Turkana complained that crocodiles were damaging the nets, the Norwegians bought the skins to defray the cost of repairs. The Turkana, having been told that they would now be paid for capturing their delicacy, bent their oars with new enthusiasm. Lodwar hospital had formerly treated about thirty cases of crocodile bite a year; now if a single one was brought in it would stir up a sensation. As time passed, Ferguson's Gulf was all but fished out. The lakeside Turkana and their Luo competitors had, as I had already seen for myself, taken to sailing across the lake to poach in forbidden waters. Largely because of the freezer project, said Clement, the British organisation's report would relate to a set of conditions which no longer existed.

What about the recipients of the Norwegian aid, what were they thinking? Clement chuckled mischievously. 'These whites brought the nets and told us to fish. We did as they said and now there are no fish left. So the whites had better find us something else to eat. It is right to take from the white. And concomitantly: the white needs nothing, so give him nothing. The Turkana has always lived by taking what he can from the environment without returning anything more than the dung of his goats. The white stepped in and proceeded to give without ever taking anything. Thus the white taught the Turkana to take more, but nothing about returning anything. Recently, some aid organisations introduced a "food for work" system to encourage people to work on potentially productive agricultural schemes in return for maize flour. The innovation has not been applauded. Several Turkana have told me the whites are introducing a new form of slavery.'

Clement's was the last white face I saw until I reached Loyapat, where I met Gerrit, a very tall, bearded Dutch missionary. I found him in a field with a Turkana man, hoeing. Gerrit was very interested in the subject of aid and had spent the whole of his working life helping the needy. However, he soon made it clear that his attitude to aid was very similar to Clement's. 'You saw that fellow in the field with me,' he said in his clipped English as we walked over to his house, 'yes? Well, he's all right now and may even stay all right. I started teaching him a couple of years ago – as a sort of example, see, so that he should grow food for his family and then the others would maybe get interested too. We'd start work at seven in the morning and sort of go on until it got too hot. Everything went OK until he started coming a bit later every day and in the end I found myself doing all the work on my own. One morning I got fed up and just stayed in bed. At eleven that fellow comes to my house and asks me why I'm not working. And then he says he wants me to give him some clothes for his children. Well, that was it. I told him what I thought of him and since then, as I said, he's been OK. But what happened was typical, really typical of these people.'

He cooked me porridge. I was briefly introduced to his pale, bored wife, who had little to say. Their two little girls aged six and seven came up to shake hands. 'They will soon have to go to school,' Gerrit said, 'and that's when we'll have to go back to Holland.'

'Will you be sorry?'

'Yes, I suppose so, in some ways. I've been here for five years now. I have grown to like the people, but what I don't like is – how to say it – their overdeveloped acquisitiveness. Another thing is that they will stop doing anything you teach them as soon as your back is turned, even simple things. I got a group together to make a fish pond, using tilapia from the river. It was very successful. All they had to do to keep it going was clean it out every now and again and channel more water into it. Then I went on leave. When I came back the pond was just a hole in the ground. They'd taken all the fish and then just let it dry up. That, I can tell you, made me very sad. I put a lot of work into that pond; I mean, it's such a good and easy way for people to get protein. You tell them that and they say yes, yes, yes – and then they forget all about it.'

'What do you think will happen after you leave?'

'I think probably the man I taught will go on working that bit of land, but the other things – yes, I feel depressed about them. And also I think that one of the reasons for the apathy of these people is that they live in constant fear. Hardly a month goes by when you don't hear shots during the night. And you understand, I'm living here alone with my wife and children, so I'm frightened. Do you know, there isn't a single goat in Loyapat? Every time someone brings in a few, the Pokot on Mount Sigir hear about it and immediately come down to steal them. And such men don't just steal; they want everyone to live in terror of them, so whenever they come to steal, they almost always kill someone too. During the past year no less than eight people have been killed by *ng'oroko* just here in Loyapat, and that's just one tiny place.'

'But don't you think this *ng'oroko* menace might also have some positive side effects? I found that from Loyiangalani as far as the Kateruk there was very little fodder grass. But once I got past Katillo, particularly between here and Kaputir, I saw plenty, as well as signs of animals – even buffalo and elephant. Don't you think that having areas free of goats helps the land to recover?'

'That's certainly true from the game point of view. There's now a herd of about seventy elephants between here and Kaputir and they are increasing. In fact it's astonishing that no one's been shooting them. But the other thing that's happening is that what was once good pasture is being overgrown by trees, particularly acacia. Some of the acacia are even resistant to arboricides and the only way of getting rid of them is by fire. So the longer this insecurity goes on, the poorer the people will become. The Turkana are pastoralists and it is very difficult, close to impossible, to get them to change their lifestyle. They don't like innovations. The fish pond was my last attempt to introduce one. I was in West Africa before I came here. I liked it better there, because people were more receptive and adaptable. But here . . . maybe I will go back to West Africa one day.'

Ten miles on, at Amolem, Richard the policeman showed me round an agricultural scheme on the banks of the Wei Wei River. About two hundred acres had been allocated to individuals to grow maize and sorghum. Water was being pumped from the river into channels with distribution supervised by the local agricultural officer. The FAO maintained the pump and supplied free diesel. What would happen if the FAO withdrew these services? 'Ah,' said the policeman, 'that is the question to which no one yet knows the answer.'

He introduced me to Carol, a tall bespectacled young American Peace Corps member, who was teaching the Amolem women basket weaving and poultry raising. She told me the American couple who were in charge of the irrigation scheme had asked her over and would like me to come too.

Dinner with Josh and Diana was like a night-stop on Mars. I stepped off the bush track running parallel with the river into a landscaped garden of trim lawns and carefully tended flower beds around a bungalow of substance. Bright electric lights illuminated a path leading to a glassed-in veranda. Josh, thirtyish, black-browed and sporting a fastidiously trimmed beard, welcomed me into his world of parquet floors and Swedish furniture. The walls were hung with Turkana dolls threatened by decorative sprays of Pokot arrows. The hazel-eyed, ash-blonde Diana led me to a carpeted living room, where I sank into a soft corduroy armchair next to a side table with an ice-cold beer on it. A sensation akin to jet lag overcame me.

The food came on metal platters to be eaten off ceramic plates, each on its separate orange raffia mat to protect the surface of the Meru oak table beneath. There were several courses, of which I can recall only the salad. The occasion was to welcome an FAO official, Henry Jimson, who was about to take charge of the agricultural scheme in Katillo. The conversation soon veered full tilt into shop. I listened and did justice to the salad; I had not tasted a tomato for a month.

Henry had just arrived from Sudan. Before that he had served in Bangladesh, Sri Lanka, Mali and Indonesia. Josh had also been in Sri Lanka. What happened to the rice project there? Well, it's still going on, but you know what the government people are like there. It's an uphill task to keep everything moving. Met John Parry on the way out. He'd just come in from Indonesia. Oh yes, I've heard it's much better there. Well, the system's a shambles, but I must say there's no comparing the officials with the ones in Sri Lanka. John said he had no trouble at all. And of course the exchange situation is a lot healthier too. You get a better deal, have a much higher standard of living. What's it like here, then? Well, you can see we have a decent house and all the usual stuff. Shops are a bit of a problem; you have to go all the way to Kitale for the slightest thing. But the human factor is almost impossible to deal with. Waste of time, really. I hear Newhouse is getting a transfer to Rome. Yes, he's done well for himself, but Sven Petersen and Guiseppe Calvarini both said it was unfair that Parry hadn't landed the job. I mean, with his experience on that big fodder scheme in Malaysia, the sugar thing in Somalia and the enormous efforts he made to get the fisheries off the ground in Malawi, he should have been the obvious choice. But it was Newhouse's report on Ethiopia that clinched the deal in the end. Where do you think you'll be posted to next . . . ?

'Sorry about all the FAO talk, Tom.' Josh's voice startled me out of my reverie. 'But you know we're all FAO and when we get together that's what we tend to talk about. Tell us about your trek.'

He was being polite, and I reciprocated. But I bored them. The environment I talked about was the wrong sort for them. Theirs was their home, their particular way of life and the greater ocean of bureaucracy in which they swam. They had little more reason than Etirai's clan to be interested in my experiences. The purpose of their presence was to improve the lives of people like Etirai through the implantation of technical infrastructures about the workings of which I knew next to nothing.

Josh had only three more months to serve at Amolem, after which, he said, the FAO would relinquish control over the scheme. 'What about the diesel supply and the pump maintenance?' I asked.

'Ah,' Josh replied, raising high his bushy eyebrows, 'that's the 64,000 dollar question, isn't it?'

Gerrit's fish pond immediately came to mind.

That night as I lay on the floor of Richard's hut I remembered the people I had seen in the camps for destitutes south of Lodwar. In particular I remembered a woman who had visited us from the camp at Kapoloqur. Middle aged and looking very unhappy, she told Sam and Sayya that she and her spindly legged five-year-old son sitting dejectedly beside her had not eaten for two days. I gave her a packet of maize meal, and the child smiled when he saw it in her hand. 'We live here on the food brought by the government,' the woman told us. 'Only a very few of us have any goats left. Most died in the drought and disease took the rest. None of mine survived. Once you have nothing, how can you get anything? The food lorry is supposed to come here every fortnight, but now we have had nothing for a month. We are beginning to starve. Three of our old ones died last week.'

Recalling that I had seen sorghum being cultivated in the Kerio valley, I asked her why no one was cultivating here now that it was raining. 'We have no way,' she replied despondently. 'No seed and no implements. And you can see for yourself what the soil is like – there isn't even any grass.'

At the time I could not think how that woman could be helped other than by hand-outs of food. But now I knew that while she and others like her languished and starved, the grass between Katillo and Loyapat was waist high. Had it been possible for them to be moved there and aided with a re-stocking scheme, they would have built themselves a village of grass huts in a day and resumed their normal lives, once again fully independent. It was not possible only because the Pokot would soon take the livestock and turn them into destitutes again.

All through that land the Turkana cowered in terror of the Pokot. Here now, at Amolem, the stage was identical; only the actors had reversed their roles. That night the Pokot inhabitants of the village were sleeping rough in fear of the Turkana. And almost everywhere, ever since leaving Baringo, I had hastened on with fearful men each day and slept beside fearful men each night, myself afraid. Fear had assumed the proportions of a mass neurosis in this part of Africa, narrowing minds, clouding vision, sapping energy and darkening the horizon.

Njaramba was right in asserting that the spectre of fear could be fought only with the weapon of education. But what is the relevance of education when, after a few years of sitting in a classroom, you are either dragged away to be married off by force to an illiterate or given a rifle to shoot someone in order to make off with his cattle for bride price? Education, like project development, can only succeed in the presence of security. Without security it turns largely into wasted effort.

From Chemolingot, after a night spent in the safety of the police compound, we reached Loruk on the border with Tugenland in a single march. After that it was just a short walk to Baringo. The donkeys had shrunk to skin and bones. My socks were stained with blood. I was glad to be out of Pokotland.

That evening we celebrated in the bar of the tour drivers' lodging at Kampi ya Samaki. Beer stood before us on the table for the first time since leaving Amolem. The occasion was a light-hearted one, but even here fear had followed us out of its homelands – at least as a topic of conversation.

Lobun pointed out that one of my most serious shortcomings throughout the journey was that I had failed to take danger seriously enough. He reminded me of how a few days earlier north-west of the Chepanda Hills I had wanted to spend the night by a water hole. The area around it had been empty of people and cattle. There were lions and armed Pokot prowling about, Kasyaluk had said, and so I was overruled. We had camped instead by a settlement. Then I had complained that I was sick of all the talk about danger and the need to camp near settlements. 'The trouble with you, Tom,' Lobun went on to say, 'is that you have never experienced what it's like to be under attack. The closest you ever got to it was when that fellow pointed a rifle at you. It was only because no one had ever done that to you before that you didn't think he would fire. But I've seen men like that shooting members of my own tribe. I have had to run into the bush with people firing guns and screaming and howling all around me. Sayya's done the same. If you'd seen what we've seen, you'd have been just as frightened as we were all along.'

'And what you forget,' Sayya added with heavy emphasis, 'is that Africans are not like Europeans. You keep thinking that we Africans are like yourself. We are not. Africans are merciless.'

I suggested to him that he probably thought like that because he had experienced mercilessness only from his fellow Africans. He was too young to have experienced it at the hands of Europeans. *Ng'oroko* had stolen his cattle. His back bore the scar of a *ng'oroko* bullet graze. He had been beaten as a recruit in the police, by a Kamba sergeant. He had been bullied by police investigating a cattle theft and locked in a cell knee-deep in water. A female relative of his, while still a young virgin, had been raped in the bush by thirty *ng'oroko* and subsequently spent months in hospital. In Ileret he had seen the mad Shangille woman whose family had been slaughtered by Turkana *ng'oroko*. Those were his experiences. Why had mine been so different? Was it because of being white?

'No,' replied Sayya, 'it's just because you were lucky.'

Epilogue

'We had no desire for further adventures, and decided to go home,' wrote von Hoehnel after arriving in Baringo. At the time of my own arrival there, I shared his feelings. But if I was to complete what I had set out to do I must follow his ghost to Mombasa. My enthusiasm was diluted by familiarity with what lay ahead, but the knowledge that the bicycle ride would be a picnic compared with what now lay behind me overcame my sloth.

Much of the route was along the main road through urban and semi-urban areas offering little of the enjoyment and excitement of the previous parts of the journey. My experiences were largely pale reflections of what had gone before – except for the traffic, which was almost as aggressive as the hyenas of Allia Bay. Bus and lorry drivers don't bother to circumvent cyclists by changing course. Each time the cyclist hears a heavy vehicle he must get himself and his machine off the road.

In the countryside, a European cyclist is usually regarded as a bit of an oddity or clown, but once he reaches a substantial town like Nakuru, Naivasha, Nairobi or Machakos he becomes a back-packing pauper and a damned nuisance on the road. A respectable European travels by car, or at least has enough money for a bus fare. From Nakuru onwards, therefore, my journey was a lonely one.

But if few friends materialised, a ubiquitous enemy did. Sleeping in the open bush is sheer bliss, but in urban areas thieves lurk by night, and the traveller has no alternative to seeking shelter in lodgings. These, in Kenya at least, are invariably part of a bar which, almost equally invariably, possesses a juke box to attract customers, and it stays turned on full blast until the last of them has gone. Machakos, Kilala, Emali, Makindu, Mtito Andei were all the same, and the last named was the worst, for no sooner had the music ceased than the lorries started revving their engines. My sharpest memory of all those places is one of nights of sleepless misery with bleary-eyed days to follow.

Voi was no exception. I set out from it in the morning cursing every ghetto-blaster in the world and damning their inventor to the deepest pit in hell. Five miles along the Taveta road the front wheel jammed: broken ballrace. Lifts being unavailable, I wheeled the bicycle back, got it fixed and set out again. By then it was early afternoon, and I only got as far as Mwatate. No lodgings there, and no food but tea and doughnuts. I pressed on, reconciled to a hungry night in the bush. There was little traffic save the occasional tourist minibus tearing past in a thick cloud of dust.

Deliverance came in the form of the Taita Hills Lodge, an edifice rising out of the steppe like an African Gormenghast. However, my scarecrow appearance at the reception counter aroused nothing short of astonishment and contempt. It was not until a credit card emerged from my filthy canvas bag that my request for accommodation was countenanced. Then, after wallowing at length in an enormous hot bath, I gorged on roast meat surrounded by a welter of German tourists wearing Hemingway-style bush jackets in a cavernous dining hall decorated with huge murals of Masai warriors, who stared down at us with studied indifference. No one spoke to me that evening. Even the barman was taciturn and pocketed my change without a word.

Next morning, as I wheeled my bicycle out of the portico, one of the Germans said, 'Zo, you are travelling by bicycle.'

'Not zo,' I retorted, giving the saddle a slap. 'This is actually a light aircraft.'

After a dreadful ride through sisal plantations and a grinding stretch of elephant-trodden bush track, I arrived at the village of Rukanga. It nestles at the western base of Kasigau, an immense cathedral rock of solid granite towering to over 5,000 feet above the Taita Plain. Being relatively remote, Rukanga gave me my first warm welcome since Mogotio, twenty miles north of Nakuru. I was shown round the school and the clinic, introduced to elders and – at a price – offered marijuana and garnets.

Predictably the tour led to the local bar, where it immediately transpired that all my newly acquired friends were broke. I bought a couple of rounds, after which they discreetly withdrew, leaving me behind as the only client. It was then that the landlady announced that the bar lacked lodgings. Asked for permission to doss down on the bar-room floor, she said she had a room on the premises which I could have for 40 shillings and she would put up with her sister.

As the bar also lacked a juke box, I had a magnificent sleep. Soon after dawn, however, someone knocked on the door. It was the landlady. She entered, knelt down, peered under the bed and got up again. 'Sorry if I disturbed you,' she said. 'I just wanted to check on my hen. She's sitting on eggs and the chicks are due to hatch today.'

I reached Mombasa in the afternoon of 4 December 1983 just as a partial eclipse of the sun was shrouding the town in darkness. An appropriate happening to mark the journey's end, I thought. But when the streets brightened up again, I was overcome by a feeling of anticlimax, of being suddenly deprived of all motivation and momentum. What next?

Suddenly I remembered something I had promised myself four years earlier. It was that if I ever reached Mombasa I would celebrate the event by going to the veranda bar of the Castle Hotel and having a bottle of cold Tusker beer. And that is precisely what I did.

Glossary

baraka	(Swahili) a blessing, prosperity, abundance.
baraza	(Swahili) place of public audience or court of law.
boma	(Swahili) defensive stockade or fence usually constructed of acacia branches. During colonial times in Tanzania *boma* also denoted an administrative headquarters.
bwana	(Swahili) master, Mr or sir.
chang'aa	(Swahili) Nubian gin, a potent, maize-meal based colourless spirit, illegally distilled in Tanzania and Kenya.
choromchoro	(Tanzanian Swahili slang term) smuggling, black-marketeering and racketeering: also see p. 16 of text.
debe	(Swahili) four-gallon tin used in the distribution for retail of paraffin and cooking oil; once the original contents have been consumed, the container is used as a measure for various types of produce.
ejoqaa	(Turkana) greeting: Is it well? The reply is *ejoq*: It is well.
gitete	(Kikuyu) bottle gourd: according to Kikuyu tradition in the nineteenth and the early part of the twentieth centuries, when a Kikuyu man went on a journey he would take with him a *gitete* filled with gruel as his food for the day. Whoever the traveller stayed the night with would replenish the *gitete* for the next day's travelling.
habari	(Swahili) news, component of Swahili form of greeting: see *jambo*.
hamna	(Swahili) term commonly used in Tanzania denoting 'There isn't any': in Kenya people tend to say '*hakuna*' instead.
hongo	(Swahili) toll, tribute, blackmail or bribe.
hoteli	(Swahili) term used to denote restaurant or teahouse throughout Tanzania and Kenya. Small hotels offering accommodation are called 'guest-houses' in Tanzania and 'lodgings' in Kenya. In Kenya, of late, many establishments have begun springing up calling themselves 'bar, board and lodgings, hotel and day and night club'.
irio	(Kikuyu) 'food': the standard Kikuyu meal consisting of boiled and mashed potatoes, peas and maize. The other standard dish, *githeri*, is boiled beans mixed with tomatoes, onions and small pieces of meat.

i-sampurri	(Masai) basket: word from which the name of the Samburu is derived: see p. 145 of text.
jambo	(Swahili) the abbreviated form of greeting, meaning 'How do you do?', and, as in English, the reply can again be '*Jambo*', but quite often it is '*Mzuri*': 'It is well'. Alternatively '*Jambo*' may evince the reply '*Habari*': 'What news?', in which case the reply is again, '*Mzuri*'. A person greeting several others says, '*Hamjambo*' – again meaning 'How do you do?', or, more commonly these days, '*Jamboni*'. The standard reply in both cases is either '*Hatujambo*' – 'We have no news' or 'We are well', or '*Mzuri, habari yako*' – meaning, 'We are well, and what is your news?', to which the first speaker again replies, '*Mzuri*'. When one group of people greets another, both the greetings and the replies are given in chorus: '*Hamjambo*' – 'How do you do?' – '*Hatujambo*' – 'We are well' – '*Habari zenu*' – 'What is your news?' – '*Mzuri*'. But also quite frequently people tend just to say '*Habari*', to which the reply is '*Mzuri*'.
karibu	(Swahili) near, nearby, nearly. Before entering a house or room, a visitor is expected to say '*Hodi*', meaning 'May I come in?', to which the affirmative reply is '*Karibu*'.
kitenge	(Swahili) a big, colourful piece of cloth that women and girls wrap around their bodies in such a way as to be held together just over the breasts. Often the *kitenge* is fastened round the waist like a man's *shuka*, usually supplemented by a blouse, but in both rural Tanzania and Kenya I saw women thus attired but leaving the breasts bare. In most cases these days, however, women and girls wear dresses, but many wrap a *kitenge* over the dress. The *kitenge* is also used as a hammock to carry babies on the hip or back.
lagga	(Turkana) water-course.
laibon	(Masai) spiritual leader.
magendo	(Kenyan/Ugandan/Swahili slang) smuggling, blackmarketeering or racketeering.
majonzi	(Tanzanian Swahili slang term) footpads, muggers or mountebanks, possibly a corruption of the classical Swahili term *wangang'anyi*. In classical Swahili *majonzi* means 'grief' or 'sadness'.
malaya	(Swahili) prostitute.
manyata	(Masai) term commonly used to denote a group of huts surrounded by a protective fence within which people live and livestock is kept during the night. The word is derived from the verb *a-many*, 'to settle', and *manyata* can therefore be correctly translated as 'settlement'. Strictly

speaking, however, *manyata* is a kraal for warriors and in that sense a protective fence is lacking. Likewise, a homestead occupied by several elders and their wives and children and surrounded by a fence is called *enk-ang*.

mguu	(Swahili) leg or wheel – plural *miguu*.
mongi	(Chagga) chief.
moran	(Masai) warrior, strictly speaking *il-murran*.
muthungo	(Kikuyu) white person, European.
muzito	(Swahili slang) a heavy person.
mwalimu	(Swahili) teacher; *Mwalimu* is the title Tanzanians have given Nyerere. Everyone else in Tanzania is referred to be the title *ndugu* – 'comrade' or 'brother'.
mzungu	(Swahili) white person, European: for derivation see p. 177 of text.
ndito	(Masai) girl, strictly speaking 'en-tito'.
ndugu	(Swahili) brother, sister, cousin, relation, fellow tribesman: also see under 'mwalimu' above.
ng'oroko	(Masai/Turkana) cattle raider: for derivation see p. 145 of text.
nyika	(Swahili) open, bare, treeless wilderness, open forest with high grass, a barren desolate region.
panga	(Swahili) machete.
seremende	(Masai/Njamus/Samburu) sweets, chocolate, bonbons, toffees, etc.: corruption of the Swahili *peremende*, itself a corruption of the English 'peppermint'.
shenzi	(Swahili) barbarous, uncivilised, primitive: *mshenzi* (pl. *washenzi*) such a person or persons. Johnson comments in his dictionary: 'Often used contemptuously by the coast native of those who come from the interior, although they are frequently more cultured and refined than the coast native!' Von Hoehnel remarks: '"*Washenzi*" is also used as a term of contempt for the natives of what the Germans call the Hinterland – that is to say, all the districts of Africa not yet appropriated by Europeans.'
shifta	(Amharic) bandit, highwayman: Richard Greenfield supposes that the term might already have been in use during the first two or three centuries of the Christian era and that *shiftas* might have been responsible for the seizure of the Roman Emperor Constantine's fleet near Adulis, the port of Aksum, towards the beginning of the third century AD. I first heard the word used to describe the Eritrean rebels when I visited Ethiopia in 1962.
shikamoo	(Swahili) contraction of '*Shika moyo yangu*' – 'Take hold of my heart': a form of greeting common in Tanzania, to which the reply is '*Marhaba*' – 'Certainly, if it pleases you': also see p. 30 of text.

shuka	(Swahili) a loincloth, fastened round the waist and usually descending to below the knee: also used as a cloak fastened over one shoulder leaving the other bare.
tanganyika	(Swahili) Tanganyika Territory was the name given by the British in 1918 to what today is mainland Tanzania and what prior to 1918 was Deutsch-Ostafrika. Somehow *tanganyika* has crept into the usage of the Turkana, Shangille, Pokot and other tribes of northern Kenya denoting 'a wild, lawless and bandit-infested territory': also see p. 143 of text.
turungi	(Kikuyu) sweetened tea without milk. Kikuyu believe the term is derived from the English 'strong tea'; however, when such tea is required in Tanzania, the term used is *chai rangi* (Swahili), 'coloured tea', as opposed to tea whitened by milk.
ugali	(Swahili) a stiff porridge made of maize, millet or cassava flour.
uhuru	(Swahili) freedom, liberty, independence.
ujamaa	(Swahili) a term which originally meant relationship, kin, familyhood or brotherhood, but was transformed by Nyerere to mean 'communal ownership': also see p. 59 of text.
ujima	(Swahili) work done with the help of neighbours, such as house-building, planting or harvesting for which no reward was expected, but the persons so helped would be expected to help the helpers under similar circumstances: also see p. 59 of text.
upepo	(Swahili) wind, breeze.
washenzi	(Swahili) see *shenzi* above.

Bibliography

Arkell-Hardwick, A., *An Ivory Trader in North Kenya*, Longmans Green, London, 1903.

Barber, James, *Imperial Frontier: A Study of Relations between the British and the Pastoral Tribes of North East Uganda*, East African Publishing House, Nairobi, 1968.

Berry, L., *Tanzania in Maps*, University of London Press, London, 1971.

Blundell, Michael, *The Wild Flowers of Kenya*, Collins, London, 1980.

Boyes, John, *The Company of Adventurers*, East Africa Ltd, London, 1928.

Bulpett, G. W. L. (ed.), *John Boyes, King of the Wakikuyu*, Methuen, London, 1911.

Coulson, Andrew, *Tanzania: A Political Economy*, Clarendon Press, Oxford, 1982.

Dale, Ivan R., and P. J. Greenway, *Kenya Trees and Shrubs*, Buchanan's Kenya Estates Ltd, Nairobi, in association with Hatchards, London, 1961.

Dorst, Jean, and Pierre Dandelot, *A Field Guide to the Larger Mammals of Africa*, Collins, London, 1970.

Dundas, Charles, *Kilimanjaro and Its People: A History of the Wachagga, Their Laws, Customs and Legends . . .* , Frank Cass, London, 1924, 1968.

Erdelyi, L., *Teleki Samu Afrikaban: Az Afrika-Hutato Erediti Fenykepfelveteleivel*, Editura Kriterion, Bucharest, 1977.

Farrant, Leda, *The Legendary Grogan*, Hamish Hamilton, London, 1981.

Fedders, Andrew, and Cynthia Salvadori, *Peoples and Cultures of Kenya*, Transafrica, Nairobi; Rex Collings, London, 1980.

Fischer, G. A., *Das Massai-Land*, Hamburg, 1885.

Freeman-Grenville, G. S. P., *The Medieval History of the Coast of Tanganyika*, Oxford University Press, New York, 1962.

Gibb, H. A. R., and J. H. Kramers (eds), *Shorter Encyclopaedia of Islam*, E. J. Brill, Leiden, 1953.

Graham, A., *The Lake Rudolf Crocodile*, a report to the Kenya Game Department by Wildlife Services Ltd, 1968 (unpublished).

Greenfield, Richard, *Ethiopia: A New Political History*, Pall Mall Press, London, 1965.

Gregory, J. W., *The Great Rift Valley: Being the Narrative of a Journey to Mount Kenya and Lake Baringo*, John Murray, London, 1896; Frank Cass, London, 1968.

Harman, Nicholas, *Bwana Stokesi and His African Conquests*, Jonathan Cape, London, 1986.

Hedges, Norman G., *Reptiles and Amphibians of East Africa*, Kenya Literature Bureau, Nairobi, 1983.

Hill, M. F., *Permanent Way: The Story of the Kenya and Uganda Railway*, 2 vols, East African Literature Bureau, 1949.

Hillaby, John, *Journey to the Jade Sea*, Constable, London, 1964; Granada, London, 1973.

Huxley, Elspeth, *White Man's Country: Lord Delamere and the Making of Kenya*, Chatto and Windus, London, 1935.

Hyden, Goram, *Beyond Ujamaa in Tanzania: Underdevelopment and an Uncaptured Peasantry*, Heinemann, London, 1982.

Iliffe, John, *A Modern History of Tanganyika*, Cambridge University Press, Cambridge, 1979.

Imperato, Pascal James, MD, *Arthur Donaldson Smith and the Exploration of Lake Rudolf*, Medical Society of the State of New York, Lake Success, New York, 1987.

Jackson, Sir Frederick, *Early Days in East Africa*, Dawsons of Pall Mall, London, 1969.

Johnson, Frederick (ed.), *A Standard Swahili–English/English–Swahili Dictionary*, Oxford University Press, Geoffrey Cumberlege, London, 1939.

Koenig, Oskar, *The Masai Story*, Michael Joseph, London, 1956.

Krapf, J. Lewis, *Travels, Researches, and Missionary Labours during an Eighteen Years' Residence in Eastern Africa . . .*, 2nd ed., Frank Cass, London, 1968.

Leakey, L. S. B., *The Southern Kikuyu before 1903*, 3 vols, Academic Press, London, New York, San Francisco, 1977.

Leakey, R. E., *People of the Lake: Mankind and Its Beginnings*, Anchor Press/Doubleday, Garden City, New York, 1978.

Matson, A. T., *Nandi Resistance to British Rule 1890–1906*, East African Publishing House, Nairobi, 1972.

Meinertzhagen, Richard, *Kenya Diary – 1902–1906*, Oliver & Boyd, London, 1957; Eland Books, London, 1983.

Meyer, Hans, *Across East African Glaciers: An Account of the First Ascent of Kilimanjaro*, trans. E. H. S. Calder, George Philip & Son, London, 1981.

Miller, Charles, *The Battle for the Bundu*, Macdonald, London, 1974.
The Lunatic Express, Macdonald, London, 1971.

Mol, Fr Frans, *Maa: A Dictionary of the Masai Language and Folklore*, Marketing and Publishing Ltd, Nairobi, 1978.

Mungbeam, G. H. (ed.), *Kenya: Select Historical Documents 1884–1923*, East African Publishing House, Nairobi, 1978.

Muruiki, Godfrey, *A History of the Kikuyu 1500–1900*, Oxford University Press, 1974.

Murray-Brown, Jeremy, *Kenyatta*, Dutton, New York, 1973.

New, Charles, *Life, Wanderings, and Labours in Eastern Africa* . . . , 3rd ed., Frank Cass, London, 1971.

Pern, Stephen, *Another Land, Another Sea: Walking round Lake Rudolph*, Victor Gollancz, London, 1979.

Peters, Carl, *Gesammelte Schriften*, ed. Professor Dr Walter Frank, 3 vols, E. H. Beck'sche Verlagsbuchhandlung, Munich, Berlin, 1943.

    Wie Deutsch-Ostafrika Enstand! Persoenlicher Bericht des Gruenders, Koehler & Voigtlaender Verlag, Leipzig, 1940.

Reid, Ian C. (ed.), *Guide Book to Mount Kenya and Kilimanjaro*, Mountain Club of Kenya, Nairobi, 1963.

Rosberg, Carl G. Jr, and John Nottingham, *The Myth of 'Mau Mau': Nationalism in Kenya*, New American Library, New York, 1970.

Teleki, Count Samuel, A Personal Diary of Explorations in East Africa, Oct. 1886–Oct. 1888, trans. from the handwritten Hungarian by Charles and Vera Teleki, Warkworth, Ontario, 1961 (unpublished).

Thesiger, Wilfred, *The Life of My Choice*, Collins, London, 1987.

Thomson, Joseph, *Through Masai Land*, Low, Marston, Searle & Rivington, London, 1885; Frank Cass, London, 1968.

van Pelt, P., *Bantu Customs in Mainland Tanzania*, TMP Book Department, Tabora, Tanzania, 1977.

von Hoehnel, Ludwig, *Discovery of Lakes Rudolf and Stefanie: A Narrative of Count Samuel Teleki's Exploring and Hunting Expedition in Eastern Equatorial Africa in 1887 and 1888*, trans. Nancy Bell (N. d'Anvers), 2 vols, Longmans Green, London, 1894; Frank Cass, London, 1968.

Williams, John G., *A Field Guide to the Birds of East Africa*, Collins, London, 1980.

Wipper, Audrey, *Rural Rebels: A Study of Two Protest Movements in Kenya*, Oxford University Press, Nairobi, 1977.

Maps

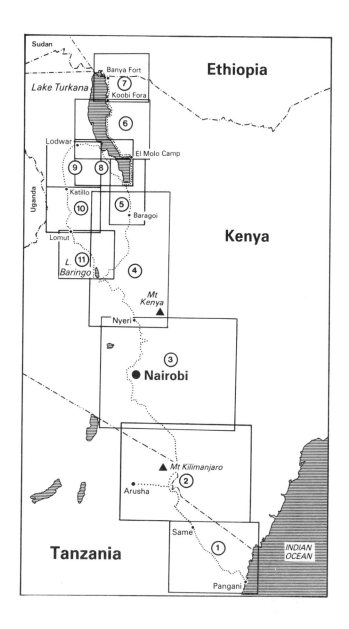

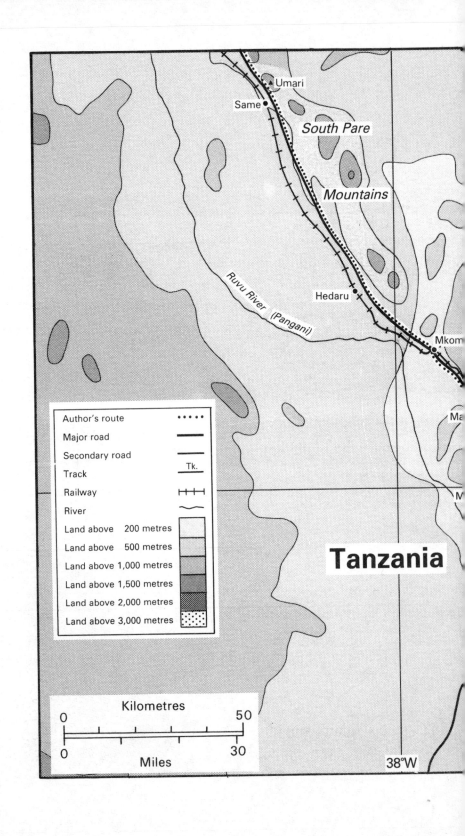

Umari

Same

South Pare

Mountains

Ruvu River (Pangani)

Hedaru

Mkom

Ma

M

M

Author's route · · · · ·

Major road ———

Secondary road ——

Track   Tk.

Railway   ⊢⊢⊢⊢

River   ～

Land above   200 metres

Land above   500 metres

Land above 1,000 metres

Land above 1,500 metres

Land above 2,000 metres

Land above 3,000 metres

Tanzania

Kilometres

0   50

0   30

Miles

38°W

MAP 1

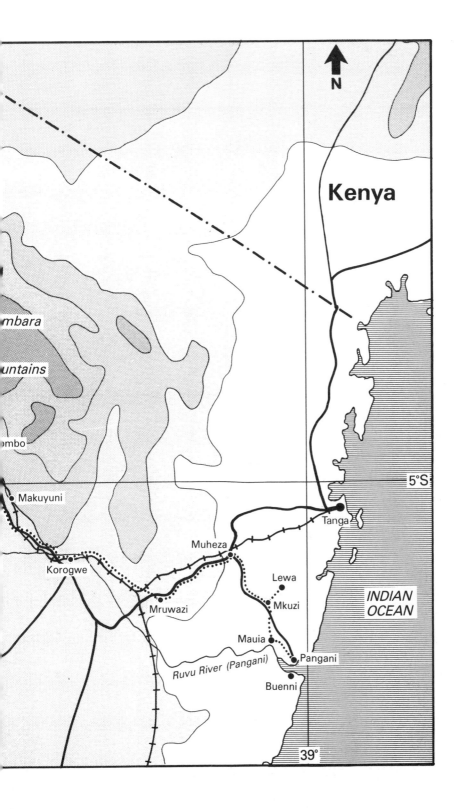

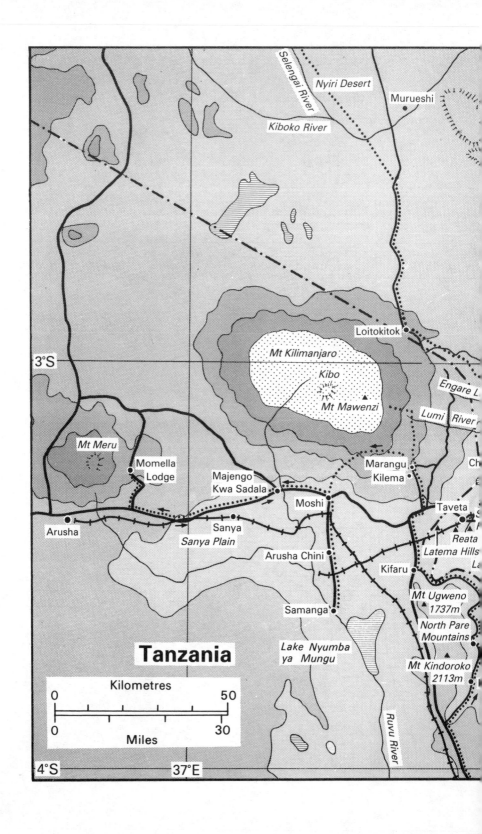

Nyiri Desert

Murueshi

Selengai River

Kiboko River

Loitokitok

Mt Kilimanjaro

Kibo

Engare L

Mt Mawenzi

Lumi River

3°S

Mt Meru

Marangu
Kilema

Momella
Lodge

Ch

Majengo
Kwa Sadala

Moshi

Taveta

Arusha

Sanya

Reata
Latema Hills

Sanya Plain

Arusha Chini

La

Kifaru

Mt Ugweno
1737m

Samanga

North Pare
Mountains

Tanzania

Lake Nyumba
ya Mungu

Mt Kindoroko
2113m

Kilometres

0   50

0   30

Miles

Ruvu River

4°S   37°E

MAP 2

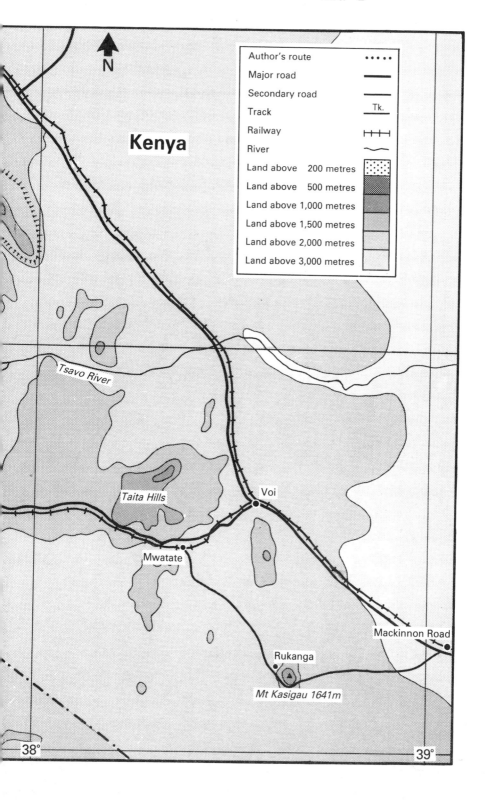

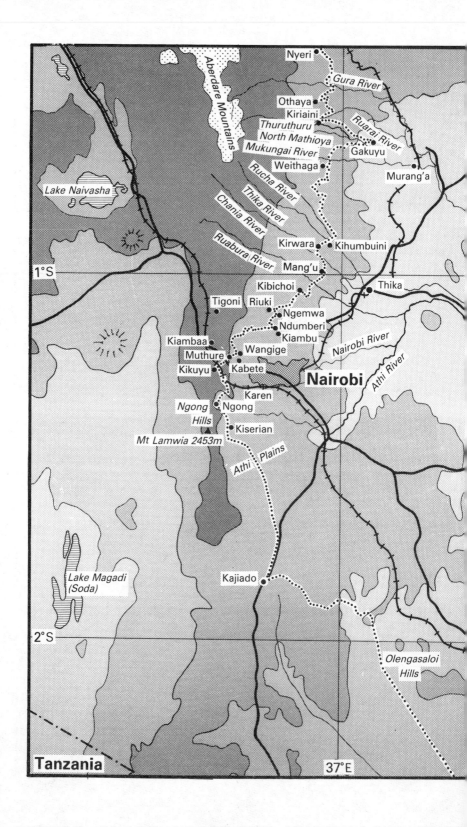

Nyeri

Gura River

Aberdare Mountains

Othaya
Kiriaini
Thuruthuru
North Mathioya
Mukungai River
Weithaga

Ruarai River

Gakuyu

Murang'a

Lake Naivasha

Rucha River

Thika River

Chania River

Ruabura River

Kirwara • Kihumbuini
Mang'u

1°S

Kibichoi
Tigoni Riuki
Ngemwa
Ndumberi
Kiambu

Thika

Kiambaa
Muthure
Kikuyu Kabete

Wangige

Nairobi River

Athi River

Nairobi

Karen
Ngong Hills Ngong
Kiserian
Mt Lamwia 2453m

Athi Plains

Lake Magadi (Soda)

Kajiado

Olengasaloi Hills

2°S

Tanzania

37°E

MAP 3

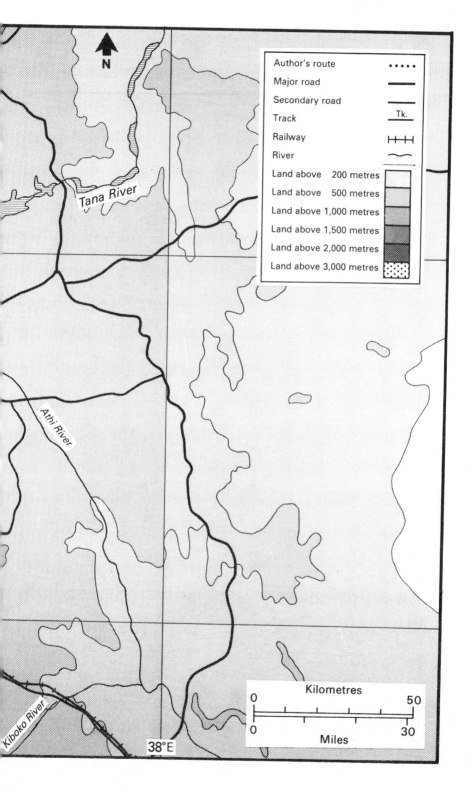

N

Author's route ·····
Major road ——
Secondary road ——
Track Tk.
Railway +-+-+
River ~~~
Land above 200 metres
Land above 500 metres
Land above 1,000 metres
Land above 1,500 metres
Land above 2,000 metres
Land above 3,000 metres

Tana River

Athi River

Kiboko River

38°E

Kilometres
0   50
0   30
Miles

MAP 4

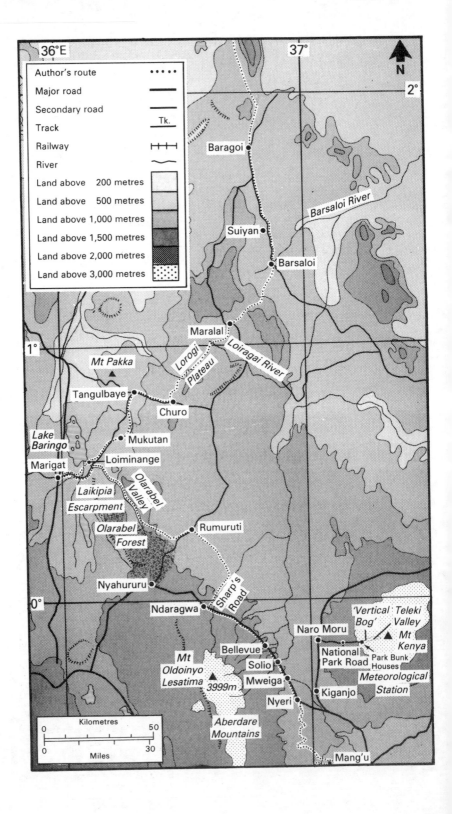

MAP 5

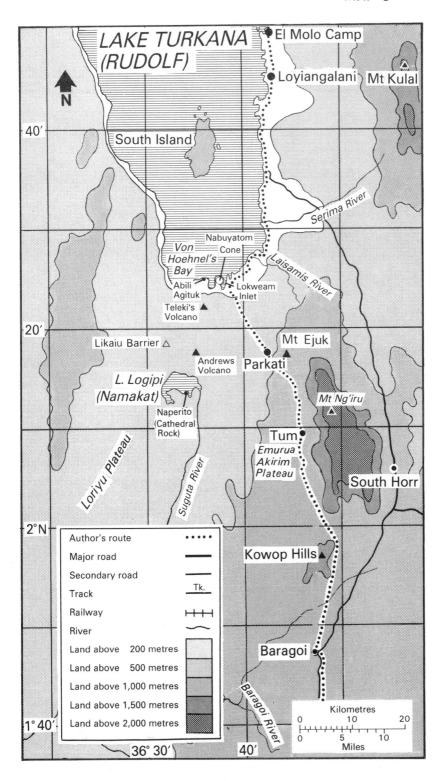

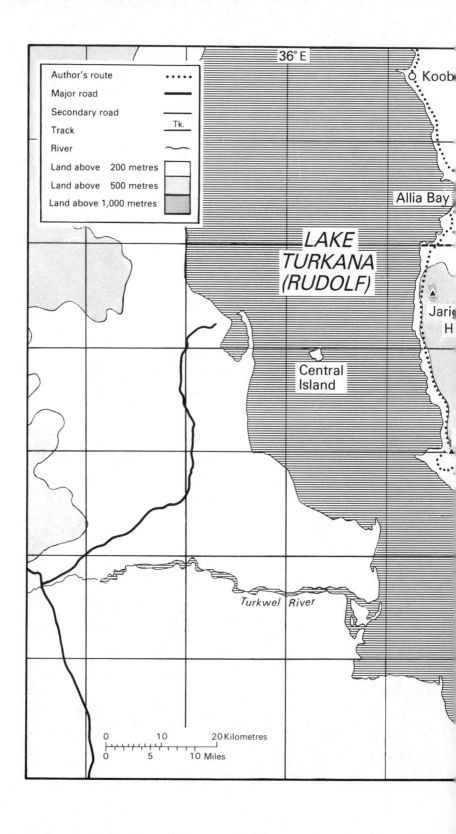

MAP 6

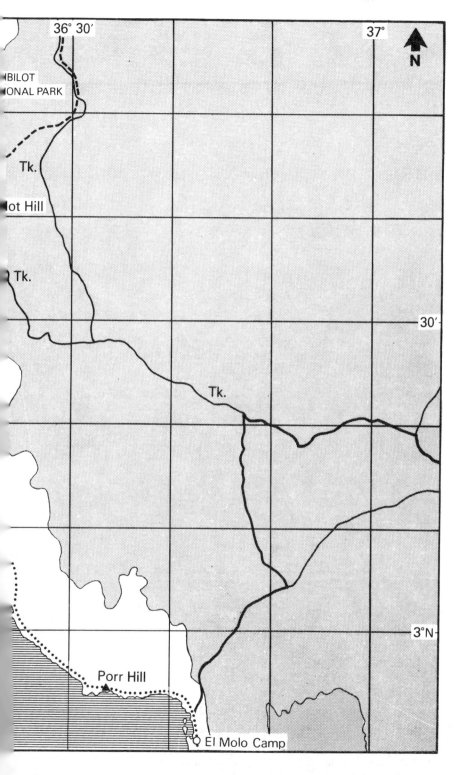

36° 30′

37°

N

BILOT
IONAL PARK

Tk.

lot Hill

Tk.

30′

Tk.

3°N

Porr Hill

El Molo Camp

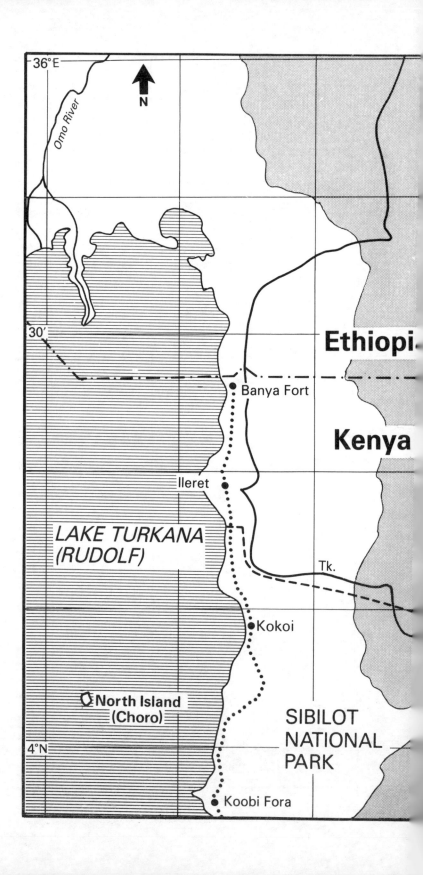

MAP 7

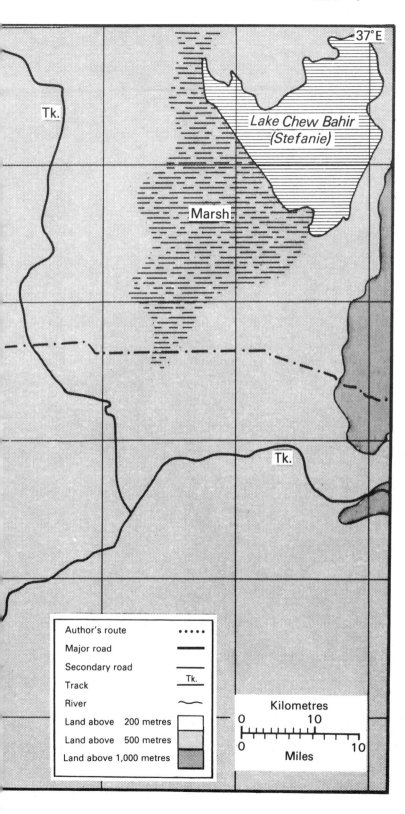

37°E

Tk.

Lake Chew Bahir
(Stefanie)

Marsh

Tk.

Author's route	•••••
Major road	——
Secondary road	—
Track	Tk.
River	~~
Land above 200 metres	
Land above 500 metres	
Land above 1,000 metres	

Kilometres
0   10

0   10
Miles

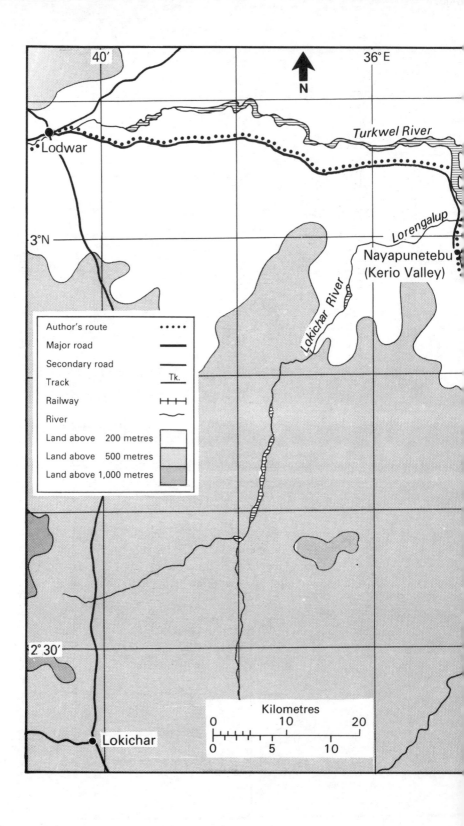

MAP 8

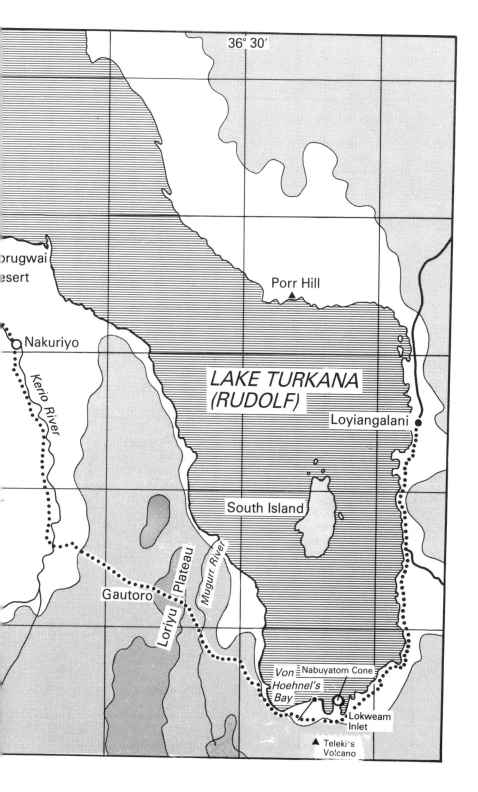

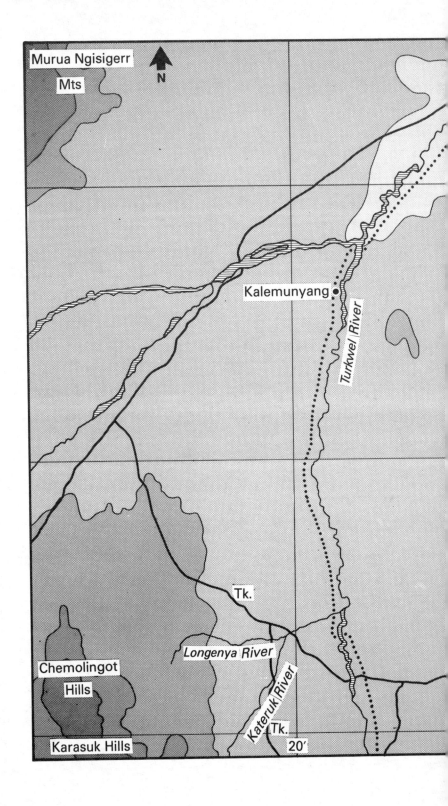

Murua Ngisigerr Mts

N

Kalemunyang

Turkwel River

Tk.

Longenya River

Chemolingot Hills

Karasuk Hills

Kateruk River

Tk.

20'

MAP 9

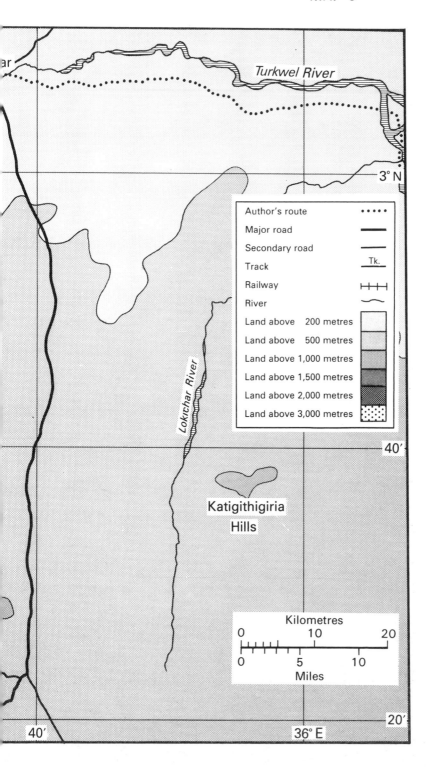

Author's route ·····
Major road ▅▅▅
Secondary road ▬
Track Tk.
Railway ┝┿┿┥
River 〰
Land above 200 metres
Land above 500 metres
Land above 1,000 metres
Land above 1,500 metres
Land above 2,000 metres
Land above 3,000 metres

Turkwel River

3° N

Lokichar River

40′

Katigithigiria Hills

Kilometres
0   10   20

0   5   10
Miles

40′   36° E   20′

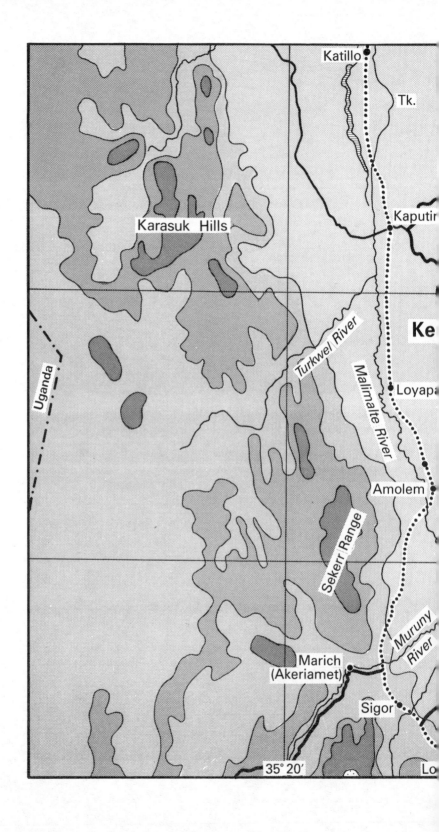

MAP 10

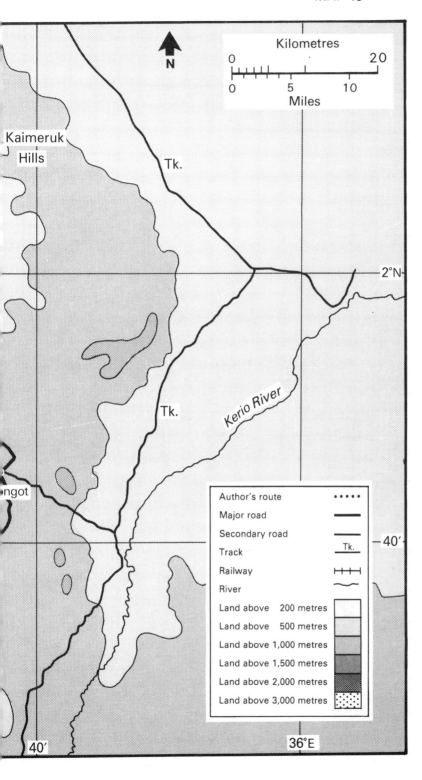

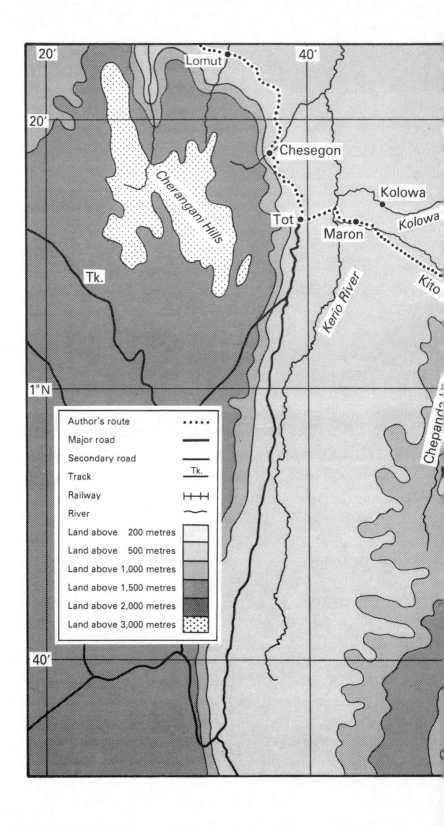

MAP 11

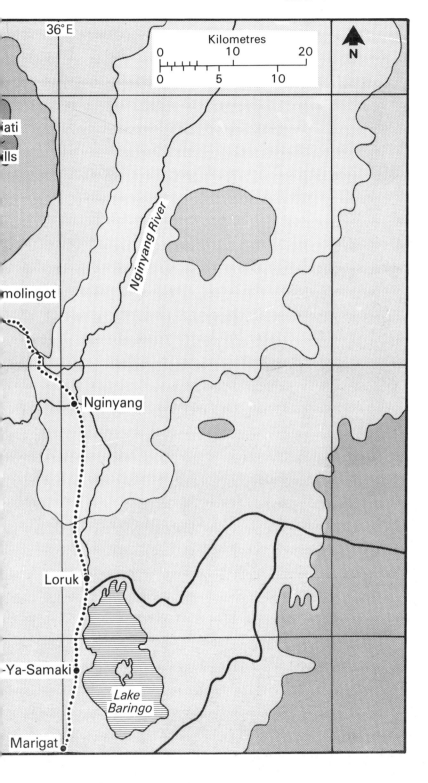

Index